Why Do I Do It?

Braiswick

Thanks to my wife for sorting out my awful *'spellnig'* and putting up with me.

Thanks also to

Adam (the Yankee Mackem) Robson for allowing me to use his September 11th 2001 reports, and Major Major (the Oriental Mackem) for his *'living the dream'* composition and *The Misfit* Cable Guy.

This book is dedicated to anyone as passionate and as bitter as I am.

Why Do I Do It?

P.D.Han

Braiswick
61 Gainsborough Road, Felixstowe, Suffolk IP11 7HS

ISBN 1 898030 30 8

Copyright © 2003 **P.D.Han**
www.author.co.uk/han

The moral right of the author has been asserted.

All rights reserved. No part of this publication may be reproduced, stored in a retrieval system, or transmitted, in any form or by any means without the prior permission in writing of Author Publishing Ltd.

This book is sold subject to the condition that it shall not, by way of trade or otherwise, be lent, resold, hired out or otherwise circulated without the publisher's prior consent in any form other than that supplied by the publisher.

British Library Cataloguing in Publication Data available.

Cover design by Dominic Edmunds

Printed in Kent
by JRDigital Print Services Ltd
Braiswick is an imprint of Author Publishing Ltd

Sunderland Till I Die!

I

"For fucks sake," the frequently uttered indecorous phrase that sums up my life supporting my football team - Sunderland Association Football Club. Over the many years I've supported my team, I've probably recited those words more than anything else. I'm no glory hunter; so unlike the stereotyped Manchester United fan, 'for fucks sake'outweighs any phrase that you could use at the other end of the spectrum, say something along the lines of 'fucking get in you beauty'.

You can't choose your football team: you see it chooses you. You certainly can't chop and change depending upon who is the more successful at any one time. Some do, but I think a *'true supporter'*, and the term 'true supporter' is one which I've discovered can be quite a controversial subject, but nevertheless a 'true supporter' will follow their team until they die! Geographical location will normally determine who you support, or you may carry a torch through family tradition, brainwashed as a child into supporting a team that may reside hundreds of miles away - such support should be admired and not shunned.

But aside from the above comments, which are just the tip of the iceberg when it comes to defining how a person develops a fetish towards a particular club, I dare say many fellow Sunderland supporters will echo my views regarding the 'for fucks sake' phrase, as life supporting SAFC is never dull, there are some ups, but more than often there are too many downs and thus the frustrating sentiments of 'for fucks sake'.

I guess having said, *"for fucks sake"* once too often, I decided to attempt to put down on paper my life and memories supporting Sunderland AFC - well over the last six or so years, as well as interjecting on another albeit recent influence in my life - the World Wide Web - and my attempts to become an Internet tycoon, you know, come up with a web site that attracts millions of visitors and makes you stinking rich.

Who am I?

Well I'm a thirty something Mackem, born and bred in Sunderland, red and white through and through. I've followed the Lads, that's Sunderland Football Club to the uneducated, since about 1982 - at least since I was allowed to go to the games, that is. I had a sheltered upbringing you see, not allowed to do anything or go anywhere, kept in a cupboard for years on end, fed bread and water until I left school and left home to find my fortune.

All right, that last bit was exaggerated a little - I got milk, not water!

I'm just a normal guy really, bitter and twisted, with a loving hatred towards the unwashed - you know - our Geordie rivals - the Mags!

I'm not as touchy as some of them though, like the bloke from Newcastle who won't eat bacon because it's red and white. Having said that, I did go through a phase where I'd not wear anything made by Adidas, because they sponsor the Mag's shirts. If I'm honest, I suppose I probably am as bitter as them, but that's beside the point and I guess the love-hate relationship most fans of Sunderland have towards Newcastle United supporters is another story.

So, where do I begin telling my tale? You could begin anywhere and at anytime, but I thought I'd start near the beginning of the birth of the Internet. It's May 1997 and I find myself on the way home from Wimbledon FC.

SAFC have just been relegated (again) after a one-off season in the top flight (again), and it's a long way back up the M1.

The way down was great. After all we were fourth bottom, Coventry were third bottom, we had Wimbledon, they had Tottenham - we would stay up and they would go down. All we needed to do was win, this way we need not worry about the Coventry result. Destiny was in our own hands. It was quite plain and simple - and quite satisfying considering most Sunderland fans hate Coventry after what they and *'Chinny Hill'* did in 1977. I personally have no memory of this, but it was us, them, or Bristol City to go down from the old First Division. While we lost at Everton, both Coventry and Bristol City, who were playing each other that day, not only had the kick off delayed - *'obviously'* to see what our result would be - but played a passing game between each other for the final ten minutes. You see, they knew that as long as they drew against each other they'd both stay up at our expense. So since then we've never forgiven the *'Chin'* or Coventry for these dirty tactics. It's a period of our history you learn as part of being a Sunderland supporter. Strange though how Bristol City have been let off the hook over the years. I guess it was down to them being the visiting team that day. But like all those who deceive in life they eventually get their comeuppance. What goes around comes around!

The week before the Wimbledon match, it was the last ever league game to be played at Roker Park. A packed house saw the Lads defeat Everton to give us a great chance of surviving the drop.

Was I there?

No!

The wife had only gone and booked a holiday to Majorca before the season's fixtures had come out.

Having regularly attended since 1982 I missed the last ever league game at Roker Park. Shame on me, but the holiday was good, even more so when the result was discovered. "We're safe," I thought, simple as that.

I could just about put up with the Cockney touts calling me mate and saying what a great result it was for us as I walked around Magaluf wearing my stripes with pride.

I say Cockneys because all touts are - aren't they? Well to me they've all got annoying Cockney accents, and I'm sure many will agree. I mean you don't come across Scottish touts on holiday in the Mediterranean now do you? Nor do you hear Scouse accents, Geordie accents, Brummy, Irish or cider drinking accents trying to tempt you into some seedy looking bar or night club on the promise of free drinks and lots of fun! The accents are always Cockney!

So here's this tout with a Cockney accent calling me *"mate"* and talking about Sunderland's *"great result?"* I'm sorry but you don't give a fuck *"mate"*, you probably don't even know where Sunderland is - it's in Scotland or it's that small mining town where people walk around dressed like they do in those Catherine Cookson TV dramas!

"Yeah I'll take that free drink and go into your pub if you look after the kids?" (I'm walking around with the little 'un still in her buggy). I mean, do these people actually bother looking at those they approach or am I supposed to grab his voucher, head into the bar and leave the bairn unattended outside?

"Err, yeah, awright mate," he says, and turns his attention to someone else.

Now back to the Wimbledon game, and I remember being in a pub in Piccadilly Circus having a drink with some friends I'd travelled down with.

We'd actually tried to get into numerous pubs but each one refused entry because we were wearing team colours. Oh yeah like Sunderland fans have a thug reputation - the stripes are red and white, Mr Doorman, not black and white.

Not to be outdone though, it was back to where we'd parked the car to put on our jackets and zip them up like *'anoraks'* so our stripes could not be seen, then off to try another pub.

Easy this time, and once in, off came the jackets to unveil our beloved colours. Well we had seen other red and white supporters in there, even some Coventry fans, so if they can show them off, so can we.

On the way out one of my mates decided to go over to some of these Coventry fans and says, "Good luck today chaps."

"Eh!"

"What'd you say that for, you daft twat?"

So that comment he made is in my mind on the way back up. Luck went to them as they beat Tottenham at White Hart Lane while we lost 1-0 - so that makes it his fault for saying good luck, then!

I'm starting to ponder over the coming season in Division One again. We'd be starting life in our new football ground - the big white elephant many people were calling our new 42,000+ capacity, state-of-the-art Stadium of Light, as it was to be named. But that was the last thing on my mind - too far ahead to contemplate.

Anyway we stopped at some services on the M1 just outside of London and headed for the toilets - as you do! I walked in and decided to use a cubicle even though I only needed a piss - call it solitary confinement - well I did not feel like being social at that particular moment, then again who is inside men's toilets - apart from say, George Michael!

Suddenly, in walks about thirty or so (well it sounded like thirty or so) Coventry supporters singing, *"Fuck off Peter Reid"* and all that - to the tune of our *"Cheer up Peter Reid"* song.

What a bunch of wankers.

Who the fuck do they think they are - deliberately stirring it up? It was like rubbing a puppy dog's nose in its own piss when it makes a mess on your carpet.

So me, being me, I stay locked inside the cubicle until the commotion dies down. Hey, I'm not getting involved in any tussle with anyone, let alone some Southern arseholes.

Besides it sounded like all hell was breaking lose out there with all the shouting I could hear.

I'm not the violent type, actually quite the opposite. I sort of pictured myself in a scenario whereby everyone outside was getting a good kicking, and every cubicle was being slowly inspected - you know the way they look under the door to see if they can see feet.

So picture the scene, I'm squatting on top of a closed toilet lid with my fingers in my ears, my eyes tight shut, and I'm spouting off *"la, la, la, la I can't hear you!"* in my head - that way I'll not hear them and they'll not see me and move on!

The turmoil eventually dies down and I decide to make a run for it. I'm expecting to open the locked cubicle door and have to step over broken urinals, busted pipes spraying water everywhere, and wade through the piss covering the floor. Surprisingly though it wasn't that bad as I cautiously made my way out.

On the way back to the car, I pass a coach full of more Coventry fans, and there's this old lady standing on the first step in the coach doorway. She yells over to me and starts singing *"going down, going down, going down."*

I look at her in amazement, shake my head, and walk off (I hear the coach driver shout at her to leave the lad alone and have more respect).

Respect?

Football is indeed a funny old game and a cruel one where fans take great pleasure at putting down any other supporter of any other team no matter what the circumstances - respect is often missing in this sport.

Then again if it's us Sunderland supporters putting down the Mags, the lack of respect we show is acceptable - right?

Well, that's where my story begins, a depressing start, but not unusual for a Sunderland fan - or me!

The summer would see some interesting transfer activity, the new stadium opening to the sound of a miming Status Quo airlifted in by helicopter, and the start of my adventures in cyberspace.

II

At the start of the 1997/1998 season I worked for this company called *'Bogus'*, based in Gateshead, Tyne and Wear. I'd been working there for over eight years, travelling the world for them - and on my own for most of the time - installing computer based design systems, following SAFC on short wave radio via the BBC World Service, spreading the gospel of the red and white cause to everyone I met, and letting them know that black and white were the Devil's colours.

This company doesn't exist today which is sad, it was a good place to work at, and I'd had some great times on my travels visiting places like Hong Kong, Bangkok, Sao Paulo, Beijing, Mexico City and New York.

Then again, looking back, I had some shit times like having to go to Israel during the Gulf War - the locals all had gas masks and I didn't because as they said, *"I was just a tourist."*

"Just a tourist?"

"Does that make me immune to the chemical weapons Saddam Hussein is threatening you all with?"

Then a few months after the Gulf War it was a trip to Syria where the food's crap! I had to endure such delicacies as *'shit in a bun with mint sauce on'*. Don't ask - it was some type of runny looking meat, in a bun with mint sauce on it and I got the runs from eating it.

I guess the bad trips made up for the good ones and the ones I missed due to certain stunts I pulled, like the time I got rather drunk the night before having to travel to Israel (this was a previous time before the Gulf War). I'm lying on the sofa at about 6.00am attempting to recover from a birthday party the night before, waiting for a taxi to take me to Newcastle Airport. I'm thinking to myself, "No way can I make a six or seven hour trip feeling like this."

So I make a bold decision to cancel the taxi and spend the day in bed recovering.

That night I take out my airline tickets and put them in one of my shirt pockets and into the washing machine. As I watch them spinning around, I practise my excuse to the boss.

"Oh dear, I've accidentally washed my tickets and did not know what to do." So I go to work on Monday to everyone's surprise - "You're supposed to be in Israel," says the boss.

"Oh dear, I accidentally washed my tickets and did not know what to do," I reply! They believed me though and I got let off the hook.

Shame on me once again!

Back to my job at hand though, I was presently working in the Marketing Department, and being a sort of PC guru, someone at the top decided it was time the company had a web site, so they turned to me to do it.

Now I knew nowt about the Internet at that time but as I'd dabbled in interactive CDs I was apparently the *'best man for the job'*.

I therefore managed to wangle a jolly down to London to some big Internet Exhibition going on at Wembley (little did I know I'd be back there within a few months).

I wandered around this place merely picking up a half dozen CDs with free trial Internet access packages on them and any other freebies I could lay my hands on, before heading off to Planet Hollywood for the night with a work mate that was with me.

Now I like the movies and all that, so Planet Hollywood was something I was really looking forward to visiting to see all the memorabilia on show, have a bite to eat, drink lots of alcohol, and hope that some big time celebrity would walk in.

As we sat at our table looking through the menu, the waiter comes up and as we order we get on chatting as he notices we're wearing *'footy'* gear.

"I like football," he says.

"So who do you support then?"

I'm wearing this T-shirt that says SUNDERLAND AFC DIVISION ONE CHAMPIONS 1996.

"Sunderland," I reply and I point to the lettering on my T-shirt!

"I support Millwall," he says.

So we decide to remind him of the 6-0 drubbing his team got the previous season when Sunderland hit the top of the table. That day we knocked Millwall off top spot, and as we went on to win the League Championship, Millwall never recovered from the thrashing we gave them and they ended up plummeting down the table and eventually got relegated.

"Really!" he says.

"So how many points did you get for that then?"

Hello!

There's a stunned silence as me and my mate look at each other in amazement. My mind is replaying that last sentence. "So how many points did you get for that then?" I'm analysing each word to make sure I've understood this astonishing outburst that has just been made.

"Err three!" we both reply at the same time.

"Oh," he says, and goes off with our order!

What a tosser!

I'm sorry but when you meet someone like this, is it any wonder that people get stereotyped?

I mean you've got the likes of thick Geordies, thieving Scousers, drunken Scots and dumb soft Southern shandy drinking Cockneys like this waiter, who doesn't know that no matter how many goals an Association Football team will score, you only get three points for a win! There are plenty more stereotypes from my twisted point of view, but I'm drifting away from the plot. I'm not saying that all Mackems are perfect mind you, but compared to some!

So I've got a lot of freebies from this exhibition and I take the ones I don't want to work the following Monday to begin the task in hand of learning how to use this unknown entity called the Internet with all its weird nerdy terminology and create my company's web site!

Having obtained access to the Internet and after few days of *'surfing'* around web sites with grey backgrounds and large fonts, I was thinking to myself "this is boring".

But I had a job to do, so over the next few weeks I slowly got to grips with the language of the World Wide Web - HTML - and created my first web site.

I had this wonderful framed web site with big fonts and crude animated graphics, scroll bars everywhere and any link be it text or an image had a an ugly underline or a big blue border around it. Those of you who know web site designing will understand how tacky this will have looked.

Still I was quite proud of my achievement and so was the senior management.

Basically I was now maintaining this site on a daily basis whilst doing my other marketing related jobs.

A few weeks later whilst surfing around the Internet, doing some research - honest I was - I came across this Sunderland fan site called *'FTM'*. Now I am a firm believer in FTM - you know three letters, two meanings, and one religion.

Let's be blunt here, FTM means politely *'Follow The Mackems'* but preferably *'Fuck The Mags'* - it's a football phrase that's all, tribal maybe but not hooligan related like certain footballing authorities and media like to portray it as.

I'd been a converted fan of FTM ever since I went to St. James' Park in the 1990 Play Off semi-finals. I mean if you were there and saw the pathetic efforts the so called *'fans'* of Newcastle United made in an attempt to get the match abandoned after we went 2-0 up by demolishing their own ground, well you'd be a converted fan of *'FTM'*.

Likewise the 3-1 defeat at St. James' on New Years Day back in 1985, when the only two coloured players on the pitch were controversially sent off, both of whom played for Sunderland, left a bitter taste in your mouth which is still there for many, including me, and it all adds to the cause!

I was also, in my mind, one of the first to wear *'FTM'* on the back of my stripes standing on the terraces at Hillsborough in the 1992 FA Cup semi-final, ironed on especially for that particular occasion.

After that game people were coming up to me and patting me on the back - you know to touch the FTM as if it had some magical power!

I'd also taken part in regular company social club quiz-nights and had always put together a team of misfits called *'The FTM Executive Club'*.

FTM for obvious reasons, though we often said the *'M'* meant Management.

The Executive Club bit was because as many of us on this team had travelled the world or were still doing so and we'd all been part of the British Airways Executive Club (air mile collecting and posh lounge squatting etc).

So I'm at work, surfing, looking at this *'FTM'* web site and any other SAFC web sites I could find, I mean doing some research, and I'm bored and I'm thinking we'll as I've got nowt to do why don't I create my own web site. So I did, while at work pretending to do my real job!

It was obviously going to be called the FTM Executive Club, so I looked around the Internet for some design inspiration and came across a Boots the Chemist web site. At that time, the Boots web site had won an award for the best UK site design - something like that.

So I stole its concept and put together my own little SAFC web site and hid it under some bizarre obscure URL (web site address) within the storage area of the company's web site I was supposed to be maintaining.

There now, proud as punch.

My own little corner of cyberspace, this small little web site dedicated to SAFC without any red or white in it at all?

Well, I like to be different so I went for this dirty gold colour - like the away strip of the time with a logo that resembled a door plaque - all rather *'executive'* looking in my mind!

It contained a latest news section, a letters page for other Internet users to email their comments, a links page, a credits page whereby I proclaimed myself the *'President'* and one or two other pages I cannot quite remember, oh and of course plenty of anti-Mag related stuff.

Now then, how will people find it I wonder?

Well I guess you have to be polite to the webmasters of other SAFC web sites and get them to link to you - a 'you scratch my back and I'll scratch your back' common bond.

Webmaster, now there's a term. To be honest it's corny and geeky. A person who creates and runs a web site is the webmaster, warrior, Jedi Knight, slayer of dragons, rescuer of damsels in distress, admired by many, feared by more blah, blah, blah.

Suddenly I'm this all mighty and powerful Dragon Slayer, fantastic. I'll beat those heathen black and whites with my words, and they shall fear my writings for I have the power!

So I contact as many other SAFC Dragon Slayers, I mean webmasters, that I can find on the Internet, and my FTM Executive Club gets a link to these other SAFC web sites and I link back to them.

There, that'll bring in visitors to my site, I think, I hope!

I also attempt to contact the official SAFC web site but no joy there. I guess then like now they will not ever entertain people who dare criticise the Club in any way, shape or form. Besides with a web site that has FTM in its title, something the Club despises, I was on a hiding to nothing tying to get them to link to me or take me seriously. 'Maybe one day you'll take me seriously,' I think to myself. 'We'll just have to wait and see.'

III

Meanwhile SAFC were having an indifferent start to the season in their new Stadium of Light, with the big summer signing of Lee *'spotty face'* Clark from the Mags. Well at that time he had turned away from the dark side and was therefore an adopted Mackem as far as I was concerned. Other new players to come in that summer were some unheard of defender from Cambridge (Jody Craddock), a little unknown striker for peanuts from Watford (Kevin Phillips) and a midfielder called Chris *'the axe'* Byrne!

I can't quite remember the story but an incident took place somewhere in Lancashire or Cheshire and evidence was found, allegedly - an axe - in the boot of Chris Byrne's car or something along those lines and thus the nickname. I didn't pay too much attention to the actual events at that time, as the player in question was to be blunt, shite, so when he was suddenly offloaded to Stockport I don't think anyone was bothered about it all.

The season had kicked off with us losing 2-0 away to Sheffield United in our new *'dirty'* gold away strip, which was a disappointment. You see, expectations were high that we would bounce straight back into the Premiership. I guess the opening of the new Stadium created a buzz that made you forget about the heartache of relegation a few months earlier. Likewise the sadness of Roker Park closing for good would soon be forgotten once people experienced the Stadium of Light, though many didn't like the name when it was announced. I wasn't bothered what it was called. I actually liked the name *Stadium of Light* - it sounded modern and forward thinking in my view.

I was however disappointed with the unveiling of a new Club crest, not that I didn't like it or anything, but just that there was nothing wrong with the old one. In fact I loved the old crest Sunderland had worn, so much so that I had it tattooed on my left arm a few years earlier.

I guess the new crest just came as a real surprise, especially to the bloke who had just got a massive tattoo of the old one on his chest the day before the new one was unveiled. The Sunderland Echo made a light-hearted story about it and I imagined the local tattoo parlours having a flood of enquiries from fans wanting the new crest adorned on their bodies. The tattoo I'd had done had hurt like hell. I'm sure the bloke who did it was deliberately pressing extra hard with the needle for some reason, so as for me getting a tattoo of the new crest, well that was not on my agenda at that time and yes I am a wimp!

The first home game in the new stadium against Manchester City was a special occasion without doubt. The game was played on a Friday night - a first for Sunderland AFC. This made the atmosphere even more special.

Friday nights are good aren't they? They signal the start of the weekend, time off from your average boring nine to five, Monday to Friday job that you wander through aimlessly in life. Then again you might be unemployed, or actually like your job, or maybe work on weekends, or have retired, or work shifts or something else totally irrelevant to this particular football game. But it's that time when the vast majority of us unwind and forget about the stress endured during the week. It means alcohol time. It means not having to wake up to an alarm clock. It means time off to do what you want to do. It means many things to many people, but above all it means to the average football supporter, time to prepare for the weekends game - unless it's the close season, which gets lonely and you start to suffer withdrawal symptoms. You have to go shopping with the wife instead! Or you have to do those DIY jobs you kept putting off whilst counting down to the start of the new season!

A full house on that Friday night however, put to one side the fact that we were in the wrong division and made you feel unbeatable. We won 3-1.

The kick off was delayed due to crowd congestion and some sort of ticket allocation fiasco, then all of a sudden some classical music boomed out of the sound system around the ground. "I know that tune," I think to myself - "I remember it from the opening titles of Channel 4's American Football highlights program I used to watch in the 80s."

The players ran out and the music changed to the chorus of the pop group Republica's *'Ready To Go'*.

The game was the perfect advertisement for football. Niall Quinn scored the first ever goal at the Stadium of Light and I swear he got confused as to which set of supporters he had to celebrate with (he'd joined us from City the year before if you remember).

We also got goals from 'spotty face' and Kevin Phillips. A good night that - the first time I'd ever supped beer inside my home ground! Well it was a novelty especially considering you couldn't drink alcohol inside the old Roker Park. Then again you couldn't drink anything inside the old Roker Park, unless you liked lukewarm Bovril and soup with lumpy bits at the bottom - assuming you managed to drink your way to the bottom. It was generally accepted that the Bovril was piped straight up from the bogs at the back of the Fulwell End.

Even the food inside the new stadium was great. You could now buy chips, and cheeseburgers, hot dogs and a rare speciality - pies that had taste - especially the popular chicken-balti ones. You could safely eat without worrying about getting food poisoning or feeling pounds heavier when comparing these pies to the Roker Park ones. If Sunderland fans ever wanted to get a hooligan reputation those pies could have been used as weapons, just as effective as a brick they were, unlike the new Stadium pies which were just pies, so throwing them in anger meant they'd disintegrate on impact. I will point out that this is all hypothetical and I've never thrown a pie in anger in my life.

The results over the next few weeks were very inconsistent and crowds started to drop. I was a season ticket holder in the cheap end, the family enclosure. At that time two adults could sit with one child and pay half of what anybody else paid in the rest of the ground. As most of my mates were taking their kids to the games now, I sponged on the back of one of them as a second adult to save myself a small fortune.

At each and every game it was becoming apparent that this classical music and pop tune were being played all the time. Hey this is a great way to introduce the teams onto the pitch. I guess it also signalled to us downing as many pints as possible to get to the toilets, have a piss and get to our seat before the referee blows his whistle to start the game.

It was now a home game against Norwich City on a bitterly cold windy day. The crowd was low in the region of around 30,000, which to some teams and for SAFC compared to twelve months earlier, is a pretty good attendance. The thing is inside the Stadium of Light a crowd of this size generates zero atmosphere which sort of spoils the experience if you know what I mean.

We subsequently lost 1-0 (the Princess of Wales died that night and bouncing back into the Premiership was looking many, many years away).. I can remember Niall Quinn and Kevin Phillips breaking the offside trap and between them they only had the keeper to beat. Quinny on the ball had merely to side tap it to Phillips to score as the keeper had committed himself to the big Irishman. At this time a lethal partnership did not look like materialising as Quinny went for glory, the keeper saved and the fans booed.

After losing more games like an embarrassing 3-1 away defeat by Port Vale, a large section of supporters were now screaming for Reidy's head and I too was being quite fickle and bitter and put down such thoughts on my web site.

We then lost 4-0 away to Reading.

Reading?

Where and who the fuck are Reading? Queens Park Rangers look-a-likes that's who. Where is not important, just some place full of Cockneys probably!

4-0 against Sunderland?

Christ at this rate we'll be in Division Two before long.

Time to really mouth off on my site. But is anybody reading it? I'd had no indication of anybody looking at it, nor had any emails my way saying how great or how shite my little corner of the Internet was.

'Fine, I'll make up a story and email it to myself,' I thought.

Well you can do that on the Internet. I mean when you think about it, the Internet is a scary place to be in. You are after all invisible and can adopt many different disguises, that's why it's subject to so many press reports about violation of private and personal information, age concerns and so on. Some people I've come across on the Web have got themselves so deep into alter egos they end up emailing themselves not knowing it's them - if you know what I mean.

At the end of the day, the person on the other end of the email or chat room or message board and so on is totally anonymous, a complete stranger.

This of course leaves room for your imagination to run wild and you create your own personality for them. I mean in my time I've come across stalkers, sixteen year old spotty faced anorak wearing nerds, the main character from the film American Psycho, rock stars, highly opinionated people who are *'holier than thou'*, and of course not to make the World Wide Web completely hostile, friends!

I still think it's a sad place though and a nerdy one at that, especially when people amazingly pretend to be you. You become so schizophrenic in playing the alter ego game that it may be really you pretending to be you and not someone else, yet you don't realise this now because you're so deep into your Jeckyll and Hide personality - geek!

Before creating this email I intended on sending myself, I end up talking on the phone to some guy who knew the Chairman one day at work - he was actually poaching me to do a bit of web site designing on the side, something to do with the Angel of the North statue. Hey why not?

The work never happened but while talking to him about this, he asked what the address was of the company's web site. I told him and he obviously decided to look at it while I was on the phone.

"Are you sure that's the right address?" he asked, "Because all I see is a Sunderland badge!"

Oh Shit!

Cold sweat time!

P45 time!

You're going to get sacked!

This guy knows the Chairman. "Err leave it with me and I'll see if the problem lies at this end."

Of course the problem was at this end, without realising I'd overwritten the opening page of the company's web site with the FTM Executive Club's opening page. Time stood still as I frantically attempted to connect to the Internet using the worlds fastest - not - 9,600 modem.

Modems are normally referenced by their speed. Nobody knows what the number really refers to unless you are a true geek, but the bigger the number, the faster your access would be - something like that.

So instead of rushing around the Internet accessing web sites on a racehorse, I'm trotting around on a seaside donkey.

Connecting the Internet on that occasion was like the slow motion action sequences of The Matrix - like where Keanu Reeves is lying backwards on his legs dodging bullets.

The problem was - whereas in the film the slow motion ends and normal speed resumes, this attempt to connect to the Internet stayed in slow motion.

Even the sound of my own voice in my head saying, "come on, come on, connect you fucking piece of shit," was being dragged out very slowly if you know what I mean.

But I got away with it.

I got connected, I uploaded the correct company opening page and that prompted me to look elsewhere to *'host'* my site. I decided to sign up and use AOL (America On Line), as it was in my opinion the only decent Internet provider at that time. The days of free phone calls were non-existent back then, so it meant these providers could sting you with monthly membership fees and you'd still have a phone bill to pay for on top of that, unless you were clever like me and knew how to sign up and get month after month of free trials.

I had to go around all of the other Dragon Slayers again to ask them to alter their link to my web site because the address had now changed. It was now a lot smaller than the long-winded address I had used when I first started to promote my *'creation'*. Being smaller meant it would be easier for people to remember though it was still an obscure address from my point of view. In those days you could buy your own web address or domain name, but it cost a small fortune: only for the privileged!

Anyway the Dragon Slayers made their changes as requested and without the slightest hesitation. Back then the numerous *'webmasters'* that existed were quite friendly towards one another, not wanting to compete against each other in some sort of pathetic quest to become *'the'* ultimate warrior on the World Wide Web (oh how times would change).

I had better mention here that I did all of this SAFC web site stuff secretly while at work because at that time I did not have my own computer at home. It also meant that no updating happened at the weekend, but that did not appear to bother my readers - well how would it. I'd never received feedback so was non the wiser.

I decided to email myself this letter I mentioned earlier using a false email address calling for Reidy's head. Well I think it was calling for Reidy's head - put it this way, it was not a pro Sunderland letter. I subsequently put it on the web site with an editor's comment next to it. That was me - the editor, there you see even I pretend to be someone else and was talking to myself (some say I still do, but that's beside the point).

'Will that prompt a reply,' I wondered?

IV

Next day at work, I log onto the Internet. "You've got post," says Joanna Lumley (the voice of the AOL mailbox if you did not know).

"Whoo hoo," my head says in true Homer Simpson style, someone has answered the letter I emailed myself!

Turns out to be from a guy in Southampton! That's pretty far away I guess for a Sunderland supporter. I copy his email, add them to my letters page, and add my own editor's comments. Before long I started getting other emails from other people some of whom became regular contributors offering their views as an alternative to my own comments, and more or less like me at that time pissed off with the plight of SAFC.

As well as emails from local people in and around the North East, I was also getting emails from places like Australia, Sweden, Germany, Iceland, America, Southampton, Southampton, Southampton, Southampton and Southampton. "Becoming quite friendly this guy," I thought, or is it just me always being cautious and distant, in other words an unsociable miserable bugger.

"Who emailed you today then dear?" my wife would say. "Oh that bloke from Southampton," I'd reply.

"Not *The Cable Guy*' again!" she'd say. Like I've already said, I have this knack of putting personalities to those who are merely just words from an email, call it self humour! So being the unsociable miserable bugger that I mentioned I am, I pictured this bloke wanting to be my friend, only too friendly like Jim Carrey's character in the film *'The Cable Guy'*. You see it's just me not wanting to make friends I guess, or at least not too quickly. Or was it because I'm doing this web site in secret, sort of all hush-hush so as not to get the sack seeing as I'm doing all of it while at work? I'm sort of pretending I'm not getting these emails, nor answering to them because I don't really have a semi-popular web site, even though I am and I do!

Gets complicated doesn't it?

Anyway I was getting a lot of emails not just from *'The Cable Guy'*.

I put down the reason the emails were coming in thick and fast, especially compared to the other SAFC web sites at that time due to the fact that I was becoming obsessed with this secret hobby of mine.

I'd log on every fifteen minutes or so to download any new emails I might have been sent. I'd also reply to them via the letters page straight away, thus people visiting the site would find that no sooner had they emailed in their thoughts and comments, that they would find them on the web site almost immediately appearing.

People were sending emails thanking me for providing this wonderful and unique fan's-eye view on supporting SAFC. Those who were exiled and unable to keep up to date with the events of their beloved Club now had a medium that allowed them instant access, the ability to find out results quickly and easily. I wished I'd had such access in the days I was travelling around the globe with my trusty short wave radio.

Back then it was a challenge to find out the score, trying to tune into the World Service and keep the station tuned in once you found it. Better still was having to finger your way through some foreign newspaper in the hope of finding some English football results or hope your work mates would remember to fax through the match report from the Sunday papers or Monday's Echo!

I realised that I now had a responsibility as people were relying on me to keep them informed and relying on me to get across the feelings local fans were having. Slowly this little hobby was getting serious.

I still had no idea how many people were looking at my web site so I decided I needed to get one of them free fancy web counters - a bit like a car mileometer which shows you how many visitors you've had. With that in place I started to witness single figures turn into double figures then three digits, four digits, five digits, and all in a matter of days.

These figures were however just a total of the number of times my pages had been viewed and not the total number of individual visitors to the web site. Apparently those figures were difficult to obtain, especially with a free an ad on like this mileometer I was using. I viewed the numbers as proof that I was really popular. So I start to think of how I could make some cash out of it.

The thing is I like a good moan, I love to bitch. With SAFC getting stuffed at such insignificant places like Reading, it gave me plenty of fuel to turn my thoughts and emotions into words.

I look back and think this was the catalyst from which my site got popular. People love to moan and love to read other people's moaning. I must have hit a chord venting my frustrations that people across the planet related too - well those supporting Sunderland AFC, and those who knew of my web site's existence.

Then SAFC suddenly started winning games and put together a seventeen match unbeaten run that saw them climb the table in dramatic fashion and go from limbo land to promotion contenders.

They still had a mountain to climb because Nottingham Forest and the Smoggies (Middlesbrough) were walking the league - runaway leaders.

I had nowt to really moan about anymore, well I did still find plenty to moan about, anyone can no matter how well their team is doing, there's always room for the odd dig or sly remark - it's healthy and it's human nature as far as I'm concerned.

Still though, it was great to see Sunderland winning so many games, becoming a more than just a half decent team and becoming, dare I say it, a Premiership bound team.

Anyway back to this reputation and popularity my little dirty gold coloured web site was gaining and back to that cash making idea! I decide to add a few more sections to the web site and change the layout to make it easier for people to navigate so they could look around my many pages quickly and efficiently. I added a merchandising section and offered *'membership'* to the FTM Executive Club for £10.00. For this you get your name in lights on my site, a little page about yourself, where you're from, how long you've supported SAFC, if you can complete the chant *"singing aye aye, yippee, yippee aye..."* and I'll send you an *'FTM Executive Club'* T-shirt.

Problem was I had no T-shirts!

I wasn't concerned about this though, I mean it looked good on the site and besides nobody would ever send me money through the post via a web site of all places, and one that is rather tacky looking, has strong bitter and twisted feelings towards all things red and white and black and white.

'Kerching' - the sound an old fashioned cash register makes as it pops up - a £10 cheque arrives in the post from the guy in Southampton. Oh dear, what do I do now? Kerching, another £10, then another and another. Suddenly I've got cheques for £60, so that's six T-shirts to find, make, and post, and not just to the UK.

There's one to go to Iceland, one to go to Australia, and one to go the USA.

Jesus, how much will that cost me?

Don't panic, just think of a solution. I thought long and hard - at least for five whole minutes.

The answer was simple; I go out buy a half dozen white T-shirts from somewhere like Matalan or maybe I'll pop along to Shields Market at the weekend. I'll buy some iron-on transfer paper, make a design and get my brother-in-law to print them out for me seeing as he has his own home computer.

I do visit Matalan but cannot find any white T-shirts, so I go to Shields Market the next Saturday morning, walking around the stalls on a bloody cold day looking for plain white T-shirts eventually coming across a stall full of them for only 50p each. It looked like they'd been dumped from the back of truck as there were hundreds of them piled on top of each other wrinkled as hell, with some Asian bloke standing there collecting everyone's 50p as they dug their way through the pile looking for unmarked ones. So I was doing the same as everyone else, digging my way through the pile looking for unmarked ones, though positioning the little 'un in her buggy just at the right angle to block access and give myself more room. I'm cunning you see.

Picture the scene early the next week. A bloke, who has never used an iron in his life, is standing in the kitchen next to the ironing board with a half dozen T-shirts in one hand and a few printouts (iron-on transfers) of the web address and web site name in the other hand.

The first few transfers ironed on okay, but a little overdone you could say, as after peeling back the transfer I had my web site address arranged correctly, but with an outline of an iron where I'd pressed too hard.

Eventually, and many hours later much to the amusement of my wife I had created my own *'merchandise'*.

Excellent, in the post they go and not too expensive either (even the ones to the USA and Australia).

Updating the members area with these people's profiles along with a few I made up to make it look *'more'* popular was very time consuming but it was part of the deal so I had to make sure I created these personal profile pages as quickly as possible.

I was amazed to get emails from people thanking me for the T-shirts. More amazingly was the fact that a few more cheques dropped through the letterbox.

I was now feeling embarrassed and very, very guilty. I felt I had turned my little site into a cheap and nasty shady place where people get ripped off. Instead of ironing on transfers onto cheap 50p T-shirts in my paisley cotton pyjamas, I'm suddenly ironing in a old worn out sheepskin coat, flat cloth cap, thin sleek looking moustache with a shoulder twitch onto cheap 50p T-shirts. You know what I mean - especially when I open up the inside my coat to reveal some knocked off gear to sell on the street corner for an absolute steal of a price. *"Ten lighters for a pound, get your ten lighters for a pound"*.

Pop Quiz - you're making money and providing shoddy goods, do you invest in quality gear building up your reputation as trust worthy or continue to rip people off you've never met, nor probably never will in a take the money and run stance?

I get sent another cheque from an old school friend. Now I'm not saying this prompted me to invest in quality, but I had more or less decided the iron on stuff was ripping people off. It was time to create a better design, find a local supplier, and buy a quantity of quality pre-printed T-shirts to sell instead and bin the remainder of the 50p ones.

The design had the web site door-plaque logo on the front and the words *'F@@@ T@@ M@@@'* printed large on the back. I'm not crude so it wasn't like I deliberately got *'Fuck The Mags'* printed. It was pretty obvious what it said, but from my perspective, the '@' sign was a clever way of hiding a *'naughty'* phrase by using an Internet related symbol.

Now the only supplier I could locate quickly and at a reasonable price to invest in was based in Newcastle of all places.

I had paid with my credit card in advance, so it was a case of having to wait ten working days before the order could be collected.

When they were ready I drove into the heart of enemy-territory, quite nervous about picking up a set of T-shirts, which was not exactly complimentary to those in and around Tyneside.

Subsequently when I asked for them they sort of said, "Are you Mr so and so." I immediately replied, "No, he just sent me to pick them up!" Fucking hell I thought I was about to get a good twatting.

Out comes a box with *'Fuck the Mags T-shirts'* written on in black marker pen. Well that's a blunt way to label up the box, I guess. I leave hastily back to the car and rip open the box like a kid rips opens their presents on Christmas Day.

There they were, quality T-shirts advertising my web site. No longer the *'Arthur Daley'* then I'm thinking to myself. Being the honest and thoughtful person I am, really I am you know, I post out these T-shirts to everyone I sent the shitty ones too; after all it was the right thing to do.

I borrow my brother-in-law's digital camera to take a few photos of the T-shirts - you know, front view and back view - and advertise them on the merchandise section of the web site. Potential customers could then see the quality they'd be buying!

By the way, that chant, *"singing aye, aye, yipee, yipee, aye ..."* - it ends in *"Fuck The Mags!"*

V

So the Lads were embarking on this fantastic unbeaten run, rapidly climbing the table turning the Stadium of Light into a fortress and selling out each time they played there.

Things were looking up, we were playing exciting football and the buzz, be it inside the ground, on the street, at work, or on the Internet was simply fantastic. Everyone was talking about Sunderland Football Club, and players like Kevin Phillips, the fans favourite, now scoring goals like there was no tomorrow. He was joining the prolific ranks of quality strikers that only come along once every ten years - Rowell, Gabbiadini, and now Phillips!

We played Sheffield United towards the end of this unbeaten run, at home, winning something like 4-2. I updated the web site and made a comment from an observation I made at the match, which at the time I found amusing.

As we scored our third goal I think - I had downed many pints that day - I noticed that a fight broke out among the Sheffield United fans, which to us sitting at the opposite end of the ground appeared quite amusing.

You had a bunch of them infighting, as we were effectively destroying their team on the pitch. I think I related to this on the web site due to the fact that they were pushing for a top six position, thus the game was a clash of potential *'promotion'* candidates.

Within a few hours of writing up my match report with this observation, which I found funny, I get a snotty email from a Sheffield United fanzine editor, condemning my view on this as it was not amusing to make fun of violence.

However the real reason behind this was some heavy handed stewarding being made towards those supporters.

Obviously upset that Sunderland has scored, some exchange of opinions had taken place, which led to several people being evicted from the ground.

According to this *Blade,* it was over the top stewarding and it was other fans attempts to point this out that caused, what looked like, supporters fighting amongst themselves.

It did alarm me to think that our own stewards would be so blunt with people especially when we're supposed to be a *Caring Club.* It sort of made you feel that the reputation SAFC had built up was being undermined by a few *jobs worth* employees or was it the Club's policy?

Conspiracy Theory time?

In a way though, I guess we've all had to endure heavy handed policing at one time or another when going to away games, you know being treated like lambs to the slaughter, herded into the visiting supporters' section, body searched like we're all convicted thugs and so on. To think that the staff of Sunderland AFC was allegedly acting in this manner was not a popular theory, echoed and condemned by all at that particular time, and sparking a good online debate from both Sunderland fans and from other visiting supporters.

I somewhat viewed this little episode as good business. It meant more and more people were finding the web site. Word was obviously getting around and I must be writing the right things or writing sufficient for people to want to agree or disagree with what I might be printing, or what other people were commenting on, whether Sunderland supporters or not.

I was now really addicted to all of this. In fact I couldn't wait to get to work each day to log on and see how many new emails I'd been sent or check the visitor logs from the site's mileometer.

I'm obviously making it look like I'm checking for emails from customers and visitor statistics in respect of the company's web site of course.

Weekends started worrying me though. I had two whole days without being able to update the site or add new feedback from visitors and so on.

I was getting withdrawal symptoms and needed a fix.

I started getting the shakes, became moody, and consumed more and more alcohol to keep calm.

My God, I had a problem. What do I do? Do I need to see a psychiatrist or something?

What I needed was to get set-up at home with my own computer. This would solve the problem I was having. At least I thought it would, I mean it wasn't like there was a *Computer Users Anonymous* organisation to help people cope with this addiction. I was probably the only one with this *disease* anyway!

It was simply far too expensive back then to buy a computer and I had no grounds for convincing the wife it was worth the investment.

A relative then came to the rescue.

He was a caretaker looking after a college that was effectively renewing its IT department and throwing out a lot of old equipment. Thus one night I went with him to the college and rummaged my way through this massive pile of old computer equipment until I had *'created'* a worthy system. It was only a 486 computer which at that time was good enough - like one fifth the power of say these Intel Pentium machines you can buy now, or in layman's terms, a 125cc moped compared to a 1200cc road racer.

I managed to *'permanently'* borrow my old 9,600 modem from work, as I had persuaded the boss at that time to upgrade so I could surf the web faster than a seaside donkey!

Once sorted I could check emails at the weekend, update match results and reports within minutes of each game finishing. My addiction was being satisfied twenty-four hours per day and seven days per week. Then again it wasn't a quick fix of my addiction. I was now fighting to use the fucking thing as the wife was also getting addicted - to that bloody solitaire game!

One Monday morning, I had one of the *'stuck-up'* salesmen come over to my desk, pointing at this piece of paper in his hand and saying, "Is your modem plugged into this telephone extension?"

I take a look at the number - 252.

"Yes I do believe it is!" I said.

"Right then!" he says, "That explains this phone bill".

Uh oh.

"What do you mean?" I reply innocently.

"Well I've been given this bill for £450 for the month and need to work out where it's come from".

"Well" I say, "You do realise that part of my job role is to keep the company's web site up-to-date. It does take a while to do this."

"And," I continue, "You lot keep asking me to search for this and search for that and it takes time to find the stuff you've asked for."

What an excuse!

I also point out that one of the top Directors had had me surfing one day looking for *'The Darwin Awards'*. I had no idea what he was talking about but it turns out to be another geeky site where people submit alleged true stories or what are more like urban myths about strange and unfortunate or embarrassing deaths people from all over the world had suffered.

He wanted as many stories as possible for a dinner party he was throwing, you see.

I have to admit some of them were amusing when I finally found some sites promoting this, like the Mexican farmer whose prize hen fell down a well, he jumped in to save it and got into difficulty. To cut a long story short about ten more people, each jumping in to save the previous, all drowned, but the hen survived!

There are many more like this, which some people might find amusing - or more like a morbid fascination.

Anyway these were very valid reasons for the large phone bill as far as I was concerned. I think they thought someone had been using the phone lines at work to ring up chat lines and what have you.

Now that they'd identified it was the modem though, no more was said. The phone bills were still high each month but it was all put down to these requests to search for this and that and my updating - the company web site - not my own little creation.

Well I'm sticking to that story; after all I'm not getting stung for any phone bills when I'm doing research into people's strange deaths or sometimes-even espionage.

Yes, I was actually asked one day to see if I could find a way to intercept emails and in particular those sent by the main competitor at that time, who was based in Switzerland.

I had no idea how to do this, but did put together a large report on the possibilities of it, the illegalities of it and an ex US naval intelligence office I had tracked down who offered such services - *mercenaries are us online!*

I had proposed it would cost about £100,000 to achieve this and so that idea was knocked on the head rather quickly. Too expensive is a good excuse rather than the fact it was totally against the law!

Did I say I researched into this? I deny all such knowledge. I'd rather get done for the phone bills than a prison sentence, although I'd rather not get done for anything! Time to move, swiftly back onto football I think!

VI

We had lost 2-1 at the Stadium of Light to the Smoggies earlier in the season. That game really did piss me off. I even left early because I simply didn't want to hear the full time whistle get blown and the celebration noises from those who supported *'the small town in Yorkshire'*. Besides I had to walk past the away supporters end to get across the Wearmouth Bridge and into the City Centre to get the bus home.

'Soul Glow' - a Brazilian called Emerson scored a blinding twenty to thirty yard volley that set-up their victory. What a player he turned out to be! Up for the cause until December when it started to get very cold. He fucked off to Portugal for Christmas and never came back, making the Smoggies the laughing stock they are when it comes to buying high profile payers who always leave in controversial fashion. It's because Middlesbrough is a dump, there's a permanent chemical cloud over the entire area due to the vastness of the eyesore of the processing plants that reside there and so a place where the sun never shines! I'm not saying Sunderland is a prettier place but we do get sunshine on the odd occasion when the weather is good.

When it comes to the rivalry factor, most Sunderland fans do realise that Boro are just that - as in rivals, but many will insist they are not. In their eyes they are wannabee rivals, jealous of the Sunderland/Newcastle thing and wanting to join in but as the phrase goes *"two's company and three's a crowd."* This is the reason for our piss taking *"Small town in Yorkshire"* chants. They think big, I'll credit them that, but they've never won anything in their entire history nor ever will.

The point is I hated this game and it came at a time leading up to the Reading fiasco, and hurt because not only did they defeat us in the league, but we then played them shortly afterwards in the Worthington Cup and lost. They allegedly stoned the Sunderland coach as well - charming bunch these mutants!

It was time for the return leg in the league at the Riverside Stadium towards the end of February. We had a one hundred percent record at the Smoggies new ground having played one and won one. I never went, opting instead for the beam back at the Stadium of Light. The record run of unbeaten matches had recently come to an end. Hopefully it'd be a one off! Over 18,000 people turned up to watch the beam back that day - a crowd most other First Division teams would worship for actual matches let alone via a giant TV screen with dodgy sound quality and a voice over by Roger *Tyne/Tees but not Wear* Thames!

Plenty of beer building up to the game, as usual, but then what a let down, as usual. Sunderland crumbled, and we lost 3-1, with *'ex-Geordie'* Alun Armstrong on the score sheet for them. Thick Geordie can't even spell Alan proper! We were off the pace once again as Boro along with the divisional leaders Forest pulled ever so further away from ourselves and the rest of the chasing pack hungry for automatic promotion.

As my thoughts went on the web site following this defeat, I had an interesting experience whereby I found some rather abusive remarks being made on a guest book I had put onto the site. Guest books are a joke on the Internet in many ways as far as I'm concerned. It's supposed to be an area for people to add their details and inform you of how lovely your site looks and *"Hey if you've got a moment, why not come and visit my site at www.blahblahblah.com."* It was at that time one of those *'must-have'* elements of a web site, a way to help monitor visitor numbers, and a way for the devious to collect email addresses for future spamming purposes. This is more proof of how dangerous the Internet can be. I mean you sign these guest books with genuine feeling and before you know it you get *'spammed'*. Now I like spam. I mean I don't actually like receiving spam. It is annoying. Spam is yet another geeky term used to describe the Internet's version of junk mail. You know how we've all had those wonderful Readers Digest letters pop through our letter-boxes telling us we are in line to win £50,000, or better still when you get these catalogue letters emphatically stating that seven out of the eight names shown have won a guaranteed £100,000. I can guarantee that your name is the eighth one shown! People are so gullible to such mailing tactics, and it is without a doubt a thriving industry to get people to subscribe to this and to subscribe to that, or buy this and buy that in the hope of actually winning that £50,000 or £100,000 prize draw. Thus the Internet is no different, and by leaving your email address on a web site you are opening the door for the junk mail societies of the world to send you the equivalent of that Readers Digest letter, or worse, and so you've been *'spammed'*.

Like I've already said, I like Spam, not receiving it, but the word itself. It is nerdy but I find it a funny way to express electronic junk mail, or hate mail as I often call it - not because they're offensive, but because I just hate receiving it! Today's Internet is however getting more and more under control with newer and revised legal and government legislation's that attempts to stop people from unknowingly opening the door to receiving Spam. Back then though there was little to no legislation thus if roaming surfers found your email address, you could end up receiving who knows what in you mail box, from *pity me* letters, the ones where someone has hit the bottom, lost everything he owns, and wants you to send him $25 to help rebuild his life - if he's hit the bottom how the hell is he emailing? There are also the ones that have somehow unknowingly signed you up to porn sites. I mean there's nowt better than opening your Internet mail box to be hit with email subjects like *click here for big titties*, or *cock-sucking online, visit now* and so on.

But back then people kept on signing these guest books. So I had to jump on this bandwagon and install my own FTM Executive Guest book. I therefore apologise if you ever signed this and ended up getting *pussy-licking* web site emails sent to you. I hold no responsibility if you left your email address on my web site at that particular time.

Now this hat trick of Boro defeats got me wound up one day when a Smoggy supporter decided to invade my guest book and post comment after comment after comment along the lines of *"three times, we beat the Scum three times"*. Strange, how he or she referred to us as Scum. It's not the politest of terms but one which most hard-core Sunderland supporters use to describe the Mags. So for us to be called Scum was somewhat unoriginal. However it was nevertheless annoying so I deleted them all.

A short time later I looked again to find the same messages posted back on, so I deleted them again, but they kept on appearing. I kept on deleting them and so this little game continued for quite a while. In the end this person started to post comments like, *"can't take it can you?"* and *"Where's your freedom of speech? You're just bitter"* and so on.

Well at that particular moment I couldn't take it, I was bitter, and as for freedom of speech, well I guess I'll just upset a few and say that although I do firmly believe in freedom of speech, especially on the Internet, there are times when that boundary is crossed and it gets too personal or too bitter, at which point I throw freedom of speech out of the window in favor of censorship. In my opinion it's called protecting your investment if you know what I mean.

Anyway this was getting out of hand, so I really did *throw the dummy out of the pram* as the saying goes and traced his IP address. This is another geeky thing you can do on the Internet. Basically no matter what you do online or whichever web site you visit, you always leave behind a signature or a footprint, so you can be traced. It's like a telephone number, which basically refers to you and your activity when online. I discovered this person's IP address pointed to some college on Teesside. So I assume it's an unemployed Smoggy with nowt else better to do than *'flame'* a Sunderland web site. Flame? Well that's another term. Self-explanatory really as in flames covering something like the way this person was smothering my guest book.

I decided to get nasty and email the college to inform them that someone was abusing their systems and posting derogatory remarks on the Internet. What a two-faced thing to say, because here was I abusing my position at work, running my hobby and getting all high and mighty about someone doing something that I was also doing, and doing so on a daily basis.

However it must have worked because the postings stopped. So if you know of someone who got kicked out of college in the Teesside area for Internet abuse way back in 1998, then it was probably my fault!

It also proved to me just how popular my site was becoming. I mean to find so called *rivals* now wanting to *destroy* your web site was sort of a compliment, in a roundabout way. It also meant I'd have to be more alert to ensure such flaming and other unscrupulous activities did not continue.

VII

Following the Boro defeat, we had to win against Nottingham Forest or we'd be something like nine or twelve points adrift which at this stage of the season would not see us being able to win promotion by default.

I hadn't been to an away game since Wimbledon and an opportunity arose to go to Forest.

One of my work colleagues had been invited to go evaluate some fancy interactive training software at Leeds University. He said he could only make it on one particular day and told my boss that he needed me to go with him due to my expertise - yeah right. The only day he was available just happened to coincide with the game against Forest.

The company agreed that I should go with him so we borrowed a company car, which meant we'd save some money by not having to pay for petrol. Having obtained match tickets pretty easily, we decided to try and evaluate the software as quickly as possible, giving us plenty of time to reach Nottingham.

So we did just that and probably too quickly and too embarrassing for the University bloke who was showing us the software. You could say we hurried him along a little too much.

"Would you like me to explain that again," he would say.

"No thank you," we'd reply.

"Would you like to go through this section by yourself and I'll pop back in about thirty minutes to see how you're getting on."

"Oh we don't think that is necessary, after all we'll be taking a copy to evaluate back in Gateshead."

And so having made sufficient excuses it was back to the car, decorate it with red and white scarves, a massive FTM Executive Club banner across the back window and down the M1 towards Nottingham.

We stopped at the first services we reached to do a *Batman and Robin*, dashing from the car into the toilets to change from our suits into our other uniform - red and white stripes and jeans!

As we drove down we talked about all possible outcomes of the game and where that would leave us in the table, whether Boro would lose that night and so on. Then on the radio Republica's *Ready To Go* started playing. Up went the volume to fucking deafening levels. So here's this little white Ford Fiesta bouncing its way down the M1 with two grown men singing their heads off to this Sunderland *'anthem'* - surely that was a sign, an omen of good things to come that night.

We got to Nottingham pretty early, parked the car somewhere safe, so we thought, well more like somewhere cheap rather than safe, and walked around looking for a pub that would allow away supporters in. We found it courtesy of the cricket ground close to Forest's City Ground, and as usual it was heaving with red and white supporters, so full in fact we had to stand outside to drink. Now it wasn't exactly warm considering it was March so you could say the beer was most definitely *'refreshingly'* cold, but the shivering was soon forgotten once the alcohol started to work its magic and the singing levels increased.

As we headed off to the ground our voices were already hoarse, but that wasn't too much of a problem for us. I started taking photos on my brother-in-law's digital camera, which I'd borrowed so I could play back the events of the game on the Internet the next day.

We got inside the ground to find our seat was in the first row. "Please don't rain," I'm thinking. It didn't and as the game got underway fortune went to Sunderland in what turned out to be an incredible performance by all the players on the pitch that night. We won 3-0, totally outplaying the home team and with news filtering through that the Smoggies had lost, made it a perfect evening in terms of results as far as our promotion aspirations were concerned. I have no idea who scored, well I guess I could have researched into it, but I don't think there's a need to cover every game I reflect on in such detail.

On our way out of the car park this dodgy looking bloke all in black tries to stop us, my mate starts winding down the window to see what he wants. I tell him to wind it down only a little as I lock my side of the door from the inside whilst leaning over my mate as quickly as possible to lock his side of the door, though he pushes me away and does it himself. The bloke is pointing at the driver's side front wheel saying we've got a puncture. Fuck off! We've got no puncture and we all know it.

"If we've got a puncture just drive round the corner and we'll have a look there not here," I say.

I was quite nervous, I mean this bloke might have been the Kurgan from Highlander, wanting to steal the car and take it for a joy ride with me still in the passenger seat screaming like that bird in the film as he drives around the streets of New York like a lunatic to the sound of Queen's *'Hammer To Fall'*, only I'm me and this is Nottingham, England, but that didn't mean this bloke wasn't the Kurgan!

My mate starts pulling away. The Kurgan then grabs hold of the door handle trying to open it. He gets a face full of gravel as we wheel spin off engine roaring loudly as we make our escape - if we didn't already have a puncture we probably have now! We do stop around the corner and guess what? No puncture! Then I turn on the radio and playing on some local rock station is Queen's *'Hammer to Fall!'* Now how fucking scary and spooky is that I ask you?

We realise as we drive home that we've just been involved in an attempted car-jacking incident. That would've been clever if the car had been nicked. How would we explain that to the boss next day at work or however many days it took us to get back home and back to work?

Could you imagine the scene?

"Nottingham! You were going to Leeds; how the fuck did you end up in Nottingham? Clear your desks and get out!" We decide that we'd tell no one about this and never have, though I guess I have now haven't I?

It was the early hours before I got home, and I headed straight to my computer. I was focused on getting the digital camera images I'd taken at the game onto floppy disk so I could get them formatted correctly and onto the web site. The problem was the computer was in the bedroom thus the wife wasn't too complimentary about my activities having disturbed her sleep and all.

"Turn the light off will ya? What are you doing? Do you know what time it is?"

"Yeah but I need to do this."

"Oh for fuck's sake who gives a shit about the football and your poxy little web site you spend more time doing that than you do with your family."

Nag, nag, nag.

Then again, I think am I spending too much time doing this? Why do I do it? After all, what am I getting out of it apart from self-satisfaction? Then I think of the emails and other correspondence I've received from exiled supporters thanking me for giving them such an insight into supporting SAFC. Well it's not exactly making me rich, which I guess has always been a hidden motive, but at least there are some who do give a shit!

I transfer the images as quickly as possible and get into bed to receive the cold shoulder. No favours tonight then!

Next day at work I frantically start formatting the pictures I'd taken so they could be viewed on the web site. "Have you got a moment?" says the voice of the Sales and Marketing Director over my shoulder looking at the computer screen, which is full of football images. I panic. You know how your heart misses a beat and you can feel your face going bright red? My throat goes dry and I can feel my legs turning to jelly. I then switch off the PC. I don't know why I did that - the old hardware reset - maybe by removing them from being visible he will forget he's seen them. I make up an excuse that the computer had frozen or hung-up on me so I had to reset it. He never commented which was a good thing. He was actually leaving the company that week so was probably no longer bothered. A few months earlier though and I would have been in deep shit if he'd caught me doing that then. He wasn't exactly the nicest of Directors either. I mean if you drew a little square moustache just under his nose he'd be the spitting image of Hitler. He was affectionately known as *'Seagull'* because of his ability to shit on you from great height. If he had not been leaving he would have most certainly shit on me from a great height that day. I guess I could've of reminded him about the Darwin Awards research he'd asked me to do if he had picked up on what I was doing, but he didn't say anything so I didn't mention the Awards (which after all had nothing to do with my daily duties, just like these football images I was processing).

Eventually, and after being very discreet following this little episode, I get the images on to the web site. Within an hour or so I start receiving thank you emails from exiles and one or two from those who had been to the game the night before. Well I guess that's another job completed, another satisfactory conclusion, the first of the *'independent'* web sites to produce numerous images from the previous night's match - a memorable match at that, one which may yet be the turning point for SAFC with luck!

I then feel withdrawal symptoms all of a sudden. It's been such an intense session to get these images online that once they are up there I feel sort of empty, not knowing what to do next. In reality I should simply have had a rest, but I'm addicted remember, so that was out of the question. I should have turned my attention to do some real work, the type of work I was getting paid for, but I didn't.

Now I was somewhat bored with the look and feel of the web site but thought it best to wait until the end of the season before doing a re-design. So I decided to pay a visit to all the other SAFC sites to see how far behind they were in terms of content and popularity - quite childish really - but I felt I was the most popular site out there on the World Wide Web and wanted to make sure I was number one in my own bitter and twisted mind. I discovered a new site that wasn't exactly on the ball with layout but it had its own message board being used by quite a few SAFC supporters. I had come across message boards before on my surfing *'adventures'* but hadn't found a free *'plug-in'* like the guest book. "I must get one of these message boards on the FTM Executive Club," I think, "maybe I'll try to get one with the end of season revamp I'll be doing."

I notice that this new site did not have a link to me so I contact its Dragon Slayer to ask if I can have link. He agrees if I link to him, so I do just that, he'll do the same for me and everyone is happy. I occasionally start to post on the message board as I recognise people's names on there as being some of those who have contributed to the letters page or posted on the guest book of my site. In those early days people would normally post using their real name, or nickname, and stick to that name and not other aliases. Eventually this message board would become a major factor on the Internet regarding SAFC fans and a very dangerous place for the naive. A place where I'd find myself being a target for abuse and for being impersonated. This would be my own fault though, I mean I'd been so cautious for so long towards people I'd never met, I probably became too friendly towards too many in the end, especially towards those who can only be considered as obnoxious arseholes who would take great pleasure in pretending to be you and saying all manner of things to cause trouble and discredit you - you know who you are! I've already touched on this earlier regarding these Internet schizophrenics and their Jekyll and Hyde personalities. I guess the behaviour of people towards others is one consequence of the World Wide Web and in particular when you put yourself on a pedestal. You then become a target for those who have only one thing in mind, to bring you down! That however is another tale for another time.

VIII

Sunderland were now enjoying a mini-revival, which was a massive boost to the Club and the fans. The emergence of winger Allan Johnston during this period provided another boost. Having recently saved our blushes by grabbing a very late equaliser at home to Birmingham, he was about to perform a similar feat this time against Portsmouth. The game marked the first match my eldest daughter attended and she only agreed to this outing because pre-match there was to be some dance thingy to the classical music piece that the team runs out to each and every home game.

There had been a scramble by the Dragon Slayers to find out what this music was called. Anyway the wife, being the cultured one in the family, knew what it was. So I got it on the site as quickly as possible. I did look on the Internet to check first though, just in case she was trying to make me look stupid by putting up the wrong info. That is one advantage of the World Wide Web. It is a great place for information as no matter what it is you might want to look, for no matter how obscure, you are sure to find a site with the information you want eventually. I remember being asked back then what the Internet was like and I sort of described it as more like your local newsagents than your local library, where you can browse through as many publications as you want at your leisure finding snippets of information here and there rather than reading a complete novel. I'm not saying this is a correct way to describe it, but I think it does sort of sum it up - or at least it did back then as far as I was concerned.

With the information confirmed, I'm now not only ranting about SAFC, whilst being very anti-Newcastle, but I'm now cultured you see with a feature on Ukrainian composer Sergei Sergeyevich Prokofiev, who wrote a ballet in 1935/1936 called Romeo and Juliet, based on the William Shakespeare play of the same name, from which one piece of music, being the one that Sunderland runs out to each home game, was titled *Dance of the Knights*.

Impressed? I am!

As I got this out first, I claim responsibility for everyone now knowing what this music is called and who composed it. Well, put it this way, it's nice to think I made people aware of it.

The Portsmouth game I went to with my daughter passed by with her mostly watching the crowd, not being able to reason with the chanting and shouting people were doing, and totally oblivious to the fact that there was a football match being played in front of her.

After eighty nine minutes or so, Johnston scored a blinder from the edge of the box to give us a 2-1 victory putting us back in the hunt and continuing a mini revival of victory after victory. *'Magic Johnston'* was thus born.

It was from this point that I suddenly realised we had a winger with class and skill not seen since probably the days of Leighton James in the early 80's. Allan Johnston was young and fresh compared to Leighton James who was in the latter years of his career when he joined Sunderland. People were now talking about *'Magic'* Johnston rather than Allan Johnston and so I thought why not create a tribute web site and try to get some feedback from the player in question. I felt like I was turning into a web design guru, so I knocked together the *Allan Johnston Magic Web Site* within a few bored hours at work shortly after the Portsmouth game. The thing was my job in the Marketing Department then, was boring. There was nothing special to do. The company wasn't being marketed in any way, shape, or form, you know the way a Marketing Department is supposed to. In fact there was more marketing going on in South Shields than there was in this company, so what else was I to do? I simply kept myself busy and made it look like I was working on this and that and so justifying my job - there was a threat of job cuts in the air as orders were dropping like flies.

I added a guest book to *'Magic's'* site, which within hours was full of comments from people saying how wonderful the guy was and referring to the recent Portsmouth goal, which to some was *'better than sex!'* I felt good; if people were using it then I had surely achieved a goal by providing a place previously missing on the Internet.

There was already a tribute web site to Lee Clark and an Alex Rae web site run by some closet Spurs supporter who really got on my nerves at times because *"he knew a footballer,"* and thought that made him better than any of us Dragon Slayers. He was now suddenly a SAFC supporter. Well fuck you mate, 'cos Colin Pascoe was at my wedding and Rueben Agboola once barbecued me a mushroom! He's probably a Wolves supporter now whilst still in the closet about Spurs. I decided to write a letter to SAFC for the attention of Allan *'Magic'* Johnston to see if I could get some content from him and to let him know there was a site in honour of him.

Meanwhile, as the end of the season got closer and closer, one of the three teams pushing for the automatic promotion places was bound to slip up. So out of Nottingham Forest, Sunderland, and Middlesbrough, guess who it was that did just that? Yep, Sunderland.

A night match at home to Queens Park Rangers in torrential rain, in which I got piss soaking wet walking over the town bridge, saw us lead 2-0 with twenty minutes to go. Final score 2-2.

A few days later, an eventful match at West Bromwich Albion saw us lead 3-2 into injury time, even though we were down to ten men following Mickey Gray's sending off for a bust up with then Albion winger Kevin Kilbane. Final score 3-3.

Four valuable points lost at the death!

It wasn't over though. It was still mathematically possible for us to go up automatic even though there were only three games to go.

Myself and the lads who went to Wimbledon at the end of last season decide we should attempt to get tickets for the last game this season, at Swindon.

If we won all three games we would go up, no matter what the Smoggies did. With the final game being on a Sunday, and due to the distance from Sunderland to Swindon, we decide that we should make a weekend of it, travelling down on the Saturday and staying overnight. Finding a guesthouse was the easy part. The difficult bit was getting tickets.

We needed four tickets, but found out to our horror that the allocation SAFC had been given was already taken. We'll have to get tickets in the Swindon end we decide; besides there are bound to be a few more Sunderland supporters doing the same.

So I phone up Swindon Town FC and enquire about tickets. Unfortunately my accent gives the game away and I'm informed that they do not sell home supporter tickets to people from Sunderland, and that the away ticket allocation has sold out.

Shite! Foiled at the first attempt. Not to be outdone, we then get the Chairman's secretary with her posh voice to phone up Swindon's ticket office. Foiled again, they will post out, but not to a North East address, just locally.

Then one of my mates remembers he went to college with a Lad from Swindon. So he finds his number and calls him up for the first time in about seven years. Never mind how am I and how are you we tell him, just get the fucking tickets. His ex-college pal agrees and sorts them out - just like that, using his local address to fool the Swindon ticket office. All we need to do is call him when we arrive in Swindon and he'll drop them off. Excellent, and typical of Sunderland supporters, no matter how impossible it looks, we always find a way to get what we want - more or less!

I advertise the fact that the FTM Executive Club will be on a tour of Swindon - it sounded like a mass convergence of some secret society! It was secret all right, just me, though it sounded impressive on the Internet. *'Cable Guy'* emails and invites me to stay in Southampton as it's only about an hour's drive from Swindon. He sends hotel details, pub and restaurant guides all within walking distance of his house. Well, thanks but no thanks, we'll be staying in Swindon I inform him. Phew, I panicked; I mean I might have gone to stay with him only to find he's some sort of psycho or misfit. Then again he might turn out to be a canny bloke, just really friendly, unlike me the unsociable, unfriendly, miserable git. He asks if there are any spare tickets and I say no but next time I'll try to get him some. I had no idea why I said that nor what it really meant, maybe it was my way of trying to lessen his despair at me not staying with him.

The week leading up to the final home game of the season against Stoke City the phone rings. I'm in the bath so the wife answers. All of a sudden she's screaming at me to, "get out of the sodding bath!"

I leg it through to the phone in my towel and she's standing with the phone in one hand and a bloody great smirk on her face.

"It's Allan Johnston for you!" she says, still grinning like a nutter. "Piss off!" I reply in disbelief, snatching the phone from her.

"Hello" I say. "Hello," replies this Scottish voice, "It's Allan Johnston here."

If I'd been wearing pants I'd have shit them!

A Sunderland player is ringing me!

Me!

"I got your letter," he says, and continues saying something I cannot remember, not because of a poor memory, though I do have a poor memory at times, but probably because I felt so nervous, like a silly lost girly fan of some teeny bopper pop group meeting their idol.

He continues talking but I'm not listening. I'm in awe of the fact that here is a footballer you really admire taking the time to phone you up for a chat!

He then says he'll donate one of his Scotland international jerseys to give away as a competition prize on the web site.

I'm flattered by his gesture but cannot help but say that I'd be inclined to keep it myself. I'm sorry but this was my way of getting some reward for the efforts I've been making in running my sites.

He agrees, saying it would be his way of saying thanks for doing the tribute site for him and we subsequently arrange to meet after the last home game of the season against Stoke City.

I come off the phone and feel proud as punch. Fuck me, a professional footballer has just phoned and spoke to me. I tell my mates and we all gather around the player's entrance after the Stoke match like a bunch of groupies.

Out he comes, and I have to say what a pleasant, polite, and quietly spoken chap he was too. You know how some footballers - no names mentioned - come across as being right arseholes with their attitude, looking down on you as if you're not worth the effort, well *'Magic'* was certainly the opposite of that.

He poses for photos with us, signs autographs for my mates, their kids, and me then he gives me his shirt, signed on the sleeve.

We all say our goodbyes then ask him to remember that a bunch of us were off to Swindon, so at the end of the game when the players go over to clap the Sunderland fans to remember to clap us in the Swindon end.

"You'll get your heads kicked in sitting with them!" he jests. I laugh - a false laugh - as I picture myself surrounded by shaven-headed thugs wearing white-shirts, braces holding up their knee length jeans and Doctor Marten boots with which they would do the kicking. They're surrounding me and asking in their cider-drinking accent if I like hospital food.

A shiver runs down my spine as I shake my head and return to normality, then off home as quickly as possible with my prized possession. Next day after a visit to Ikea for a decent frame, it's hung up in the dining room pride of place much to the dismay of the wife - 'cos it didn't match the colour scheme!

Two games to go and six points out of six is the requirement. The live match on Sky TV against Ipswich was vital. As we lost 2-0, automatic promotion was over. I even threw my stripes at the TV in a fit of rage!

I mean we could still do it at Swindon but now had to rely on the Smoggies slipping up. It sort of spoilt the planned celebration weekend we had in mind. As usual with supporting Sunderland AFC it was going to go down to the last game of the season!

IX

It's the Swindon weekend and the first time I've travelled overnight to watch the Lads. Hopefully it'll turn out to be an enjoyable journey that would result in Sunderland gaining promotion.

Of course it's out of our hands because we're third in the league behind the Smoggies, but if we win, and they don't, we'll be promoted back into the Premiership at their expense.

This time last year four of us had travelled to Wimbledon for the last match. This year we were three 'cos the daft twat who had wished the Coventry fans good luck was not invited to come with us. We banned him because it was his fault that Wimbledon beat us. He was a jinx, simple as that! Call us paranoid if you like, or maybe just superstitious.

I'll admit to being superstitious, for example I must wear my colours to all games I attend, but never the away strip, only my red and white stripes. I guess that's not too bad a superstition to have really. I mean I know one Lad, who never wears colours, but must wear his red and white pinstriped boxer shorts when he goes to a game. I've no idea how old they must be, but the one occasion he did show me them - and I stepped back at the time - easy, easy, no funny ideas now - they were quite worn out. I assume he does wash them though!

I try not to wash my top until either it's too smelly, or too dirty 'cos I've split beer on it, or we lose a game.

There's also this supporter I heard about who loves eating chicken balti pies, especially the ones inside the Stadium of Light, you could even say he's addicted to them. Anyway every time there's a crunch match and he eats one, the team loses. So he often finds himself with the dilemma of really wanting a pie but fears eating one will mean the team will lose that particular important game, but he cannot resist due to his addiction.

There's a lot more people I know with strange superstitious habits. I dare say everyone has one even if they don't realise it.

About half way down to Swindon we stop near Stoke just off the M6, for a bite to eat and some refreshments. We get talking to a Stoke City supporter in this quaint little pub - better than the motorway services and a damned site cheaper. Stoke were apparently playing Manchester City the next day and defeat for City meant relegation into Division Two. We've all been there and know what that feels like!

I think Stoke were also on the verge of going down too or had we already sent them down the week before when we beat them 3-0 at the Stadium of Light? I don't remember exactly, but anyway, we wished him luck as we set off to complete our journey.

You see you can wish football fans luck when there is no direct influence on your game or your team, it doesn't mean I'm two faced now does it?

Arriving in Swindon late afternoon we slowly found our way to our digs for the night. After unpacking, showering and dressing to go out for some food and beer, we wait around for about an hour until the ex-college pal of one of my mates turns up with the tickets for the game.

It would have been fun if he hadn't turned up with them. What a wasted journey that would have been. We'd have been hanging around outside the ground wandering up to all and sundry saying, "Got any spare tickets for sale mate?" - you know the way some homeless person you always see asking for any spare change you might have. Well they annoy me, I mean don't get me wrong here, I'm not getting all high and mighty taking the moral high ground in terms of the homeless issue we have in our country. I'm merely making a comparison that's all.

So there we were four dodgy looking blokes with *'foreign'* accents *'dealing'* on the street as shifty looking envelopes exchanged hands. With that bit of business out of the way it was off out to the nearest curry house.

After eating we decided to walk into the City Centre to see if we could spot any other Sunderland supporters. At first we felt we were the only ones there. It was quiet and calm. However, turning a corner we were met by the wonderful site of a pub bouncing to the chant of *"Cheer-up Peter Reid"* and full of red and white football strips. Suffice to say we stayed there until closing time.

Coming out of the pub was funny though as we found ourselves in what looked like a war zone. Sunderland fans don't cause bother but for some reason as we all headed back to our overnight accommodation, we had to run the gauntlet of about twenty police vans and about two hundred police officers in full riot gear with a dozen or more Alsatian dogs wanting to rip us to shreds.

Not one Sunderland fan caused any bother so why the police were there in such huge numbers is beyond me - I guess they cared about us or thought we were all Newcastle United supporters. Then again word might have spread about my advertising on the Internet about a secret society known as the FTM Executive Club being present. Well, here I am, Coppers! The FTM Executive Club in all its *'single'* glory! Come and get me!

Next morning after a lovely full English breakfast, we start a brisk walk towards Swindon Town's ground, stopping off on the way outside this pub, which wasn't open yet but was surrounded by thirsty hoards of the red and white cause. The pub opened within the next half hour and, it was inside for more alcohol leading up to kick-off time.

I didn't actually drink too much in there, too much the night before you see, so I didn't feel exactly one hundred percent if you know what I mean. The atmosphere in the pub was electric, as you'd expect, everyone thought we could beat Swindon and that lady luck would stay with us, and Boro would slip up.

One of my mates has this superstition that if he and his missus has sex the night before an important game then Sunderland will lose. He was therefore full of confidence telling us about this superstition that he believed we should all adopt in future, so as to give added strength to the players! Work that one out if you can!

It was now time for the game so off we set.

As we approached the ground we witness for the first time the infamous Swindon Magic Roundabout. At the time it was named after Allan Johnston as far as I was concerned due to his magic ability to *'run rings around the opposition,'* so I had to take a photo of it for Magic's web site. Now if you have ever had the pleasure or have been unfortunate enough to visit Swindon you must have had to endure the Magic Roundabout.

According to the locals until September 1972, there was only one Magic Roundabout and that was the children's television program featuring Dougal the dog, a hippie rabbit called Dylan and the spring-loaded Zebedee amongst others. Apparently before the building of this road layout, the area had been a motorist's nightmare failing to handle the volume of traffic, which converged on it from five directions. Then again it still is a motorist's nightmare from all accounts.

The new roundabout simply combined two roundabouts in one - the first a conventional clockwise variety, and the second, which revolved inside the first, would send traffic anti-clockwise. Does this make sense? I don't know who exactly invented this road layout but they were obviously pissed when they drew it up.

Imagine if you can a roundabout surrounded on the outside by something like another five mini roundabouts in the shape of a 50p piece. There you have Swindon's Magic Roundabout (or apparently a multi-mini roundabout as it is officially known) a masterpiece of road engineering or just a joke?

It was interesting watching all these cars navigate around such an over complicated road system. Surely one big roundabout would have done, or just multiple sets of traffic lights to annoy the hell out of you like we have in Sunderland would be better. You have to see it yourself to believe it, it is quite a sight - in fact an eighth wonder of the world maybe!

Crossing it on foot was fun too, the road is quite wide and you've now got a few thousand Mackems, most of them drunk, attempting to cross this roundabout system like kids lost in a maze - you know - totally bewildered as how to get from 'A' to 'B' without bouncing off the bonnet of an oncoming car!

You had to cross it because on the other side stood the County Ground - home of Swindon Town FC. We got across without incident and there stood the ground before us, or four cow sheds, all very antiquated, very small - in fact my garden shed is bigger than this, it has a window and a door!

We were all wearing colours, but we were sitting in the main stand - which would be full of Swindon fans. We therefore hid our colours by wearing jumpers and sweatshirts and jackets so we could get into the ground unnoticed.

We were walking but not talking - our accents would give us away - and none of us could do the straw chewing, cider drinking drawl of the local countryside farmer accent.

It's weird when I look back because it was fuss over nothing, but I felt like an enemy solider undercover brushing past Swindon fans and dodging eye contact with the police just to get past the first hurdle, which was handing over my ticket and getting through the turnstiles.

I'm now some secret agent in World War II, having successfully infiltrated myself behind enemy lines, I'm close to the point of handing over secret documents that will help the Allies defeat Hitler's armies!

I sneeze, people look at me - was my sneeze a Northern sneeze or a countryside *'cider'* sneeze - can they tell the difference? I take a tissue out of my pocket, part of my colours are exposed for a moment.

Did those German sentries notice?

No, I walk on by; they salute (I'm dressed as an officer you know, full uniform, iron cross, jack boots, monocle - the works). I salute back and carry on with the task in hand.

We arrived at our gate and waited in a small queue moving forward towards the point of no return.

Would I make it?

Would I slip up at the end by opening my mouth and speaking in my strong Mackem accent?

Would I even help end the war?

The ticket is handed over, ripped, stub returned, turnstile unlocks, and I'm in.

We've all safely made it inside the main stand, which resembles the old Main Stand at Roker Park, so it's upstairs first to find our seats.

We sit down, there's only a few hundred in the ground, the ends behind both goals slowly filling up with SAFC supporters.

A few dodgy looking straw chewing characters sit in the row in front of us. We wait a while chatting - our accent becoming apparent to the locals sitting near us. A bunch of school kids take to their seats about five rows behind us.

The place if filling up nicely, both ends behind the goals now swarming in a sea of red and white. Sunderland songs start getting louder.

Right then lads, off with the jackets and off with the jumpers and sweatshirts. Why not show off our colours, it is after all a warm day so it was getting uncomfortable sitting there all hot and bothered.

A few finger pointing and one or two gasps take place as we stand there proudly in our colours, then we spot a few more Mackem's in the same stand as us. Well we're not alone. The police and stewards notice us but show no concern towards us.

The game then starts. I guess it was about ten minutes into the first half when Kevin Phillips scored a spectacular volley from the edge of the box. Goal. We jump up and to our amazement about three quarters of the main stand we're sitting in jumps up.

Jesus!

Both ends behind the goals are going mental. Three quarters of the stand we are in is going mental and half of the stand opposite us is also going mental.

Fuck me, there's more Sunderland fans here than Swindon fans. We have completely invaded this town and taken over. The allies have indeed won the war.

What was all that fuss about? Why panic about getting into the ground acting all suspicious and hiding my colours under my coat?

The number of fans here astounded me. I mean it must have been a huge embarrassment to be a Swindon Town fan that day. Can you imagine going to the Stadium of Light to find that thirty-five out of the forty thousand there are visiting supporters? It's totally dominating, intimidating, and there is nothing you can do about it.

If I remember rightly we then went 2-0 up.

At half time we were in the Premiership as news from the Riverside came in that the Boro game was goalless. That put us second at that point and automatically promoted. They would have to take part in the lottery that is the play-offs and not us.

An announcement came over the tannoy that the Swindon players would do a lap of honour after the final whistle if the Town fans stayed in their seats to clap their team, and for the team to show their gratitude to their meagre support.

The second half started and the noise generated by all of us Sunderland fans ceased. Boro had scored, and not only had they scored pretty quickly into the second half from what I can gather, but they scored twice. You can imagine Bryan Robson in his dull voice telling the Smoggy players that those Mackem bastards are 2-0 up and to "get out there and finish the job." You could see disappointment in our faces. We were winning this game but it meant fuck all. We were heading towards the lottery now. The ends behind both goals fell silent.

The game suddenly turned into a midfield passing game between the Sunderland players. The Swindon team couldn't get the ball and when they did it never lasted very long. They did pull one back very late on and a small cry of goal celebrations went out from the minority of home fans watching the game. They can score another two for all I care now, as it makes no difference to our final league standing. You couldn't see Boro losing.

This deafening silence by the Sunderland faithful obviously affected the team. I guess they must have known it was all over and automatic promotion was not to be.

Boro went on to score four goals I think, and as news of each one came through, these school kids behind us started chanting "Boro, Boro, Boro." God that was annoying, I mean they're only kids but you want to turn around and shout, "shut the fuck up you little brats".

The game slowed to a snail's pace and I wanted to go home now. Weekend spoiled. "Boro, Boro, Boro," the children kept singing. I'm gritting my teeth yet I'm saying in my head over and over again, "Fucking hell man you fucking little fucking bastards".

Full time does eventually arrive and that's it, all over. But it's not all over because we do get another bite of the cherry. It's play-off time. We know we're third, but who will end up sixth. Looks like Birmingham we believe at that time. Well we are a good team now and shouldn't fear anyone. The play-offs start with the two-legged semi finals and as far as I can remember supporting the Lads, Sunderland had never lost a semi-final (Stamford Bridge 1985, Newcastle 1990, Hillsborough 1992), so Wembley bound it would surely be!

Now as for the Swindon Town players doing a lap of honour, well that never happened. You're talking about a football ground three quarters of which contain the away team supporters who on full time invade the pitch.

So we join in.

Everyone is chanting and you sort of feel cheered up. "We want Reidy! We want Reidy. We want Reidy!" is being bellowed out by everyone and lo and behold he appears in the directors box holding a microphone and makes a speech which I couldn't hear as it came over all Charlie Brown school teacher like "whah, whah, whah, whah".

I can imagine the Swindon officials thinking, "Fucking Mackem bastards spoiled our planned lap of honour!" whilst at the same time counting the cash on what was probably record gate receipts.

The police did not intervene as maybe they had realised we were from Sunderland and not Newcastle, and the pitch invasion was not meant as an act of violence. Slowly but surely everyone made their way out of the ground and it was a slow walk back to the car and the long journey back up the M6.

I pictured the Swindon players locked inside their changing room shitting themselves until we've all left, then they would embark on their lap of honour, but the ground is empty. The problem is they don't realise this probably because it's what they've been used to all season!

Outside the ground, we had to re-negotiate the Magic Roundabout again, and I decide to give my wife a call though I got a mouthful not having bothered to call her until now! I forgot - honest I did!

Eventually back in the car we find out we're playing Sheffield United, first leg at Bramall Lane. *"Do we go?"* is the topic of conversation.

Well this time I find myself in the back of the car on a long journey home from watching the Lads not as depressed as I was twelve months earlier.

I've got lots of digital photos of the weekend to put on the web site and a lot of comments to make about the game and the events as they unfolded.

Likewise the season was not over. In a way it had just begun with four teams about to do battle for the honour of playing in the Premiership.

Sunderland against Ipswich at Wembley was to be the bookies favourites. I was worried, failing to beat Ipswich a few weeks ago cost us the chance of automatic promotion, or was it when Kevin Phillips missed a penalty resulting in a 0-0 draw at home against Swindon earlier in the season? Oh how those two points would have come in handy today!

We attempt to take a break at some services on the M6 near to where we'd stopped on the way down. Manchester City had been relegated at Stoke and their fans had completely destroyed the services. It was a sad sight, I mean we've all been there and suffered relegation to the lower divisions, but we've always held our heads up high and not caused damage, like these City fans had. "Just like the Mags," we said, looking back at the time they smashed up the Bigg Market and its poor defenceless telephone boxes because they had failed to win the Premiership. Anyway I was rather desperate for a piss but we were not allowed to stop, so had to drive another thirty odd miles to the next services. It took about twenty minutes to reach the next set of services but the pain from wanting this piss made it last a lifetime. I was in absolute agony, and the stretch of road between the service stations had no turnoffs, nor did it present any opportunity to stop the car on the central reservation for urinary relief. At this point I became an expert at the Lotus position. You could say I turned leg crossing into an art form. How many different ways can you cross your legs? Just then as if by some cruel quirk of nature, the heavens opened and it started to bloody rain. Each raindrop that hit the window was like a hot needle being stabbed into my bladder as I frantically tried not to think of anything liquid related. "Fancy a beer mate?" asked one of the lads. "Don't be fucking stupid," I reply "I want nowt from you unless you have a spare pair of trousers with you," you see, at this point I had considered just pissing myself as the pain was now unbearable and I was sure my dick wouldn't fit in the top of an empty beer bottle.

"Thank fuck!" I remember shouting as we finally pulled into the services. I don't think the car had even stopped properly before I jumped out and hurried as fast as my crossed legs would carry me to the bogs. On reaching the urinal I couldn't open my fucking zip then when I did I couldn't find the fucking thing, it had shrivelled up so small that tweezers would have been handy. So there I am, dick in hand, waiting…. and waiting…and waiting…and…. nowt! I'd waited that fucking long to go that I think the piss had been absorbed back into my body. "Shit, isn't that toxic or something," I'm thinking, when suddenly… Niagara fucking beautiful fucking Falls! I swear that to this day I have the world's weakest bladder because of that!

It was the early hours before I finally got home. I went straight to bed but couldn't sleep.

My head was thumping, full of noise, but there was no noise if you know what I mean. I could hear noise even though it was silent – it was a deafening silence that kept me awake as I reflect on a quite amazing season, though it wasn't over yet!

X

I frantically spend the next day formatting over thirty or so digital photos I'd taken of the weekend's trip, and get them onto the web site as soon as possible. Following the success of the Nottingham Forest images I put online, people would be expecting more of the same, or so I thought.

The Internet was now a hive of activity with people both disappointed following our failure to win automatic promotion, yet at the same time excited about the play-offs. With our record over the season we were surely the stronger team and therefore we'd not only be off to Wembley, but we would win promotion through the back door. First though there was the minor task of defeating Sheffield United in the semis.

Now, up until that point, I had never missed a semi-final in my time supporting Sunderland AFC, having been to both legs of the Milk Cup semi-finals against Chelsea in 1985, the 1990 play-off semi-finals against the Mags and the FA Cup semi final in 1992 against Norwich. The '85 semis were an event in themselves. Having taken a 2-0 lead at home from two Colin West penalties I made my way down to Stamford Bridge with the official travel club, after about three postponements following bad weather, and under the threat of all out war!

If you remember the first leg ended with the Chelsea *'fans'* ripping up half the seats in the Main Stand Roker Wing only to throw them at their own supporters! The media picked up on this and so for the return leg, Chelsea chairman Ken Bates banned all television cameras from being present.

We went 2-1 up early in the second half, which prompted all hell to break loose as the Chelsea *'fans'* rioted. I always remember this fat bloke - a Chelsea supporter - running around on the pitch attempting to twat Clive *'Flash'* Walker, our then star winger, who was also an ex-Chelsea player. There were about a dozen or so police on the pitch attempting to catch this bloke who shouldn't have been difficult due to his size and lack of speed, yet somehow they couldn't. Amongst all of this commotion, the players appeared to stop playing to watch what was happening, while at the same time dodging another copper galloping around the pitch on a horse to get the other Chelsea *'fans'* back into the stands. I swear what happened next is true and it's one of those stories I always bore people with because I've been telling it for years. In fact it's one of those stories you tell your grandchildren if you know what I mean.

You had the majority of players, including the referee, in the Sunderland half, while in the Chelsea half, you had Clive Walker avoiding a fat Chelsea fan trying to twat him one, who is avoiding a half dozen or so coppers, the Chelsea goalkeeper, and Colin West. The referee had not stopped the game while all this was going on even though the players had sort of stopped playing. However someone decided to pass the ball to *'Flash'* who then belted off down the wing, crossing the ball towards Colin West. As the ball came over into the six yard area a copper appeared from nowhere and flicked the ball onto West who headed it into the net to score putting us 3-1 up and on our way to Wembley! It was an amazing sequence of events. I mean can you imagine a copper with his *'tit'* helmet still on flicking it onto Colin West to score! Bloody marvellous!

We, the Sunderland fans, were kept inside the ground for almost an hour afterwards before being escorted back to our coaches, many of which had been smashed up. Unfortunately, there was no other alternative transport available which meant those supporters who had travelled down on these coaches, had to travel back up in them even though the windows were smashed! I was worried as I looked for the coach I'd travelled down on because at that time, I'd just bought myself a sheepskin coat (they were fashionable back then, as was my pink jumper and mullet hair style), but I hadn't actually paid for it. I was worried the coach I had travelled down in would be smashed up, my sheepskin will have been nicked, and I'll be a few hundred quid out of pocket, whilst at the same time bloody freezing on the way home. But as luck would have it the coach was undamaged so at least I was warm on the way home, unlike some other poor buggers. I was still a few hundred quid out of pocket though as I still had to pay for the coat!

Anyway that game made you wonder what prior knowledge Ken Bates must have had, in order to ban the television cameras from the ground so the scenes of violence couldn't be shown!

Fast forwarding in time to these semi-finals, and for some reason I just did not fancy going to Bramall Lane to watch the first leg against Sheffield United. I really cannot recall the reason why I chose not to, but I didn't. The match wasn't even on television to watch either, so it meant I had to huddle around the radio to see what advantage we'd take into the second leg. We lost 2-1, and so that meant we had to score two goals more than Sheffield if we were to reach the Wembley final.

The game that night was buzzing, and extremely atmospheric due to an unearthly fog that descended around the Stadium of Light. It turned out however to be a very memorable 2-0 victory, 3-2 to Sunderland on aggregate, and in many parts thanks to keeper Lionel Perez who pulled off a late double point blank save similar to Jimmy Montgomery in the '73 Cup Final against Leeds. Perez was not the best of keepers, a typical vampire in a way - you know the type - scared of crosses - but he'll always be remembered for this one outstanding moment. After the final whistle, a lap of honour, and scenes of jubilation, my mates and me formulated a plan of action to get tickets for the final.

The next day at work this plan of action was finalised. We decided we would start queuing up for tickets from around 4.00 am onwards, taking turns to stand for one hour. It meant we had to draw straws to decide who would stand first, and then hand over to the next person and so on until the ticket office opened. I got 7.00 am to 8.00 am, but hung around as it was just too exciting.

We'd studied the Wembley plan and went for medium-priced tickets - we wanted seats and not those benches that occupied the first dozen or so rows that were so low to the ground you'd find you were squatting rather than sitting. We got a row of *'proper'* seats, split via an aisle, but that didn't matter. What mattered was that we were off to Wembley again, this time to face Charlton who had surprisingly put out Ipswich. We felt so confident Sunderland would do it though. The amount of goals the likes of Kevin Phillips had been scoring meant we would surely be in the Premiership at the start of the next season.

With the tickets sorted, the next task was how to get there.

A friend of my brother-in-law had a coach we could use with a driver, so I phoned him but he wanted over three hundred quid. Fuck that, so we sweet-talked the Chairman's secretary who organised a hire coach - a sixteen seater, insured for five named drivers for forty quid. Now that was more like it - a bargain! There were twelve of us so we put out the word that there were four spare seats. They were snapped up, even though two people at that time had no tickets, but as long as they paid their share of the coach and petrol no-one was complaining.

Meanwhile on the Internet, the buzz that was flying around prior to the semi-finals was now reaching fever pitch, and I quickly jumped onto this by creating a special Wembley guest book. The amount of messages that appeared on there building up to the match itself was incredible. People were saying how easy the game would be, supporters of other teams were signing it wishing us good luck, Charlton fans signed it with *"may the best team win,"* but most of all the begging messages that appeared dominated. When I say begging messages I mean people wanting tickets, unable to get hold of them.

It became *touts are us* online, not that I had any profit from any illegal transactions that were taking place mind you. People from all over though were attempting to get a ticket. I had struck up a canny relationship with this guy from Pennywell who was now living in California. He'd emigrated out there having fell in love online - how romantic! He was however a follower of the *'FTM'* religion and related to my way of thinking. Somehow though he managed via email, fax and telephone to get a ticket from the Club with some sort of sob story, which you've got to give him credit for, considering it would turn out to be a trip that would cost him in the region of about two grand. I told him I was going and I'd meet him on the steps of Wembley way. I also arranged similar rendezvous' with other people - some of which had bought my FTM Executive Club T-shirts. I also received an email from *'Cable Guy'* who reminded me that I had said I'd get him tickets if I could, not that I could remember ever agreeing to such a thing, which I did point out, besides SAFC's allocation for the final had sold out. Maybe he was referring to the gesture I made after he asked for Swindon tickets. I knew it'd come back to haunt me one day but not this soon. A day or so later I found out that a batch of two thousand tickets had arrived at the Stadium of Light - unadvertised, which meant I could have got him tickets, but I was lazy and did not. I guess I couldn't chance buying fifty quid tickets for someone I'd never met. To this day I've never told him I could have gotten him tickets, and I don't think he ever went, sorry if you're reading this Neil!

I now had one FTM T-shirt left and I had jokingly offered it to Alex Rae who spent an hour one night on his web site's chat room courtesy of *'Closet Spurs Boy'*. I remember asking him if I gave him the T-shirt, would he wear it under his stripes and that if he scored would he lift his shirt over his head to reveal the T-shirt so that I'd get a shit load of free advertising. He said yeah, he would, it wasn't as if he was going to get selected for the game anyway. However I got another tenner from a young lad who then started complaining about not receiving his T-shirt quickly enough. He sent the cheque one day, expected the T-shirt the next. Then he started whinging by signing the Wembley guest book saying, *"where's my T-shirt, I've been ripped off,"* and so on, over and over again which was annoying as it degraded this popular area at the time. For fuck's sake I've got a full time job, wife, kids, mortgage and so on, give me a chance will you? Next thing, he's designed his own SAFC web site and wants a link from mine and wants it now! The email I receive is followed by another one, then another one, then another one, every five minutes, wanting to know why I haven't linked to his site. Did I say I was ever-online twenty-four hours a day and seven days a week? I decide to look at his site out of curiosity. What a fucking joke! It was one long red page, with fonts the size of the screen, full of meaningless comments. You could say it had the world's longest vertical scroll! Imagine if you can sticking together loads of sheets of A4 paper vertically and writing one letter per page;

WELCOME TO MY SAFC WEBSITE

You have a total of twenty-two letters and four spaces, thus twenty-six sheets of A4 paper and therefore the very, very, long vertical scroll.

Was this kid for real?

Well he was only fifteen and, I guess he was showing enthusiasm, so I set up a link for him. It was his funeral when people looked at it and laughed!

On the Friday night of the play-off finals weekend I decide to do something daft and dye my hair blonde like Lionel Perez for the big day out. I also visit a local sport shop to get some lettering put on the back of my stripes. I go for FTM EXECUTIVE, as it'll be publicity for my *'popular'* web site I thought. Someone else was getting his shirt done with the words PHILLIPS 35 TODAY. Of course it meant if Super Kevin Phillips were to score in the final he'd take his goal tally to thirty-five and break Brian Clough's post war goal scoring record for Sunderland, for a single season, which would be some achievement. At that moment however I couldn't care less who scored as long as we won the game.

I buy some blonde dye but having brown hair it turns an embarrassing ginger colour - not that I've got a problem with people who have ginger hair, well actually I do if you're called David Corner or Ian *'Scarface'* Wallace and other such ex players who were *'worshipped'* due to the curse of the useless red headed footballer to play for Sunderland AFC.

There was also this ginger-headed kid at school who was, to be blunt, a tosser, and for some bizarre reason decided not to like me, resulting in years of abuse. Then there's Chris Evans but then everyone know he's a wanker, and an annoyingly rich one at that who'd probably sue the arse of me for having the audacity to call him a wanker!

There is one other person I can think of, one which unfortunately springs to mind as I write all of this, though I'd be getting a little too personal. Besides that's a chapter in itself - if not a book - and one that has really got nowt to do with football nor the Internet!

Anyway, I have to suffer this weird colour until the next day when it's a dash to the shops to bye some peroxide, which fucking stung like hell, but it worked, though some of the blonde was a bit yellow!

I pack up a sports bag with some spare clothes, food, and a four pack of Lambtons beer, then it's off to bed but I'm not tired. Insomnia starts to set in as I lie wide awake in the darkness thinking about what the next day holds, a quick shag later however I'm sound!

XI

6.00am, May 25th 1998. I'm waiting on Chester Road to be picked up. I'm a designated driver on the mini bus we've hired but not until we reach Ferrybridge services, at which point off come my jeans and on go my black Sunderland shorts. I'm now behind the wheel on the road to victory!

Oh, I suppose I better mention the reaction to my new hair, which had mixed responses from *"it suits you,"* to *"you're mad,"* and *"are you gay?"* One of my obsessed mates starts going on about his no sex before a big game superstition by checking with all the adults on the bus, that nobody shagged their missus the night before. He is content that his superstition is on target. Then he asks me. I hesitate and he goes ballistic, "Oh no man, you didn't, you didn't did you? Oh no!"

"Hey man come on, me shagging the wife won't stop the Lads winning today," I say.

We reach Wembley safely and with plenty of spare time.

Out comes the Lambton's now that my driving duties for the day are done. After the beer runs out, we head down Wembley Way to find an Off-Licence for more cans and wonder where the Charlton fans are? I mean we've been here an hour, the place is swarming with Mackems and only Mackems.

We end up standing on the steps of Wembley Way - me thinking I'll bump into the lad from California and all that. I mean there's fucking thousands of people in red and white on Wembley Way so the chances of spotting anyone is very remote. Maybe someone will relate to the FTM EXECUTIVE on my stripes and tap me on the shoulder to say hello, either that or twat me one!

We spot Eric Gates and Marco Gabiadinni hanging out of a window above the hospitality area. The *"ole"* chants start and so on. Then we spot the legendary Charley Hurley followed by Soccer AM presenter Helen Chamberlain - she's a fit bird in real life like. We shout over to her - "Not going to be depressed today are we?" Her team Torquay had been in the Third Division Play Off Final a few days earlier and had lost. She was then on Soccer AM the next day dressed in black in a state of mourning. What we shouted over was just to cheer her up as she is (or was) a closet Mackem apparently.

Time's up though hanging around loitering and so on, so we head inside the ground. We find our seats, brilliant view Royal Box side about twenty odd rows up facing the corner flag and an aisle seat. There's this little old biddy behind me sitting next to this fat bastard. She comments on my hair by saying something like "Eee, Hello Lionel". I take off my shades, put them in my bum bag that I had on which was keeping my money safe - well I was wearing just my SAFC shorts so had to have somewhere to keep my beer money, then it's back under the concourse for a while – well actually until kick off.

More beer, this time draft, warm, headless pints in plastic containers. After a while and the usual visits to the toilets for a piss, we notice how the floor is becoming rather wet. A stale smell is in the air too, then we realised what it was. There's that many people drinking beer and what have you, and that many queuing for a piss that the bogs are overflowing. So here we were ankle deep in piss, drinking piss and trying to get getting pissed!

As for the game itself, well the first half is a distant memory to me; after all it was 1-0 to them and the same old story. The Sunderland fans had out sung and out numbered the opposition yet we were losing as usual. Likewise I didn't like the fact that we'd obviously lost the toss for wearing our home strip and had to play in the dirty gold coloured top and blue shorts.

Quinny scored the equaliser early into the second half and it was at that point one of the most unbelievable and memorable moments of my life. I cried. I mean here I am thirty plus years of age, crying at a football match. Those who know me know I am a sponge in real life - that is I have the ability to absorb emotions and never show them. At this moment however I bubbled - with joy though. I'd been to Wembley in 1985 for the Milk Cup final and saw Sunderland lose and fail to score. I'd been to the Play Off Finals in 1990 and saw Sunderland lose and fail to score. I'd also been to the F A Cup final in 1992 where guess what, yep Sunderland had lost and failed to score.

Now however my team had scored and it was pure bliss. In fact I get a lump in my throat just thinking about it. It was an emotional occasion for more than just me. Sunderland hadn't scored at Wembley since 1973 and I dare say very few of the Sunderland crowd were around then to witness that goal.

I was only six when Ian Porterfield scored Sunderland's *greatest ever goal* that won us the FA Cup against the then mighty Leeds United. I didn't even see the game, too busy playing outside with my Action Men, riding up and down the street on top of my Scorpion tank. That was a toy; by the way, you didn't think I owned a real one did you? It was a tough piece of shit when I come to think of it, toys that just don't exist anymore.

Today it's all games consoles. Kids simply stay indoors and never get outside to experience true living. I remember once getting this email that was titled *'If you're not smiling by the end of this, then what were you doing when you were young?'*

It sort of listed things from your youth like Cops and Robbers, Cowboys and Indians, playing football with a tin can, Chopper bikes and Top Trumps - remember if you placed these in your bike spokes, you had transformed it into a motorcycle. It also asked *'do you remember when dog shit was white?'* and referred to the likes of nettle stings, earwigs and yellow snow! Then there were real television programmes like The Double Deckers, Vision On, Rhubarb and Custard, Swap Shop, Tiswas, and Dr. Who - that is if you were allowed to stay up to watch Dr. Who 'cos it was scary as shit.

It also reminded me of making very important decisions like who goes first in the game you're playing by ranting *'ip-dip-dog-shit'* and issues of race which at that time meant arguing about who ran the fastest.

The point I guess I'm making is that the vast majority of people celebrating Quinny's goal hadn't witnessed Porterfield's, I'm not suggesting they were all outside playing with Action Men, but that this was the only goal they were witnessing Sunderland score at Wembley full stop.

As the pandemonium of the outrageous celebrations subsided, I realised that I was in row one. My seat was in row twenty something, yet somehow I'd managed to leap my way down the aisle to the front. I legged it back up to my seat to give my mates a hug followed by the old biddy and the fat bastard sitting behind me.

Kevin Phillips then scored his thirty-fifth goal of the season. It broke Brian Clough's post war goal scoring record for a single season. For a split second I thought of that bloke who had gotten PHILLIPS 35 TODAY printed on his top and how ecstatic he would be.

However, and more importantly Sunderland were winning. Fuck me my team, the team I've always supported, my fucking football club is winning at Wembley. I was off down the aisle towards row one again jumping on any fucker who got in my way, back up to hug my mates, the old biddy - I think I kissed her on the cheek and the fat bastard - yes I probably kissed him as well.

Fucking hell, this was heaven, my voice was gone, I'd lost my shades too, but who cares, Sunderland were winning.

Someone got substituted and on came Danny Dichio. A ball came over and all he had to do was a diving header and it would be 3-1. Flamboyant twat went for a scissors kick and put it wide. Bastards. Then Charlton pulled it back to 2-2 Bastards. Both of their goals had come from Clive Mendonca - fucking bastard. Mendonca was a Sunderland lad as well and not very popular all of a sudden.

Quinn scored again, 3-2 to Sunderland. Fucking hell my emotions are getting torn apart here, but down the aisle it was again, back up, hug my mate, the old biddy and the fat bastard.

Five minutes to go and Mendonca gets his hat trick. Bastards. Bastards, bastards and again - bastards. He decides however to celebrate (allegedly) by putting his two fingers up at the Sunderland crowd. What an ignorant fucker. To do that to people from your hometown is a disgrace. Since then he has become a hated figure in certain quarters, has been referred to as a *'gypo'*, and to many is an unwelcome site. Personally, I think he's a tosser. I can respect all footballers regardless of who they play for, well apart from Alan Shearer, but not those who cannot act professional enough. By all means wind up the crowd, but not by putting up your two fingers, especially to those from your home town. That gesture meant he told me and you to fuck off. Can you accept that? I know I cannot.

Then it's full time, 3-3, and so another thirty minutes of football to come. One of my mates little boy is crying his eyes out. I go over to see what's wrong, and he's upset because he wanted Sunderland to win. He was looking forward to us playing Liverpool and Manchester United the next season, as he really wanted to see Michael Owen and David Beckham play amongst other Premiership superstars. I felt really sorry for the little fella. I mean it was an emotional rollercoaster for everyone and something a kid should not have to endure.

"Don't worry," I say, "We'll do it in extra time."

Now extra time is a blur, though I do remember two things from it. First of all we scored to make it 4-3 with about five minutes or so remaining. I was at that point physically and mentally drained and like many around me did not have the energy to celebrate. No bouncing off down the aisle this time. Likewise no kissing the old biddy nor hugging the fat bastard. I did wish at that point that the golden goal rule applied. Then semi-final hero Lionel Perez rose to claim the ball from a corner. Charlton defender Richard Rufus who had never scored for the Addicks jumped to meet the ball. As he had a crucifix in one had and a clove of garlic in the other, the vampire keeper we had in goal flapped. Rufus scored. 4-4. The referee blows for full time. It's a penalty shoot out.

The mate I'm sitting next to along with his two kids gets up and says, "Right I'm off." It was too much for him and he just couldn't bear watching the penalties being taken. So he fucked off leaving his kids behind! They were about fifteen and thirteen so don't go calling social services. I mean it wasn't like they were little kids he'd just abandoned. I don't blame him in a way, he did have a dodgy ticker so it was probably fuck off out of Wembley or it'll be some sort of seizure.

The penalties were taken one after another in the goal in front of the Sunderland supporters. I just stood there silent with my hands behind my head, turning each time to express a sign of relief to the old biddy and fat bastard.

Vampire Perez was fucking hopeless at attempting to save them. Sunderland's penalties were spot on apart from when Chris Makin fluffed his shot but luckily the keeper dived the other way as it trickled into the net. One thing I do remember about the penalty shoot out was the one Kevin Ball took. Now we all know how Bally was such a hard bastard. If there was any pressure on taking a penalty he never showed it. He just marched to the penalty spot like a man possessed, placed the ball and just blasted the fucker as hard as he could straight down the middle. Now that's how to take a penalty. I never rated Bally as a player - well a defender yes but not a midfielder. I'm sorry if this upsets some but it's just how I feel about the bloke. He was however an influence on the pitch which in hindsight was taken for granted. His influential hardness both on and off the pitch would, in time, be sorely missed.

There was also Alex Rae's penalty. I wondered if he would have lifted his shirt to reveal an *FTM Executive Club* T-shirt if I had given the one I had left to him.

Then up stepped Michael Gray, and the rest is history. At the time, I will say I had this gut feeling, the same type of feeling I got when Gareth Southgate took England's penalty against Germany in the Euro '96 semis. I guess what I'm saying is I had an inkling he'd miss.

After he missed I just sank into my seat. I put my hands over my head and sat there staring at the ground looking at my feet.

I heard the Sunderland chants, the *"One Michael Gray"* chant, the *"we love you Sunderland we do"* chant, and other rallying calls the fans belted out to hide their disappointment. I remember people climbing over me to get out as I just sat there not moving. I then saw my lost shades on the floor under the seat in front of me. I mean there I was sitting isolated at Wembley refusing to acknowledge anyone else's existence, lost in my own little world not knowing when to look up or when to move and feeling happy all of a sudden because I'd found the shades I thought I'd lost. Talk about a screwed up head, I mean the shades were insignificant really, I'm heartbroken, mentally shattered, totally and utterly devastated but now I'm happy that I've found my shades! I still don't move though and still sit with my head in my hands. I remember someone tapping me on the shoulder quite angrily saying something along the lines of "Get up man, show your support for the team." Fuck you, you fucking wanker. Who are you to tell me what to do?

The old biddy leans over on her way out and says something like, "Never mind son, I'm sure we'll do it next year, Are you a season ticket holder?" I have no idea why she said that, but I replied yes I was and yes I'd be there next season - so fuck you whoever you were tapping me on the shoulder and telling me to stand up and be proud or whatever. I am proud but I don't have to stand up. If I want to fucking sulk, I'll fucking sulk whether you think I should or should not, I don't give a shit!

I sit there for ages. I'm telling myself I should move but my legs just won't let me. They are glued to the ground. I know I should move because everyone else might be back at the bus waiting to go home. I imagine the television cameras zooming in on my blonde head with some sarcastic comment being made from the pundits or abuse and laughter from happy Geordies watching the game in pubs and clubs back in the North East. Worse still I imagine the Newcastle media taking a photo of this lonely devastated Mackem and printing it on the sports pages as they gloat about our defeat. And yet in some strange way I was hoping they would zoom in on me on television or take my photo for the newspapers, I'll have my fifteen minutes of fame, albeit for the wrong reasons.

Eventually I do decide to stand up and go. At this point, Wembley is almost empty. Well most Charlton fans are still in the ground celebrating while the song *'Tubthumping'* is being repeatedly played in the background, but the Sunderland end resembles a ghost town with litter blowing about and a few tumbleweeds rolling by.

I put on my shades so as not to make eye contact with anyone and walk out, oblivious to anything or anyone. I get back to the minibus where there's plenty of discussion going on, a few tears and one or two drowning their sorrows with alcohol. I couldn't and wouldn't talk to anyone. I think we were probably somewhere near Nottingham before I opened my gob and then it was something like 'bastards'.

"About time you fucking spoke," one of my mates said. "Hey man, it's not our fault you miserable bugger, you can talk to us!" said another. So I take a deep breath and start talking - I can't remember what about though. Thankfully no one pointed their finger at me and said it was my fault for breaking the no sex before an important game superstition.

As it got dark, silence falls, people start to fall asleep, the kids are already sound and I wondered at that time if they realised what today's game would mean in the history of football. There were less than a handful of games played at Wembley that had the *'legendary'* tag applied to it like say the '66 World Cup Final. Today's events would join such ranks, though at the time that was little consolation.

After undressing and climbing into bed in the early hours, I find myself staring in the darkness at the ceiling. As usual I cannot sleep, my eyes are heavy but won't close. I've got a headache once again due to that bloody annoying deafening silence, then my head starts playing *Tubthumping* over and over again.

"I get knocked down, but I get up again, you're never gonna keep me down".

Once again Sunderland had been knocked down but would they get up again after such a traumatic day?

XII

I think it's really difficult to look back at the play-offs and remember it fondly as it was more or less torture. Many people that day will have aged considerably with the stress endured. It's little consolation when analysing the game and realising just how much positive publicity SAFC gained from the event. We became in a way everyone's darling - you know, the neutral's second favourite team.

It was the morning after the *'event'* and it's a quiet household. I'm up early for some reason. The kids are still in bed, so is the wife. I make myself a cup of tea and flick on the television. Fucking hell, they are showing Mickey Gray's penalty. God I could have done without seeing that so soon.

I turn off and sit in silence, thankful that I took the day off work so as not to face the Geordies and whatever shite would be pouring out of their gobs. Then again the main reason for taking the day off was to dye my hair back to brown, so while everyone's in bed I pop out to the local chemist and grab some ordinary brown dye. I get back and my wife, bless her, helps me get rid of the *'peroxide-Perez'* look, and back to the *'me'* look, while being sympathetic to all that had taken place twenty four hours earlier.

I decided not to update the web site, it was just too early to put anything coherent down in writing, in fact it would take me about four or five days before I did, and when I did I simply wrote amongst other things, *"Why me? Why did this have to happen to me? I've done nothing wrong and simply don't deserve such heartache."* I wish I'd kept a backlog of the stuff I had written then, I'd have preferred to publish word for word what I said and I guess the emotions I'm trying to express now would have had more impact, but I never backed anything up, I do now, but not then.

Normally the close season is a barren time without football. I'd have preferred there to be no more, the season had taken its toll on many, myself included. However it was the summer of 1998 and there was more football, the World Cup Finals in France.

From somewhere I found a burst of energy and with the Internet being quiet due to lack of football prior to the World Cup starting, I began looking around for inspiration to re-vamp my site.

First off I took a gamble and went out and bought myself a new computer. Well I didn't actually buy it, I wasn't exactly flush, never have been. I had sold out of the T-shirts I was selling on the site but there was little profit in it really, so it was a buy now pay later computer, or rather buy now, worry about how to pay for it later.

I cleaned up the computer I had got from my brother-in-law and sold it for about one hundred and fifty quid, not bad for zero investment. With a new computer sorted, a new web site was my task and over the next few weeks I designed what I consider one of the best ever home pages for a Sunderland web site. I used the Florida Panthers ice hockey web site for inspiration, using a black panther image to relate to our black cat association, and Florida because I was off on holiday to Orlando in the September - which had worried me as I imagined I would miss home games against the likes of Man. Utd or the Mags, now it was to be something like Bristol City and Oxford so I could bear missing non-entities such as these! It also incorporated imagery of Magic Johnston as I attempted to combine his tribute web site into this new version of my main site.

I also re-launched my FTM Executive Club onto some new free web space I had found. The Internet was now getting cheaper as companies were providing access without having to pay ridiculous membership fees. It still cost to connect but just a local phone call. Daytime surfing was a non-starter - unless I was at work, and so I burned the midnight oil for a while until the new site was ready to go.

Apart from looking different, nothing had changed, except now I had a message board - in fact the same message board I had discovered a few months earlier. I had built up a good email relationship with its Dragon Slayer, a lad from near Manchester, who may not have seen eye to eye with my style of writing about SAFC, but agreed to make his message board mirror the look and feel of my new version, but on one condition. I had to give him my away ticket vouchers which was not a problem for me, I hardly travelled away anymore to watch the lads, home games only, apart from the end of season games of recent years like Wembley, Swindon, Wimbledon, Burnley, Man City to name but a few of the more *'eventful'* ones.

My days of away travel ceased once the bairns were born, you see I found that there were more important things in life than just football. Football has and always will be a part of my life, but it takes second place to other things from time to time, besides I've managed to visit over forty different stadiums in my time which is quite an achievement and one I'm proud of, though one or two of these don't exit anymore like Ayresome Park, Leeds Road and the Baseball Ground (Middlesbrough, Huddersfield and Derby County for those of you with poor memories).

I launch the new web site and receive mixed responses from my audience. Well the vast majority are, to be honest, in awe of my creation, which without sounding pedantic was simply a masterpiece. There were one or two who moaned for some reason, *"not as good at last seasons site!"* or did they simply mean they don't like change, probably falling into the category of those who refused to embrace the move from Roker Park!

The World Cup starts rolling and for once I can sit and watch the games on television, totally unbiased, marvelling at the skilful nations, enjoying the spirit of those nations who were shite, and the surprise package, which in my opinion was Morocco, and a player called Mustapha Hadji. It was in the papers that Reidy had gone over to the World Cup to scout for new talent and I prayed he'd buy someone with the skills of Hadji, especially when it was reported that he had watched the Norway v Morocco game in which the lad played a blinder. In my view we were a strong team capable of going one better than last season but needed strengthening in one of two areas such as defence and midfield.

However, before any new blood arrived, some old blood departed, the major one being Lionel Perez to Newcastle United of all teams. Semi-final hero to final zero and now a Skunk! And I dyed my hair in honour of him?

His replacement though was this Dane called Thomas Sorensen, the new Peter Schmiechel the press were saying, if that's the case then that'll tighten up the back, and the arrival of defender Paul *'pies'* Butler, signalled that Reidy was on the same wavelength as me. Come on Peter I thought, only Hadji is missing.

As the World Cup got into the knock out stages England faced their usual penalty shoot out exit, and it brought back the memories of Wembley once again, though this time it didn't bother me. I guess I was now over the heartache. Now you can tell which players are penalty takers and which ones are shit scared, avoiding eye contact with the manager so that they are not selected to take one. When the Mags David Batty stepped up, you could see his body language mirrored that of Mickey Gray, in other words he did not want to do this and sure enough he missed. England were out!

I can't really remember much else of the summer, the fixtures came out and you couldn't help but look at Charlton's as well as ours. Their first away game was against the Mags that should have been us I thought. We had an opening day fixture at home against QPR - oh the reality of Division One football again.

Prior to the start of the season I received an email from a lad who ran a web site for Watford fans wanting to get an opinion on how I thought Sunderland would do over the coming season and also how Watford would fair. I said we'd walk it and Watford could possibly scrape through via the play-offs. I wish I had followed up such statements with a few quid at the bookies, little did I know these comments would come true.

There was now an air of optimism amongst supporters and people were counting down to the start of the new season. A talented midfielder was still a requirement as far as I was concerned. I hoped that Sunderland would gamble, splash out, and buy big.

I was at work one day and I was thinking about the World Cup that had recently ended, when I suddenly remembered how impressed I was with the Moroccan midfielder Mustapha Hadji. I'd also witnessed on the message board one or two others mentioning this player as well.

I then came up with a cunning plan for a brilliant wind up. It had occurred to me whether or not the likes of Sunderland and other *'official'* media ever read *'piddly'* little web sites like mine. I also wondered if a single person could start a rumour, make that rumour grow until it hits the press, hits the Club and forces them to either deny it or suddenly think about investigating the rumour to the point where if it were a player, and they were impressed with that player, they'd sign him. Are you still with me? I therefore decided to start a rumour that Sunderland were going to sign Mustapha Hadji.

I started by doing some research, hunting around to find out as much as I could about the player, where he played at present, his international record with Morocco and so on.

Then I created an alter ego to use on the message board called *Mohammed El Tumatchi* - what a great made up name, and posted on the message board that Hadji was going to join Sunderland, and his cousin - Tumatchi's cousin - who lived in Casablanca, had a newspaper cutting that confirmed the interest (Mr. Tumatchi was a student in Leeds - well that's how I portrayed him).

A wave of responses followed this posting with people actually believing it. Eventually though I was put on the spot and asked for proof of the newspaper cutting. I therefore set about creating a false email address so I could email people this newspaper cutting rather than post it on the message board. It sort of gave added proof that the Tumatchi character was in fact a real person with a real email address.

I then searched the web for a picture of Hadji. I found one on a Moroccan sports web site. The picture had some French text below it. So I took a snapshot of this page and cropped it down to a reasonable size. Next I deleted some of the French words (God knows what they said but then again I don't speak French so who cares), and replaced them with words like, *"Sunderland", "Peter Reid", "Stadium of Light"*, and so on.

The image was looking good, but my character, Tumatchi had said it was a newspaper article and that his cousin in Casablanca had sent the clipping by fax to him in Leeds. So using some clever image manipulation I turned this coloured image into a photocopy and added some *'noise'* - to make it look dirty.

Next came the best part of all, emailing the file to some fellow Mackems (though they might be annoyed now that I've confessed). Anyway, this emailed image eventually found its way back to me, the real me that is, via my real email address, so pretending to go along with all of this I subsequently placed this newspaper-clipping image onto the news page of my web site. I asked this sales assistant at work who was in fact French to translate this fax I'd received via email just before I put in on my web site and bizarrely, the sentence I'd cropped and changed at random actually made sense, more or less saying that Sunderland were about to sign Moroccan midfielder Mustapha Hadji from Spanish club Deportivo La Coruna.

Within a day the rumour machine had gone out of control. Hits to the site went through the roof. The hits to the message board also went crazy and before long, the wind-up appeared on Ceefax, Teletext and in the Sunderland Echo, it may have even made it onto TV but I'm not aware of this.

Mission accomplished? Maybe, I had proved that many Sunderland supporters like myself wanted a big name signing yet Reidy denied all knowledge of this and laughed it off. The wind-up was over though it maintained some momentum for a few weeks to come, even managing to find its way onto the web site of the Spanish club that Hadji had played for.

You never know, I mean you could start a rumour and watch it grow to a point whereby it reaches the player involved and he looks into this club *"Sunderland"*, sees how passionate the fans are, how great the stadium is, how almost perfect the team is and decide, *"I'd like to play for them"*.

I still have the copy of the Sunderland Echo with the back page headline of *"Reid: No Move For Hadji"* - I hope the Echo doesn't mind me re-printing their comments; "Rumours that Sunderland are poised... to sign Moroccan World Cup star Mustapha Hadji were quashed today. It's news to me" he said. He's not a player we're after." (July 17th1998).

Sunderland fans from across the country rang the Echo yesterday to inquire about the story in a Moroccan newspaper which suggested Peter Reid might be moving for the player.

The tale was also publicised widely on the Internet.

Peter Reid, linked to many players after taking in several World Cup games, today killed speculation.

"It's news to me" he said. "He's not a player we're after."

Internet wind-ups like this have been tried many times since, but the media can only be fooled once and I was that person who fooled them first. People say it's wrong to build up the hopes of others, but that was not the intention. I didn't mean this to cause friction nor make people look like idiots for believing it. It was merely a stab at having some fun with some serious issues tied to it. I mean many still don't find this funny; I still do just as I did back then. If I was the only one who did find it funny then call me Andy Kaufman, maybe I am the *Mackem, man in the moon*.

At the end of the day though I had increased the awareness of my site no ends, I even got a mug shot of myself in the local newspaper one night to further promote the site and my attempts to attract some sponsorship.

I simply had to get serious now. Here I was, Dragon Slayer to an extremely popular *independent* web site attracting thousands of visitors each day and giving the likes of the official SAFC web site a run for its money yet I'm not making a penny out of it. I was still doing all of this out of the passion I had for SAFC, but such was the popularity that you simply cannot ignore looking at ways of trying to make some cash out of it, call it just reward for the efforts I've been making.

Unfortunately when you've got FTM in the title of your web site people back off wanting to advertise or sponsor you, thinking you're a hooligan! I'm not a hooligan, yet I simply couldn't bow down to pressure from anyone and streamline the site to make it more commercially viable. I had to balance up if I wanted to be middle of the road or still harsh with my opinions. I'm stubborn and so stuck to my principles and kept on reporting in the style that had made the site the success it was to begin with. In other words the season would start with me running this *'massive'* web site with no income being made from it, well not yet!

XIII

The 1998/1999 season kicks off with a tight win over QPR at home in front of a sell out crowd. Hooray! However the victory is marred by Lee Clark getting stretchered off with a broken leg or something like that. Boo! Put it this way it was an injury that would keep him out for quite a while. That to me meant we were now missing a key player in the midfield. "Go on Reidy," I started thinking again "Go and buy Hadji, you know all about him now!"

The following Monday at work everyone is told that within the next four weeks around a quarter of the workforce would lose their job. Falling sales meant inevitable redundancies. Well that's just great. I mean deep down I'd known for months that things were not well and for months most of the stuff I'd done at work revolved around my little hobby rather than actual marketing related tasks. I therefore assumed that I'd be one of the *'sacked'* staff. To make matter worse the announcement of who will be made redundant was to take place right in the middle of my holidays. Therefore I'd be swanning around Disney World not knowing if I'd return home to a job and my secure income. As I started preparing for the inevitable, concocting my curriculum vitae, looking in the papers for anything that required few skills, I found to my horror that I had no insurance on the mortgage. Thus if I became a *'Government Artist'* - drawing dole - I'd somehow still have to pay the whopping mortgage every month. Fuck! How was I going to do that? I'll tell you now I had many a sleepless night leading up to the holidays not knowing if I'd have a job or if I'd end up getting repossessed. On top of all that I've just gone and bought a buy now, pay later computer - how was I going to pay for that as well?

The day before my holidays start I go to see the boss and plead with her to tell me if I'll have a job when I come back. As far as I'm concerned the Company knew by then who was going and who was staying. Unfortunately for me the boss simply wouldn't say or rather said she simply did not know. So I asked if they'd send me a letter so at least when I got back after my holidays I'd know straight away if I still had my job.

With that bit of business over I set off home, packed and flew out to the USA. I decided that this cloud hanging over my head would not spoil the holidays and it didn't. It also signalled a well-earned break from the Internet, though I wondered what reaction people would be having now that my site had suddenly ceased to be updated. I hadn't told anyone in cyberspace that the site wouldn't be updated as I was off on holiday. That to me was like shouting *"hey Mr. Burglar I'll be away for the next few weeks, help yourself!"*

As usual when you're on holiday you have to walk around showing off your colours as much as possible. I'd basically ensured that every T-shirt I had with me was SAFC related – am I sad? I even had an argument with this *'Yank'* one day about who Magic Johnston was. You see I was wearing this T-shirt that had Magic Johnston emblazoned all over it and for some reason this native assumed that he was some basketball player, not a soccer player, and that it was spelled Johnson. Sorry it's football not soccer. I really hate that term and it's annoying when you watch television nowadays and see the panellists refer to it as soccer rather than football. Soccer is some stupid American term as far as I'm concerned, a term for them to distinguish between what is real football compared to what they consider to be football - or *'gridiron'* as we call it, which I can only assume is just as annoying to them as soccer is to us.

I can remember the day we visited the Magic Kingdom. Now that is the centrepiece of Disney World and so one has to wear one's red and white stripes when walking around this fine fantasy environment. However you'd be damn lucky to keep your colours on for more than an hour. The humidity in Florida is quite simply unbearable and our football tops are just not designed to allow your body to breath. You end up walking around with the most uncomfortable amount of sweat dripping from your body, while your face burns. But I had to get my photo taken with Mickey Mouse whilst wearing my colours. Don't ask me why, it was just something I had to do. I managed to keep my shirt on until the photo was taken but that was it, too much, no more, I just couldn't stand wearing the thing another second. I'd probably lost about three stone in weight with the sweat. My stripes were hanging down to my knees and the short sleeves looked like baggy long sleeves. In fact I was so skinny after just one hour in that humidity all I needed was buckteeth, a spotty face, and some jam jar glasses and I would be the stereotypical Internet geek.

I therefore buy a cheap white vest and a baseball cap to shield my already lobster face from the blazing Florida sun - oh and some deodorant - I fucking stink like a Skunk with the sweat I'd produced!

A few American style burgers later and I'm back to my normal self, an overweight beer bellied geek!

Later that evening still in Disney World, I take out my stripes and deodorise them so they smell like a Mackem and not a Skunk and put them back on. It's amazing how cool it gets on an evening and how the humidity drops. Everyone is waiting to watch this fireworks display and I end up standing next to a Mag for some bizarre reason, whilst behind me I notice this bloke with webbed hands and gills, in other words a Smoggy.

"Heard the score today?" says the Mag in a friendly tone. "No" I reply abruptly, "Yoos won sivin nowt".

"You what?"

"Sivin nowt."

"Seven nil? Who?"

"Yoos man, agaynst Oxfad."

"Oh, really!" I say. Is this bloke pulling my leg? I mean here's a Geordie being friendly towards a Mackem, or maybe the body odour from my stripes is making him feel at home and he's totally unaware that I'm wearing red and white. Then again he has just told me that the Lads have won seven nil against Oxford United, or is this what happens when you go on holiday, the rivalry factor dissipates and its a case of we're all from the same part of the world and so become patriotic. We're not Mackems and Geordies anymore, we're English - put the kettle on!

Well assuming he is telling the truth, I was now on a mission, one which, should I choose to accept it, is to find an English newspaper the following day. So instead of lazing around the pool having a relaxing day off from the all day theme park sessions, it's off on a twenty mile car journey to this *kwiki-style-mart* where I'm informed they sell the News Of The World.

And sure enough they do, and indeed the lads have won 7-0 - but without Kevin Phillips apparently - now there's a thing!

As the holiday ended, that dark cloud hanging over my job back home resurfaced. I'd managed to put a mental block on it so as not to spoil the holiday, but now it was well and truly on my mind as we flew back home. That was a journey and a half as well. Flying over the Atlantic towards America is basically travelling back in time, you gain at least five hours, so even though you will be jetlagged it doesn't feel so bad, yet flying back towards the UK, you're travelling forward in time, and it really does screw your body up. It's just so uncomfortable flying long haul, even more so when you've got kids to keep entertained, and a drunken Geordie in his black and white top, drunk no doubt due to his fear of flying, incoherently attempting to talk to you, while you are politely trying to ignore the filthy heathen.

We get home early in the morning and basically we all go to bed for a few hours as we are really drained from the flight. The suit cases are just dumped unopened in the dining room but before climbing into bed, I quickly scour the mail to find the letter from the company telling me if I'm still employed or not.

Nothing, the bastards didn't even have the decency to write to me to tell me if I've still got a job. That was great, I'd have to phone later that day which was totally undignified from my point of view, and ask if

I'm still working. I related it to Oliver Twist saying, "Please Sir, can I have some more?" only it'd be, "Please Sir can I come back to work?" What made it worse was I knew my boss wouldn't be there. If she'd kept her job she'd be in the Far East at some exhibition, meaning I didn't have a clue who to call. I decided I really needed to get some sleep so I'd worry about it when I woke up and felt a bit more refreshed.

A few hours later I dialled work, I knew a lot of my friends might have been made redundant. I decided not to call reception but the direct line at my desk. That meant whoever picked it up would be a survivor from the same department I was working in and I guessed if anyone knew if I was still employed it'd be the people I work with, in other words my departmental colleagues.

Sure enough one of them does in fact answer the phone and basically starts spouting off, so and so and has gone, and so has this person, and that person. I attempt to interrupt him but he's not listening to me. If I were in a cartoon I'd be sticking my hand down the phone so it comes out at his end and slaps him one on the face. Finally he says, "Oh, and you need to speak to the Chairman, hang on I'll put you through."

"Hang on a minute!" I say, "The Chairman?" "Yeah," he says. "So is my job safe?" "I've no idea, all I was told was when you phone in you need to speak to the Chairman."

Oh so they were expecting me to phone! "Well," I say, "you better put me through."

God I was shaking at this point. Here I am Homer Simpson about to talk to Mr. Burns high up in his ivory tower.

"Hello my boy, enjoy your holiday?"

"Err yes Sir, Mr. Chairman Sir," I say nervously in a grovelling tone. "Well the good news is you're still working here, when are you back, tomorrow?" "No," I say "not until Monday," - today was Thursday. "Ah right, not to worry, well anyway boy, you're being transferred to IT, you should fit in fine there with your computer skills. See you Monday."

"Oh," I say surprisingly and that was that.

I came off the phone not knowing if I was happy or not. The way I saw it was I'd been dropped or at least my job had, and as someone in IT had taken voluntary redundancy, I'd been shifted into an obvious vacancy.

Well I guess that means I can keep the site going as well and with that I logged onto the Internet to view the backlog of emails I suspected I had.

Sure enough there was a mountain of correspondence to go through, many of which were pleading with me not to close the site. It became apparent that the lack of updates during my holidays had gotten to people in a big way. They had suffered withdrawal symptoms, the same type of symptoms I'd experienced many a time during my online addiction spells, but symptoms I had not endured during my holiday thankfully.

I was being blamed. "Why have you closed the site? How dare you! We rely on your updates," and so on. Hang on a minute, there's a message board people are still using, yet they're moaning about me not updating what I refer to as *'news'*, when it's really just my opinions I'm putting online and mostly bitter and twisted ones at that.

I was really surprised that people had missed these comments I'd been making, so much so I felt the need to apologise whilst pointing out that I wasn't in the habit of letting every Tom, Dick or Harry know when I was going on holiday.

I then realise there is no message board. Where the fuck has it disappeared to? I email the Dragon Slayer who runs this message board, and ask what's up. When I do get a reply he explains that he thought I'd closed down the site and so removed the link. "Well thank you very much," I reply sarcastically, "I was on holiday." Anyway he restores the link and my site starts getting back into gear.

I then read a very interesting email, a proposal from another fellow Dragon Slayer that would change the way SAFC would be reported on the Internet and move me one step closer to my online millions - not!

XIV

My '*new*' masterpiece is less than two months old when I receive an email from a fellow Dragon Slayer, whose impressively titled *If You Hate Newcastle* web site had been giving my FTM Executive Club a run for its money - probably down to me being on holiday and without the *number one* site being updated daily, people turned to the *number two* site for daily updates.

Both of our sites actually shared the same message board, and his email is asking me to close down my site! No way! However, he wants to close down his site as well and close down the message board site, combine our three *talents* into one, creating, and launching a new site for Sunderland fans, the likes of which had never been seen before, with a massive back room staff of feature writers, thousands of pages, and of course including the juicy bits from our current sites.

It was an interesting idea and one, which fitted in with my philosophy of running a site that would generate income. I reckoned this was the next step towards reaching that goal and if it meant sharing the spoils with one or two others then so be it.

We were all of a similar age, having around fifty plus year's experience supporting SAFC. This meant we had a gold mine of information, views and opinions to share with the rest of the Internet community. We decide the best way to achieve this is to meet in person. So prior to the next home game we meet inside this pub in the City Centre, which isn't there anymore - it got closed down in some sort of drugs bust I think. It was a quiet pub, although very dark and very dingy, but ideal to meet and discuss issues in private, especially for three Internet geeks. I'm not saying that we were sat there in a secluded corner wearing anoraks and discussing nerdy things like the size of our hard disks, but we blended in well enough not to be noticed. The only downside to meeting in this pub was the dirty old men who started to frequent the place, smelling of piss, wearing suits that were probably over thirty years old, full of beer stains and God knows what else.

It was when they started serving free buffet food on the bar that the attraction for the dirty gits was too much and they simply took over the pub digging their dirty hands into plates of chips, sarnies, crisps, and anything else put out on the bar top for anyone to sample.

You could be standing there talking to someone and from out of nowhere a hand would appear between the two of you, grab a handful of chips from the bar your leaning on, then disappear just as quickly as it had appeared, leaving behind the aroma of piss, thus forcing you to move away from the bar and stay away only returning when you wanted a re-fill - then it was bottles only. I don't care how well they washed out the pint glasses; I couldn't drink out of something some smelly old git had his lips to.

I guess these dirty gits were simply immune to disease, probably because they were riddled with it themselves, but if you or I dared taste say a chip, you'd end up with food poisoning and within a few hours start getting severe stomach cramps followed by vomiting, diarrhoea, and so on. It wasn't the food that was poisoned mind you; the problem was with the germs these bastards left on everything they touched whilst grabbing handfuls to consume. Then again the chips were swimming around in grease looking very unappetising whilst the sarnies, although cut into nice triangles, were made with what looked like stale bread they were that hard.

Eventually, after a few meetings, and hundreds of emails to one another the three of us come up with *'Project-X'* and a launch date of Christmas 1998. It left us with about three months to complete the new site and close down our current ones. We decided to continue updating our own individual sites until the new one was complete. This way we could *'surprise'* the Internet audience when the time came to reveal *'Project-X'*.

We knew what it would contain in terms of content and what additional people we'd be approaching to ask if they'd like to contribute, but we didn't have a name. Of course I wanted to call it the FTM Executive Club but this was a collaboration of three people, thus it was agreed the name would not reflect anything that resembled our current web site names.

I came up with a handful of possibilities from *These City Lights*, to *A flute for 50p*. I also thought of *The Promised Land* which was SAFC's aim, *the promised land* being the Premiership. Then there was *Wise Men Say*, but of course that may have upset those who ran a paper-based Sunderland fanzine of the same name in the late 80's and our audience may have thought that we were the same people.

I wanted something that could be abbreviated like the *A Love Supreme* fanzine, which was known simply as *ALS*. Then it struck me, *Ready To Go*, we could be known as *'RTG'*. That had to be the name. The players ran out to the song of the same name every home game, it meant if the site became huge, every time the players ran out to this tune people may sub-consciously think of the web site.

Sunderland's goal was to reach the Premiership and so the catch phrase *Sunderland AFC: Ready To Go* said it all from my point of view. After a few rounds of online voting, my fellow Dragon Slayers or web partners agreed. The race was now on to design a site, add sufficient content, and find staff to contribute in time for Christmas.

One of our planned sections was to be totally Mag orientated - a section we'd initially call *McGeordie*. We'd have to find, and persuade a Newcastle United fan to write articles for us, slagging off SAFC and all that is red and white. We knew it would be controversial and would upset Sunderland supporters, but we also knew there'd be a morbid fascination to read what this Mag would be saying about SAFC, thus it would be a popular section.

The Mag we approached to do this for us was running his own successful site albeit for NUFC fans. Initially he was apprehensive about collaborating with a bunch of Mackem's. In fact after an initial email from me to him, he backed off due to my *FTM* related web site title by stating that *FTM* was a phrase he associated with clueless arseholes at best and violent psychopaths at worst. *FTM Executive* to him meant even worse - violent, clueless arseholes in suits - the Fourth Reich!

All of this was a bit rich considering this person would refer to Peter Reid and all Mackems as *Monkeys* or *Simians* and a bunch of *SMBs* - Sad Mackem Bastards - apparently - which is no better or worse than the *FTM* phrase. All very two-faced if you ask me. But his loss, and although our launch date would pass without a Mag writing for us, we'd still have a Mag's section up and running, the initial content was written by me! Yes, I confess that for the remainder of the season this new Ready To Go web site's very own *McGeordie* creation as we called him was yours truly.

Now that was a strange task to have to perform once a month - the idea was to have certain sections updateable on a monthly basis, so when it came round to having to write anti-SAFC stuff from a black and white's point of view, I found it to be an unnerving experience, very schizophrenic, a bit like cross dressing if you like, something you simply wouldn't dream of doing, yet here you were doing it. Don't start getting any funny ideas that I was writing this shit in stockings and suspenders mind you, I'm merely expressing a comparison of how it was that's all.

At that time it was almost impossible to slag off Sunderland due to the incredible season they were having which made the task easier to carry out. I doubt I could have done such a thing a few years earlier or a few years later when we were shite or being relegated again.

Still it's one of those things you have to do if you want to set precedence and have a top class web site read by millions. It's a dirty job, but someone had to do it!

A month or two before *Ready To Go* was unleashed on the unsuspecting Internet audience; a gathering took place. Now this wasn't an arranged fight between a bunch of immortals wielding swords, chopping off each others heads and shouting, "There can be only one," but simply an arranged meeting between a bunch of fellow Sunderland supporters who frequented the World Wide Web and had built up friendly relationships with one another.

I could say we were a wide and varied bunch of nerds meeting up which included the likes of Obi Wan Kenobi, Marty Feldman, Beaker from the Muppets, Vic Reeves, Dick Van Dyke, Skeletor, and Christoper Biggins. But that's probably taking the piss a bit too far and insulting a good bunch of lads. In fact those that met up prior to what was a home game against Barnsley were not your stereotypical Internet geeks but ordinary Sunderland fans that had access to Internet technology be it at home or at work - that's all.

I was invited to go alone which was fine by me, as I wanted to meet up with Neil, the lad from Southampton who I'd referred to as *The Cable Guy* due to my paranoia. Neil had become a good friend as far as I was concerned; he had in a way contributed to the partial success of my old FTM Executive Club and was an ideal feature writer to join 'Project-X'.

Having met up with this varied bunch of fans, a lad who called himself *Cockney Mackem* because he supported Sunderland but was, in fact, a Cockney, *The Thief of Bad Gags* as he liked to be called on the Internet mainly due to the bloody awful jokes he'd post on the message board, and a lad who called himself *El General, Mad Marc, Supreme Leader of the Red and White Army* and believes to this day he was behind the Hadji wind-up. Sorry mate I've already confessed to that one.

Anyway I had to drag Neil out of the pub everyone had met up in and into our dirty dive to meet my new web partners and basically offer him a position as a feature writer, explaining what *Project-X* was, when it would go live, how it would make us rich, and if he'd keep mum about the whole thing until it was launched. Being ex-army he was up to the task swearing not to discuss this new site with anyone, well he said he would but then he'd have to kill them afterwards.

From what I can gather this gathering set a standard and even now many Sunderland away games will attract a gathering of Internet buddies most of which frequent our web site - I have to say 'our' web site rather than mine I guess from this point onwards - its comforting to know that you've achieved something if you bring together a group of strangers who then become friends. Considering these people live across the country and around the globe it's like electronic pen pals, blind dates without the dating if you know what I mean.

XV

As Christmas approached it became apparent that it wasn't a case of if Sunderland were going to be promoted, but when. As I had predicted, Sunderland were walking the league, having sustained only two league defeats to date and would only suffer one more during the rest of the season.

In fact it was to turn out to be one of the sexier seasons you could possibly imagine being a Sunderland fan. Is this what it's like all of the time for the Cockney Manchester United supporters?

I could easily write two or three chapters concentrating solely on Sunderland's record breaking 1998/1999 season, but I don't think there is any need to. Everyone knows how our total points tally set a new record which hasn't been bettered and that we took easy points off every team in the league.

Peter Reid was a saviour, a genius, a masterful tactician, and transfer *'wheeler and dealer'*. Not only were we playing an orgasmic 4-4-2 formation with crosses being whipped in from wingers Magic Johnston and Nicky Summerbee, but we were scoring goals like there was no tomorrow, and not just from *'Super'* Kevin Phillips and Niall *'Disco Pants'* Quinn.

For the latter part of '98 Quinny was out with a bad back and Phillips had been out since I was on holiday having suffered a broken toe in the League Cup. Deputising were back-up strikers, Danny *Disco* or *Donkey* – depending upon which side of the fence you stand - Dichio and Michael *The Shopping Centre* Bridges, who showed that they could fill the boots of our two main strikers quite easily.

What was getting me excited was the fact that by Christmas we were in the semi-finals of the League Cup and that signalled another visit to Wembley. My superstition of never losing a semi-final meant we were dead certs to be heading off to the twin towers again.

However, some clever shit emailed me to say that my comments about Sunderland not losing a semi-final were incorrect and started listing numerous semi-final defeats from the depths of SAFC's history.

I did point out after this snotty email that I was still correct in my assumption as what I said referred to my time supporting Sunderland, therefore since 1982 Sunderland had always reached the final if they made it to the semis.

Up the road at Newcastle, Ruud Gullit had bragged about the Mags' sexy football. To be honest if they were playing sexy football, I'm at a loss to describe how we were playing. Sexy football at that time in the North East of England was summed up in one word - Sunderland.

Just before the last game of the year, we launch Ready To Go, simultaneously closing down our respective sites at the same time late one night.

People would still visit our old sites but we had anticipated this by putting up online *"this store is now closed"* notices, followed by *"you can find our new store at"* and pointed people to our new web address.

Ready To Go was initially living on yet more free web space and under a pretty poor address, one that would be very difficult to remember, but at that time it was still the norm, as no one was offering domain names or web space cheap enough.

Our audience were impressed with the new site, its design, its plethora of information, club history, statistics, Mag baiting and of course the good old reliable message board.

Initially we'd attract just over seven thousand individual visitors in our first month. That alone was a great achievement. My FTM Executive Club was probably getting just under one thousand per month, so seven times that amount for this new combo site was gauged as a sign of success. Then again if that was a success, I'm not sure how to gauge the following month, which saw us attract forty thousand individual visitors, which was an incredible jump. Well, that was it; we had achieved a number one record. The mission wasn't accomplished yet though as there was still no income.

Shortly after our launch, we started to receive some pretty heavy criticism from a few of the remaining Dragon Slayers who were still doing their own SAFC things on the Internet.

One in particular was becoming more than just a scratch, more like a nasty rash. It appeared that this kid, and it was just a kid, some back bedroom fifteen year old, was disgusted that he had not been asked to be part of our collaboration. You cannot be asked to join something if you have nothing of any value to offer now can you?

However, this kid wouldn't let it lie, just like the time he bought my remaining FTM T-shirt and it wasn't delivered yesterday so to speak, he went on and on and on, sending emails, posting abuse on our message board and rambling on his own site. Talk about the dummy being spit out of the pram, this was a mini Keegan losing his rag like the now infamous *'I'd just love it'* television interview. Only I doubt this child had curly hair, actually I doubt if he'd reached the age of puberty by then.

I found it complimentary really, as we had our very own Internet stalker, no matter where you'd be or what you'd do online; up he'd pop, having a pop. Affectionately we christened him *'Kerching'*. I'd be checking my emails and *'Kerching'*, there's a message from him drivelling as usual about something insignificant. I'd look at the messages on the message board and *'Kerching'* there he'd be, moaning, and trying to prise people away from our site and onto his *'effort'*.

I even got to install some real time instant messaging system, which you could say is like a cross between your email, a message board and a chat room. It's a simple system that allows you to talk to someone, well type to someone instantly, receive replies instantly and so on. No sooner had I installed this program and got it up and running, mainly so that I could discuss development issues with my partners, when *'Kerching'*, he'd found me. Go away and shag a bird, lose your virginity please then you might just grow up! The rash was getting worse; I'd find my nickname being used on the message board posting complete garbage and utter drivel that I hadn't written; yet it was signed by me. I was now once again being impersonated online and I was getting annoyed.

I'm all for competitiveness on the Internet, it's healthy and keeps your mind ticking over looking for new ideas and ways to keep your audience entertained when they visit your web site, so much so that they want to come back to your site time and again.

I will admit the conception of Ready To Go killed off all forms of competition from any other remaining Dragon Slayer. In fact from our perspective, the only real competition was the official SAFC web site and our aim was to supersede its monthly audience so that we could proclaim ourselves the number one web site, be it official or independent. That way we might just attract some sponsorship, or someone wanting to take advantage of our massive audience and advertise on our site. It'd be the step towards the elusive online millions I'd dreamt of. I assumed my partners felt the same as me.

I guess in a way the train had left the station and *'Kerching'* had been left standing on the platform and felt left out, not that he was ever in our plans, but for some reason he thought he should have been and thus started a one man verbal war, sorry a one kiddy verbal war against us.

His crowning glory was a newsletter he put together which got too personal for my liking. You know how on the web you have your online nicknames and so on. I mean nobody calls you by your real name, especially your full name, yet this newsletter was an attack on all three of us who ran Ready To Go, commenting that many supporters he knew who were online, felt that the launch of our site in December 1998 killed off all forms of competition between the independent Sunderland AFC web sites.

Yes, well I've already admitted to that.

He also reminded people of the *'Gatherings'* which took place between Sunderland-based fans, and those exiled who were coming up to watch the lads play and that these *'Gatherings'* as he put it, were used as excuses for the three minds behind Ready To Go to come up with ideas for the new site. There was only ever one *'Gathering'* and only ever one person we wanted to meet with to discuss ideas. As far as he was concerned, those who ran the *'smaller'* web sites were understandably annoyed at the fact that three people who were once so friendly, could do this to them. He then stated that the fact was we were never friendly. His line, *'Is it fair? Hell no, it's not fair!'* was a bitter resentment. He even dared to suggest that the three of us should be taken to court for breaking rules of competition. On top of this he then blabbed that I was in the Sunderland Echo advertising my old site.

So?

Your point being please?

His actual comments were a lot stronger than I've mentioned here, and in my opinion personally insulted us all.

The bottom line was that as he bragged about his newsletter being read by a few hundred people, he was inadvertently advertising our site for us, and driving more traffic our way, making us even bigger. Rather than biting back, we just let him rant on as much as he wanted. Our monthly audience figures were on the up and would remain so regardless of how much he slated us. To keep him in line though we deleted his messages from our message board. The message board existed for people to crack on about anything and everything with the main emphasis being football and in particular SAFC. When *'Kerching'* popped up he'd be simply moaning, having another dig at us and trying again to get people to visit his site. It degraded the standards of the message board and presented us with just cause to remove his drivel.

He never gave up though and started frantically communicating with some of the remaining Dragon Slayers, begging them to join him and create a combined web site. Now then, hadn't that already been done? It set a new trend whereby anything Ready To Go would do, our *'spammer'* or *'cyber-stalker'* would copy in one form or another, which was again amusing, yet complimentary that we had set a measure from which everyone would look towards for their own inspirations. However, it also meant that we were coming up with new ideas on how to keep the Internet audience entertained, which were then simply being copied. We'd have to keep on our toes to make sure this didn't get out of hand.

People may think I'm being a little harsh here on what was just an immature kid playing pranks upsetting a group of grown men. We'll if you haven't worked out how much of a bitter and twisted person I am by now; you haven't read the book properly now have you?

The thing is when you are personally attacked and insulted, you fight back, not in a threatening manner, I'm not like that, but you do what you have to do to protect your investment. It is something I have always done since I first started doing my thing on the World Wide Web and this incident would not be the last either.

In time *Kerching* would calm down and stop being a thorn in our side. Much stronger and weirder people would take over that role, though one by one they'd all be a flash in the pan, here today and gone tomorrow.

XVI

February 1999 was to be an eventful month, on the pitch, online, at work, and personally. A poor January saw SAFC dumped out of the FA Cup as usual in the early stages, along with a semi-final first leg defeat in the League Cup, whereby we were taught a lesson in Premiership football by Leicester City. In fact, although SAFC lost only three league games all season, one of these was between the two Cup-tie defeats and so we lost three games in a row that month. I was actually off work sick with the flu but there was no way I was going to miss the semi-final. I had a one hundred percent record to maintain. So I trundled off to the Stadium of Light, coughing and snotting and spitting phlegm to watch the Lads under perform.

We knew we were Premiership bound but that night there was a gulf of class between Leicester City and us. We could turn it around in the second leg, though they'd have to do it without me. I wanted to go, but couldn't as I had a date with a man in rubber gloves! It's not what you think - you see – I had taken the brave decision to have the old 'snip'.

The wife and me had decided that two kids were enough, that she should stop popping pills, and that the time had come to do something permanent. Now the choices were either a), she has the old tubes tied, spends days in hospital, and then remains unable to clean the house, bend down to put the dirty clothes into the washing machine, and can't drive me to the games for weeks on end, or, b), I get the snip. After she'd sent me on a huge guilt trip to the tune of *"you haven't felt pain till you've given birth,"* and *"you want to try passing a bowling ball through a hole the size of a polo mint,"* I agreed to option b). This would prove to everyone that I really was the caring and responsible chap they all thought I was, or so I reckoned.

Anyway I had settled nicely into my new job in IT, being basically a fire fighting technician, fixing software, fixing hardware, removing the scourge of ever increasing email viruses, and keeping the company's web site up to date.

It was now very difficult to find time to work on Ready To Go. I now had a proper job that kept me quite busy. It was a case of in first thing, check my emails, possibly do some updating, then off to fix this and that before having time maybe by lunchtime to log on again to see what's been going on. It was a good job, the addiction I'd had the previous year had gone otherwise I have no idea how I'd do what I was supposed to be getting paid for rather than what I wanted to do.

I had informed my new Boss that I needed time off and explained why. As expected the last day at work before the operation was one long piss take. I arrived to find a large pair of scissors and a watermelon on my desk. Those who sat around me then started blowing up balloons and popping them with whatever sharp instruments they could find. There were even one or two stupid Geordies doing monkey impressions in front of me as if my bollocks were to grow out of proportion. "You'll be like Peytar Reid," they'd say. "Fuck off!" I'd reply!

No matter what they tried I was unaffected. It was nothing to fear. It was a simple twenty-minute operation. So what if I'd be fully awake, I'd have a few days off resting so as not to get bollocks the size of the watermelon my work mates had affectionately bought me. I felt quite brave doing it fully conscious.

I informed my partners I might be offline for a week or so as I'd be using both hands to gently cup my bruised balls. I guess one of the advantages of being in partnership with others is that you know *'your'* site will be constantly updated without you. There was no worry about any juicy gossip or transfers coming in that you'd miss as the three of us were covering each others' responsibilities for times when one or other of us would be on holiday, or unable to update the site or other reasons, like me for example having a vasectomy!

I've got this knack of not worrying about anything until the very last minute, so it wasn't until the morning of the operation and I'm shaving my pubes in the bath that I start getting nervous. You have to shave them because of the nature of the operation - you don't want any stray curly pubic hairs getting stuck inside your body you see.

It was a Saturday, luckily an away game, so I wasn't going to miss anything, well apart from the return leg in the semi-finals but at least it was on Sky so I may not be there in person, but I'd see the action live and my excuse was enough in my mind not to affect my superstition regarding semi-finals.

At the *snipping clinic* I was really starting to shit myself and tried in vain not to show it, though I reckon my wife knew as I tightly held her hand in the waiting room.

It was late afternoon; I was the only bloke there. The wife was still trying to reassure me when this door opened and out came this fella, white as a sheet, walking as if he'd ridden a horse for a fortnight. The man with rubber gloves followed him out and shouted my name. The wife and me followed him back through the door into an *interrogation room*. We had to sit under this big white light bulb and swear to Almighty God that we didn't want any more kids and that we had made this decision together. This was what we both really, really wanted, honest!

I then had to follow a nurse into the operating room. The man with rubber gloves asked me if I wanted the wife to come in with me. "Why no man, I'll be fine," I said, what I really wanted to say was *"hold me"*.

Once in the other room, the nurse told me to strip, at this point I asked her if I should keep my socks on, stupid twat! As I climbed onto the table wearing only a T-shirt (and my socks) the nurse starts painting my genitalia with brown antiseptic paint using a cotton wool ball. At this point I am desperately trying not to get a stiffy. "Don't be fucking stupid," I'm telling myself, "I'm a happily married man and this is only some good looking blonde in a nurses outfit gently stroking my bollocks with her soft peachy hands, I'm too fucking scared to get a hard on."

"You look nervous," says the Doctor. "You can change your mind".

Like derr!

"No," I said, "there's no going back now."

"Well don't worry," he replied, "I've done twelve today already without any problems."

Fucking marvellous, I thought, that makes me unlucky thirteen!

Suddenly I feel a sharp pain in my groin as this rather large needle was thrust into my body.

Within minutes the doctor is saying, "Can you feel this?"

Feel what!

The anaesthetic had worked its magic, and that was that. All I felt was a strange tugging sensation, which didn't bother me.

What did get to me though was the snipping sound of the medical instruments. I had no idea what was going on, I couldn't feel a thing, but that sound was driving me crazy.

Within no time it was done. I slowly got up, grabbed my bandaged genitals, and slowly eased them into the tight little pants I had been told to bring, and then finished getting dressed one handed. I left the operating room in slow motion in fear of something below splitting or popping out or whatever else my imagination was coming up with.

I got home and lay on the settee, watching the footy results coming in. Sunderland had won - so that was comforting. The bairns came back from my parents and the little 'un jumped on me. Oh that hurt! I hadn't felt anything until then. The anaesthetic was obviously wearing off and I don't know if it was the little 'un jumping on me or some allergic reaction but I suddenly felt like I was going to pass out. I crawled into the bathroom as quickly as I could to throw up.

The next few days were spent in bed. I refused to move as I could start to feel some swelling. The wife was a tower of strength often lending words of support and sympathy like, "get off that bloody settee you big girl's blouse," and, "for goodness sake man, pull yourself together." But I recommend to any bloke having this procedure to ignore their other half and have as much rest as possible so as to avoid melon balls.

These idiots who walk in, get the op, walk out, then go back to work, or out on the piss, or start doing some DIY because they are *'men'* and they have to show that there's nothing wrong with them, deserve all the swelling they get.

Having said that, I forgot all about the operation while watching the semi-final second leg. We went 1-0 up, I jumped up to celebrate the goal and it felt like something did pop. The pain was sudden, sharp and immense. I slumped to the floor in agony, though I was still happy that SAFC had scored. I'm not sure if the tears were of joy or pain. Football wise it meant 2-2 on aggregate and that the return to Wembley dream was still on.

However Leicester equalised, it ended 1-1 on the night, 3-2 to them overall and my semi-final superstition had gone!

I went back to bed - sore. I had to go back to work the next day and knew there'd be more piss taking from the Geordies with their simian impressions. Then again I could actually relate to it as I crawled into bed, knuckles trailing the ground, jaw open due to the constant numbness and irritation in my genitals.

I put myself on desk duty for the next few days as I couldn't, nor did I want to lift heavy objects, or run around fixing people's computers as I was still under doctor's order to rest. It allowed me to catch up on the web site, plough through the backlog of emails and see what shit *Kerching* had dug up. He was having another go on his site, this time saying he'd received an email which was supposed to have said that the Ready To Go web site, or RTG as it was now commonly known, *"didn't reflect the true opinions of Sunderland supporters"*. Yawn.

Interestingly I had received an email the same day from someone who said that he had been talking to *Kerching* in some online chat room. Apparently, he was going to make up some false letters slagging off RTG, email them to himself and then answer these letters himself, having a pop at RTG again! So that meant negative emails, and negative replies. Now as two negatives make a positive, my opinion was simply thank you once again for the inadvertent publicity, which you're providing.

Kerching, who was more or less harmless, if not bloody annoying, was nothing compared to the next online stalker who would suddenly appear, though only briefly. This time we had to deal with a Mag, one who was to be known as *pRik*. Not content with his own Sunday Sport trashy-style Mags site, he managed to copy the entire Ready To Go web site within a few days, all images and logos included, then altered where it said *RTG* to *SMB*. That was very annoying. All the hard work that had been put into the design and layout of the site was been torn apart by another little kid, only of the Skunk variety.

Now three of us had entered into a verbal partnership to create and run the site, but following its success and the ever-increasing volume of traffic we were attracting, we had planned to take our verbal agreement one step further and make it legal.

Thus I had to endure no end of paper work that said I was not only in full time employment but also self-employed working for an Internet trading partnership called Ready To Go. Sounds great, does that mean I could call myself a Director? I guess I could call myself whatever I wanted. The paper that made our agreement legal was scary though. Even now I dread the onset of April and the self-assessment forms coming through the post. We had no income from this partnership, which makes filling out these forms a pointless exercise if you ask me, but it laid the foundations should any income come our way.

Being legal, it was decided that the site *pRik* had ripped off was a breach of copyright or something along those lines and therefore we sent a rather heavy letter via email to the company he was hosting his site on.

I cannot remember what exactly was said, but within a day or two his site and the ripped off version of RTG had been permanently closed down. He was using free web space to promote his onslaught of anti-Wearside material; therefore it left little choice for the hosting company but to shut him up.

It was online war in a certain sense. Whereas the *'Kerching'* thing was merely a war of words, this had been a skirmish, though it wasn't World War Two, nor an online Viet Nam, but more like the invasion of Grenada - over before it started.

I don't know if his hosting company issued threats to him, but we never heard of him again. *pRik* was either legally threatened or lost his virginity shortly afterwards which forced him to grow up.

About one week later however, our own site was suddenly closed down.

XVII

I may appear obsessive in the way I've gone on and on about statistics, the number of visitors to the web site, the traffic, the amount of times the pages are viewed, but that's what running an Internet site is all about, apart from the money making aspect that it.

It's nothing out of the ordinary mind you. Look how we pride ourselves on our home attendances compared to other teams - *"we've got more fans than you"* and all that, or look at how the BBC has a rating war with ITV regarding who has the biggest audience figures when it comes to watching either Coronation Street or Eastenders. I watch neither if you want to know, I may be sad but when it comes to soaps I do have a life.

Initially the Internet statistics thing was about how many people visited your web site or *uniques* as they are called. However it's the number of times your pages are viewed that's the main focus of web statistics these days. There are numerous geeky terms when it comes to this subject. I've already mentioned uniques, but there's also the likes of accesses, impressions and hits.

Most people will refer to their site statistics in hits. The thing is the term hit from the technical anorak's point of view is misleading. Imagine if you have a web page that has, say three images on it. If someone looks at your page you will actually register four hits, one for the page and three for the three images. Therefore if someone blags on about having millions of hits, you could seriously dilute that total depending upon how may images they've got on each page.

It's the impressions figure or page views, which is the more accurate measurement.

Ready To Go had jumped from seven thousand uniques in its first month to around forty thousand in its second month. The page views however made the site statistics very impressive. On average we worked out the average visitor would look at between ten and twelve pages daily on Ready To Go, that meant overall monthly we were getting in the region of about half a million page views. That was a tremendous figure considering the site had only been active for about eight or nine weeks.

This figure was on an upward curve. Before long we would be sustaining over six hundred and fifty thousand page views each month, and that's where the trouble started with our site suddenly closing.

These places on the Internet that allow you to store your web site for free, are only free to a point. If suddenly you're attracting too many visitors they will pull the plug on you.

Hosting companies that offer free space have got very powerful computers storing not only your web site but probably thousands of others as well. Each time a request is made to view a web site, the wheels and cogs inside the computer will start turning, directing the traffic towards viewing that site.

However if you've got thousands and thousands of people all looking at the same site, you could end up in an online traffic jam, whereby the cogs of the computer cannot direct the traffic quickly enough, thus if someone is asking to look at a different web site stored on the same computer, they'd be stuck at the back of the traffic jam or would be in a queue to join the traffic jam - like being on a slip road about to join the M25 at nine in the morning.

It's called *'bandwidth'* and every hosting company will have their own set of rules regarding how much *'bandwidth'* or traffic is allowed to access your site each month. It's something normally measured in Megabytes and for your average freebie web site, Megabyte allocation will be pretty low. It's a measurement these free hosting companies will constantly monitor and should you exceed their limit they will either want you to cough up money for the privilege of keeping your site on their books or they will close you down.

We never got the first option, they simply closed us down. Nothing in life is free you see and the Internet is no different.

We had to make a quick decision and spend some of our own cash to move our site to a hosting company that could handle the volume of traffic we were attracting.

We were now investing serious money but still getting no income. Yes I know I'm obsessive about money, but who isn't. When you pay for web hosting, nine times out of ten you will need your own web address. Therefore, we decided that if we're splashing out for professional hosting we should have a proper web address and not an obscure freebie one. Unfortunately the phrase *"ready to go"* is a common and catchy set of words. To our disappointment the *'.com'* and *'.co.uk'* addresses had already been taken.

However www.readytogo.net was free and so it was purchased. It was something that got us really excited for some nerdy reason. Here we were evolving to the next level and owned what was then a rarity - our own domain name. For some daft reason we thought our audience would get just as excited as we did when we switched over to our paid for hosting, dedicated domain name and massive monthly bandwidth availability. They never did so I guess it shows how sad we were, sorry, how sad I was. I won't bring my partners down to my twisted, geeky level.

Moving on from the techno-babble I've written over the last few pages, which probably bored the tits off of you, it was getting nearer to Sunderland being mathematically promoted. We were classed as a *sleeping giant*, having a massive stadium, huge support, yet promotion would be guaranteed at one of the smallest grounds in the country, Bury FC.

The game was televised live. Being mid-week and thinking I'd have no chance of getting a ticket, I watched us get promoted in the comfort of the living room. I found out the next day however that there had had been cash turnstiles open on the night. I guess if I'd known that I might have tried to go.

Still it was a great occasion and the inevitable was finally confirmed after months of waiting, we were back in the Premiership. This time you felt we had the team, the stadium, the finances, and as always, the support to last more than one year in the top flight.

Then again even if we'd finish fourth bottom, that would've be good enough in my eyes.

The next day the web site was bouncing with messages of congratulations for the Club. Of course getting carried away I wrote an outburst on the news page that basically slagged off every other team in the league, from the little boys like Bury who we'd defeated the night before with comments like *"going down"*, to teams like Wolves, who have for many years always threatened to get promoted, have spent millions, but never got anywhere, and and in my eyes would never get promoted – well not at that time.

Then of course there are obvious ones like Grimsby who I just said *"stank of fish"*, and the *"sheep shaggers"* of Norfolk and Suffolk and so on.

It was over the top and pretty childish I will admit that, but then again that's me, always the challenging anarchic type. Within a few hours I deleted the article, mainly due to an influx of emails from people condemning the slagging off of those we were leaving behind. Preferably I'd have left it on as it would have attracted a lot more hits, more responses on the message board and probably more correspondence to our letters page, thus ever increasing volumes of *'interactivity'*.

However this was no longer solely my site and I sort of thought my partners wouldn't have liked what I wrote so it disappeared as quickly at it had appeared.

Having said all that, there would be many more times when I'd get carried away and write even more over the top and controversial articles. It wasn't like I would do this deliberately. In many ways it was my feelings on the subject and the news page was not really a news page, more like reviews, gossip and editorials. At the end of the day it prompts debate. Some agree, some disagree. Some go out of there way to personally slag you off for writing such *"utter garbage"* as they put it. They'll still come back to the site to read anything new, so on that basis alone, feedback from writing *"utter garbage"* equals success.

I even pulled off another Andy Kaufman style wind-up, this time on the first of April, when I declared that I was to cease working on Ready To Go to concentrate on running NUFC's official web site. Many people emailed or posted on the message board good luck messages saying things like, *"don't forget your true colours"* and so on. One or two bitter people thought it was disgraceful to work for the heathen scum, declaring they'd rather be unemployed. Yeah right so if someone comes along and offers you a substantial amount of cash to work for your nearest rivals, you'd turn it down? I'm not talking about being offered a tenner to wear a black and white strip for the day, I mean big money.

Following on from promotion at Bury was the Championship. Again it'd be achieved away from home and this time the victims would be Barnsley. Once again the match was televised so I didn't make what is a short journey down the A1 towards Yorkshire.

With that done and dusted, all that was left was to keep winning and break as many records as possible, the first being a run of thirteen successive home victories which would equal that of the famous Sunderland team from the latter part of the Nineteenth Century also known as *"The team of all the talents"*. We drew 0-0 in a dull game against Sheffield United, but it still didn't stop the partying afterwards. It was the first time SAFC had played at home since winning both promotion and the Championship. A few of us met up in our dingy dirty old gits pub to celebrate promotion and the rising success of the web site. We'd also invited along SAFC radio commentators Eric Gates and Guy Mowbray who we'd struck up a reasonable friendship with albeit via email, and we were getting many a plug during match commentaries in return for promoting quiz nights they'd hold and other stuff.

Sure enough many pints later they stumble in, Gatesy with some bird he'd pulled - if it was your missus Eric forgive my presumption. I had to remind him in my drunken slurry voice that the FTM he and Marco Gabbiadini had performed way back in 1990 was *"better than sex"*. Subsequently I asked for his autograph which read *"2-0 FTM better than sex, Eric Gates"*. I've still got that somewhere though it's got some lager stains on it.

We had also invested in a new range of T-shirt, which we shamelessly flogged before during and after the Sheffield United game. We sold quite a few actually and though people may suggest we were ripping off supporters by making money selling stuff to fuel our web site, they were quality T-shirts and not like some of the shit that was being sold on the Wearmouth Bridge that day.

Promotion had attracted all sorts of shady characters who were selling shoddy gear. Surprisingly enough, they all had Cockney accents shouting out *"cam on sunlan fans, git yor premier bound scarves here, only a fiver, cam on"*.

Amusingly, then again fucking hilariously was one of these Southern idiots who had a load of these red and white knitted scarves with the words *"Sunderland AFC - Pride of Tyneside"* printed on them.

Fucking stupid Cockney wanker. People were walking past him either laughing their heads off or hurling some sarcastic abuse at him.

I should have bought one just for the stupidity of the item, a sure fire collectors piece even if it was slightly insulting to the people of Wearside. I doubt he was doing it deliberately, though it does show the sometimes lack of knowledge those down South have about us up North- next time do your fucking homework properly you thick twat.

That wasn't the first time something like this had happened. I can remember during the Eighties, a David Bowie concert was held inside old Roker Park. When Bowie got on stage the first thing he said was *"Hello Tyneside!"*

After selling a shit load of our own T-shirts, Guy Mowbray and Eric Gates getting free ones, a dozen or more pints, I head off home, stumbling into the house to be confronted by the evil foot tapping, rolling pin holding, and thoroughly pissed off wife.

I must admit I upset her by coming in late, especially as I had said I was only going to have a few beers. I got a quite a mouthful from her and ended up sleeping on the sofa that night.

"Don't even think about getting into the same bed as me," is one of the few comments I can remember.

It was probably a good thing as I was up most of the night talking to God on the *'big white telephone'* if you know what I mean.

We had two games remaining and winning both meant another record, this time for the largest points tally any team had ever achieved in Division One. After disposing of Stockport County away, our last game of the season would be a memorable 2-1 home win over Birmingham City.

What made the day special was not only the presentation of the Championship trophy, but the pre match rock concert by the band Republica and, of course, their song *"Ready To Go"*. I doubt the band had played in front of so many people before and in front of so many passionate about one particular song. Again I couldn't help think that it would subconsciously make people recall our web site and not just the tune that the team ran out to.

One sentimental moment during the players' lap of honour, was when fullback Martin Scott broke down in tears. Scotty had suffered in recent seasons with long-term injuries and had had little part in Sunderland's emphatic promotion. I think the injuries he had sustained forced him into early retirement, if not, he knew deep down he would not be part of Sunderland's plans the next season in the Premiership. The mass celebrations of the fans just got to him I guess and was something he would miss, it was quite an emotional moment. I have no idea what he's doing these days. I think he went on to do some coaching course as a first step into football management. I hope he's doing all right though wherever he is; he was a consistent player for Sunderland during his career.

I didn't celebrate after leaving the ground. No obsessive drinking this time, not after the ticking off I'd had a few weeks earlier. I simply went home content that the season was finally over without the worry of the lottery of the play-offs. The close season would this time be football free and time to reflect on the achievements the team had made and how I'd progressed online.

XVIII

Shortly before the season ended an Internet company that was trying to sign up the biggest unofficial football web sites -Premiership only - as part of an online network approached us. They called themselves the Unofficial Football Network - UFN, a subsidiary of some large well-known publishing organisation.

The deal was pretty simple, we put up advertising banners and in return we'd get paid something like one penny for every thousand adverts that would be viewed by our audience. It wasn't those annoying pop-up banners though. We've always avoided using such crude methods. If it annoys us, it'd annoy our audience, besides I guess anyone who has surfed the Internet and accidentally stumbled on some pornographic web site has been hit by the curse of not just pop-up banners but multiple pop-ups. You close one pop-up only for it to open up another one and you end up in a vicious circle while desperately attempting to close down all of these browser windows before the boss catches you looking at smut while at work. I'm not expressing this from experience mind you, just what other people have told me - honest!

One penny per thousand doesn't sound much, but when you're getting over six hundred and fifty thousand pages viewed each month, you can see how the income would be attractive. Of course once split three ways and once the monthly hosting fees and excess bandwidth charges were paid there wasn't much left.

I won't say exactly how much we were offered, just take the above figure as an example, not that I'm trying to hide anything, it was just pocket money at the end of the day.

It did mean we'd have to make major changes to our site, but as it was the close season, a re-vamp was an easier option - a clean slate. Unlike the previous year, this close season wasn't quiet. In fact there was very little drop in terms of monthly visitors, which meant the site had to be kept up-to-date, as much as possible whilst attempting to re-design a new version.

Being the start of the holiday period and with many of the bosses away, the mice did play! What I mean by this is I started to use this slack period at work to concentrate on the re-vamp and the inclusion of the adverts from UFN, placing them on as many pages as possible in order to help increase the potential income.

Within a week we had almost completed the re-vamp and decided to launch this new look early the next week. I put in a lot of hours over the weekend, so much so that on the following Monday I was in two minds whether or not to call in a *'sicky'* - just to have a lie in, but I went to work feeling blue as you normally do on Monday.

A phrase, *Monday morning blues* had poignant significance this time. When I arrived, everyone was told that more redundancies were to be announced by the end of the week. This time they mentioned actual numbers and from which departments. One person from IT would be sacked by the Friday. Seeing as there were only two of us in IT, it wasn't going to be easy to stomach either way.

Everything to do with the new web site was put on hold from my perspective until I knew where I stood with my real job, and so I spent the remainder of the week preparing for the worst, backing up important documentation and software I wanted, updating my CV, and collecting numerous names, postal addresses, and email addresses of potential companies to poach should I be the one to go.

In a way I shouldn't really refer to being made redundant as a bad thing. It will be to some, but its not the end of the world should you ever be made redundant. Unfortunately I speak from experience having been made redundant a few times. There is more to life than work I guess and it probably has a greater affect on those who live and breathe for the company they work for, sacrificing *'having a life'* to show they are a model employee - or an arse licking brown tongue. At the end of the day you are a number, that is all and if your number is up they will sacrifice you. I know people who have gone to work on Christmas Day and New Years day - of their own accord just to impress the bosses. I've also seen them get made redundant as well, which for some reason devastated them.

As for me, if I'm contracted to do thirty-seven hours a week and have one hour for lunch, I will work thirty-seven hours a week and have one hour for lunch. Don't get me wrong, I'm not like unapproachable or an awkward employee, I will put in extra hours when it is called for but if there is no need to, then I'd rather be at home with my family if you want me to be honest with you.

Maybe it's just me and the way I am, but my outlook on things like this is to prepare for being part of the unwanted variety, then if it does happen it's less of a blow. Better than having the attitude, *"they'd never sack me, I'm far too important"* and all that crap!

Anyway by Friday morning, all traces of me working on the web site from work had been removed and I simply sat at my desk, computer switched off, doing fuck all until I knew if it was me getting the fat redundancy cheque and P45 or the lad I worked with.

All other departments had told those who were no longer required pretty much straight away, yet IT was kept waiting for over two hours. If the help desk phone rang from someone whose PC had gone belly up or had received a virus through their email, they were told to wait until we knew which one of us was leaving. We had no animosity against each other, regardless of which one of us went.

As expected, when crunch time came the P45 was handed to me. Fair enough I'd mentally prepared so it wasn't a catastrophe. There was some worry though, I mean there's always worry when you're suddenly unemployed, you've the problem of how to keep your house and put food on the table amongst other things. Since the major redundancies the previous September, I had taken out some mortgage protection and other insurance policies, so I was covered and could discount that worrying debt straight away.

Likewise having worked for the same firm for around ten years, I did get a nice pay off, which would, by my calculations, last about six months worse case scenario.

I'd have liked nothing more than to sit on my arse doing nowt but concentrate on Ready To Go. Unfortunately, as it generated less than dole money, I had to focus on finding a new job.

Ideally I now wanted to move into Internet designing. Having your hobby as a career is sort of the ideal job, so having got home and informed my wife and family that I was on the dole, I spent the remainder of the day applying for jobs from the week's newspapers I'd kept, and sent out email flyers to potential companies who may want a bitter and twisted Mackem designing web sites for them.

I think I even posted on the message board looking for a job, though that never yielded anything apart from a substantial amount of sympathy from the regulars, which was a kind gesture.

I spent the weekend with a calculator glued to my hand comparing income to outgoings and deciding what debts could be cleared with the *golden piss-off* I'd received. I then calculated the minimum income I needed to get in order to survive. Many people I know who have been made redundant will only look for jobs that match their last salary band. I think this is slightly naive - unless you've got serious debt - because in a way when you are made redundant you no longer have a salary band and should take anything that's offered which keeps you afloat so to speak. Let's be realistic here, it's easier to secure a higher paid job while your already employed. I think this is a sensible rule to follow should you end up losing your job, not that I'm attempting to ram this idea down your throat or anything.

Seven days on from the *Monday morning blues* I'm registering in the Job Centre. Now whilst the majority of those queuing looked like decent folk there was a splattering of thickos, slappers, shell suit idiots and things in there obviously signing-on, having no intention of finding work.

I had to squeeze past people who you'd not want to touch nor associate yourself with, yet I was now one of them, taking a ticket from a machine with a number on it and watching this electronic scoreboard flash up a number every ten minutes. If it matched the one you were holding, you could see someone who had to suffer working in this place to take your details and add you to the Government's statistics.

I sat down next to this old looking wrinkly faced geezer who still thought he was jack the lad, with his cheap jewellery around his neck Mr. T style, vest to show off his muscles, tattoos of naked women on his arms, and a swallow on his neck.

"What number yer got?" he said, "436" I reply.

"I'm 435."

"Nice."

"I'm afore yer."

"Never!"

It may look as if I'm being snobby and all that but it was something I'd never experienced before and was glad when the whole ordeal was over to tell you the truth.

Then again for some strange reason I cannot explain I found myself inside the nearest sports shop pricing white polyester shell suits and baseball caps.

It was a relief to get home, though the thought of having to join the queue to sign on every other week wasn't very appealing.

As it turned out, the few hours I had suffered in there was a complete waste of time. No sooner had I got home, the phone rang. It was a bloke from this Internet Company in Newcastle. He'd got my email I'd sent the previous Friday, and asked if I could go through and see them that evening.

I jumped at the chance and drove through to *'enemy territory'* around 6.30pm to meet this husband and wife team who ran a small Internet company, which they declared as being one of the top three in the North East.

Within an hour of being interviewed they offered me a job. To this day I'm of the opinion that I was never unemployed - fired on Friday, hired on Monday!

I didn't start straight away mind you, I did have some holiday planned so ended up having a month off, which was great, I had enough redundancy money not to worry about being off for so long, could spend the first week or so taking the kids to and from school, then polishing off the new site without looking over my shoulder!

XVIX

The close season always has an air of uncertainty about it. There is always rife speculation about who'll be joining, who'll be leaving and when will the fixtures come out.

No sooner had the season finished when Sunderland went out and bought central defender Steve Bould from Arsenal. I had mixed views regarding this transfer. On one hand Reidy was being very shrewd by signing experienced Premiership defensive qualities, signalling he wanted to make sure we stayed up at the first attempt.

However it also signalled we'd bought a journeyman, way past it in terms of age and one that had the Mags posting abusive crap on the message board with references to buying wheel-chaired invalids.

The departure of Andy Melville meant we had to buy a replacement, however, the purchase of Steve Bould wasn't exactly the fans choice. As the season unfolded we would all be proved wrong.

Not long after, those much-anticipated fixtures came out and it was a tough start, away to Chelsea then home to Watford and Arsenal followed by successive away games to Leeds then the Mags. Apart from the Watford match, it was viewed as a baptism of fire, and the critics were predicting us as relegation candidates.

Suddenly and unexpectedly things started going horribly wrong. Firstly, the City was dealt a big blow when it was announced that Vaux Breweries were to close and despite all efforts to keep it alive through protests, media backing, employee buy-outs, the owners, the Swallow Hotel Group wanted the place shut.

Many people lost their jobs through this and I can't recall what stance the Club initially took over all of this after all Vaux were the main sponsors and the red and white stripes carried the Lambtons Beer logo - a quality drink brewed by Vaux.

Many people wondered what logo Sunderland would carry and concerns grew that the team would be wearing the Swallow Hotel logo on their shirts. With a new strip to come out prior to the start of the season many fans were in the mood to boycott it when launched. A suggestion appeared on the message board. The idea was that RTG should provide iron on transfers to cover the Swallow logo. I thought the idea of people wearing Sunderland stripes with the Ready To Go logo embezzled on the front, along with the words 'Don't Swallow' would be a great publicity exercise, so in jest I mentioned it on the web site. Next thing I know I get a phone call from the BBC wanting me to go on Radio 5 that evening and talk about the boycott of the new strip and the iron-on logos we were to offer. Fucking hell! You make a bloody joke and next thing I know it's factual. This seems to happen regularly, I express my opinion or ideas, as I'm quite entitled to do, and suddenly I'm getting phone calls and emails from media moguls who've turned these opinions and ideas into actual fact.

Needless to say, the radio interview never happened. We had no intention of printing logos - too expensive.

There was still going to be a boycott of the new strip in honour of those workers who had lost their job following the closure of Vaux. The Club moved quickly on this issue and a new sponsor was unveiled when the new strip came out. Everyone forgot about the rift that had grown between brewery supporters, fans, the media, and the Club.

Then a local Sunday newspaper published a picture of Sunderland midfielder Lee Clark at the F A Cup Final. Nothing wrong with that as everyone knew he supported Newcastle but as he was supposed to be a professional footballer, you'd think his commitment would extend to Sunderland AFC. However he was wearing this T-shirt that said *"Sad Mackem Bastards"* and that is what caused the problems.

There was public condemnation of Clarky for wearing such an insulting item. In fact it got so out of hand that regardless of his apology the fans demanded he never pulled on a red and white strip again. Hits to the web site went ballistic and to be honest I was on the side of the majority who felt he had personally insulted every one of us who supported SAFC. A phrase *"once a Geordie, always a Geordie"* was born and Sunderland had little choice but to sell him off as quickly as they could.

In the end it was good riddance to the spotty faced twat, who in my judgement wasn't good enough for the Premiership anyway. We'd survived without him for roughly two thirds of the season so could survive without him full stop.

It became apparent the photo was originally published on the Internet by the same bloke we'd approached to be our online resident Mag. 'Good job we didn't hire him,' was the thought that crossed my mind, I'd have had to sack him for gross misconduct.

I have to admit, I admired the publicity he got for his web site albeit black and white trash, and part of me, was slightly jealous of someone pulling off such a scoop. However his underlying agenda to show Clark the error of his ways and get out of playing for SAFC and onto better things was taking it a bit too far for my liking. Whatever victory he claimed he did his fellow Geordie no favours. He cost Clark his job, who was sold off to Fulham and became a hated figure in the Sunderland ranks.

People had worshipped him and many had bought the *"Clarkie is a Mackem"* T-shirts that were being sold in and around the ground. Many of these and a few hundred red and white shirts with *"CLARK 4"* printed on the back, were ceremoniously burnt, by those disgusted to have had anything to do with the unwashed brain-dead idiot he was.

Of course he went onto better things all right - not.

Overall it was quite an event and hopefully the last of the negative publicity Sunderland had suddenly suffered. Nevertheless, a few weeks later it got worse.

For some crazy reason I still don't understand, Sunderland sold off striker Michael Bridges, a promising youngster to Leeds United. It made no sense whatsoever to sell such talent. He was on the fringes of making it into the first team on a regular basis and one player well capable of shining in the Premiership - or so it was forecast. I hoped that the profit gained would go towards suitable replacements. As the players were leaving though, no one was coming in.

Then Allan Johnston of all people fell out with Reid to the extent that he would be snubbed for the entire season, left to rot in the reserves and forced to train by himself.

Apparently the alleged rumour is that Johnston, who had by now forced his way into the Scotland squad on a regular basis, had agreed a new contract with Reidy albeit in principle via a handshake.

Whilst training with the Scotland squad the story goes that he found out other Scottish players who were playing for other Premiership sides were getting far more money than the revised contract he'd shook on. Having told his agent, Johnston was advised to go back on his word and let the agent thrash out a better deal. However Reidy allegedly refused to entertain the agent, and if you believe the gossip, believed that anyone who agrees a deal verbally with him is bound by it.

It was quite a story and a rumour that circulated for many weeks and months. Whether this is fact or fiction I guess we'll never know, however it demonstrated what appeared to be a dark side to Peter Reid, one that worried me.

We had within a short space of time lost three class players although no one was bothered about spotty face, losing your super-sub was a bad move, but then losing your star winger was devastating. Without a shadow of doubt, Allan Johnston would have lit up the Premiership with his skill. I couldn't believe what had happened, having met Allan and spoken to him on the telephone numerous times his personality and character was that of a mild mannered gentleman. This ungentlemanly conduct could not have been his doing from my point of view.

It did however explain why recent attempts to contact him regarding the new look for Ready To Go, and the raised profile we wanted to give the Allan *'Magic'* Johnston section went ignored.

Subsequently the work put into developing his part of RTG was dropped. Talk now was of whom Reidy would buy as a replacement. Everyone considered the fact that we simply couldn't start the new season without any more new faces. Yet no new transfers were on the horizon.

As usual with a big club like SAFC and being recently promoted many wild stories about who was joining us were printed in the press. It became a transfer gossip game that even we joined in with making up daft links between this player and that player about to sign for Sunderland.

Eventually we did sign someone, ex-German international defender Thomas Helmer, but that would turn out to be the start of the farcical transfers Sunderland would be associated with all too often. Then again the signing of Danish midfielder Carsten Fredgaard a few weeks earlier was more like the beginning of the money wasting.

The season started with a weak squad as far as I was concerned, though a record-breaking fee was paid for the services of Swedish international midfielder, Stefan Schwarz, from Valencia. Then again when your record fee is four million it doesn't exactly set the world on fire in terms of the rest of the division standing up and suddenly take notice of you, worried that you're a powerful force to be reckoned with. Schwarz turned out to be a reasonable buy in the early days, but long-term injuries later in his career at Sunderland, along with rumoured managerial bust-ups, kept his appearances and contributions to SAFC at a minimum - that's how I saw it.

We were thrashed 4-0 away to Chelsea on the opening day of the new season. Again, it looked like it was going to be another one-off year in the top flight following this humiliation.

However our first home game of the season was against play-off winners Watford who were dispatched 2-0, both goals coming from former Watford player Kevin Phillips. Those were valuable points. Unfortunately I didn't get to see the game.

I was still settling into my new job you see and had spent the day with the Boss offsite, installing email software and server hardware.

He had a habit of not eating and so we had no lunch. Driving home at the end of the working day, fighting my way through shitloads of traffic across the Tyne Bridge, and towards the bottleneck of the Heworth Metro station roundabout, I started to feel very queasy and felt like I was going to pass out. I opened the window fully to get some fresh air as I fought to keep myself from fainting as I drove home.

I should have pulled over really in case I did pass out. However I was still driving through Geordie Land and if I did stop and did pass out I'd either wake up in a field stripped naked or pull away to find the car jacked up onto bricks. There was just too much traffic to pull over and so I foolishly kept on going. I got home and simply dropped straight into bed, clothes still on, shoes still on.

The day caught up with me and lack of food and liquid made me flake out. Even though I was trying to impress my new employers, from that point onwards I'd have to call the shots when it came to taking a break and having some food, even if the Boss didn't want to.

The weekend saw another home game and a stern test against Arsenal. Reidy took the bold decision to drop Kevin Phillips and play with Niall Quinn up front by himself as he attempted to avoid defeat from one of the Championship contenders.

A 0-0 result was greeted at the final white with wild celebrations - you'd think we'd just won the Cup or something.

We had four points from nine and were sitting mid-table, while up the road the Mags were rock bottom. We'd lose our next game away to Leeds United, even though we went 1-0 up. We hardly ever win at Elland Road so it was no real surprise, but we were slipping and our next game could either set us on our way or push us deeper into trouble.

It was of course the first Tyne and Wear derby since 1996.

XX

It's difficult to describe the atmosphere and apprehension I felt while walking around Northumberland Street eating a cheese pasty for my lunch the day we were playing the Mags. It was the first time we'd played the enemy since 1996. Then it was a 1-1 draw, Mickey Gray putting us in the lead before Shearer scored an obvious offside goal.

The Mags were struggling at the foot of the table - oh how sad. Then again we were more-or-less just above them. Still it gets the adrenaline pumping not knowing what the outcome would be. It's those times of the season you look forward to, but also dread. Unless you go 4-0 up within the first five minutes, you want the game over before it starts.

I'm probably not making much sense here, but unless you have this sort or rivalry, roots which go beyond football, then it's just difficult to comprehend the tension that builds up before a match between SAFC and NUFC.

Putting on my historical head for a moment, the Newcastle and Sunderland rivalry goes far back in time, beyond the one hundred and twenty odd years of North East football history. Sunderland, being the largest conurbation on the East coast of England and the biggest city between Leeds and Edinburgh, developed largely due to its growth as a coal-exporting town using the River Wear for its output. The expansion of Sunderland occurred despite centuries of stern resistance from the prosperous and dominant town of Newcastle, which was in the privileged position of possessing a Royal Charter, inhibiting the shipment of coal from nearby competing ports such as the one in Sunderland. As a result of the Civil War, the competition between the ports of Sunderland and Newcastle intensified as Newcastle pinned its colours firmly to the Royalist mast.

In part, Sunderland's attitude was influenced by its large contingent of traders from Scotland as they sided with Oliver Cromwell's Parliamentarians. The town received a battalion of Parliamentarians from Cromwell in 1642. This battalion was composed mainly of Scots. As a result, Sunderland became the centre for Cromwell's assaults on Newcastle and Durham, which had also sided with the Royalists.

The roles of both Sunderland and Newcastle in the Civil War were of tremendous significance. Newcastle was the main supplier of coal to London, if Sunderland had joined Newcastle in its support for the Royalists, the supply of coal to Cromwell's London would have almost completely dried up, and the outcome of the war may even have been different. It is not too surprising that Sunderland placed its loyalties with Cromwell rather than the Royalists, as it was a Royal Charter that limited the town's trade and provided Newcastle with a hugely unfair advantage in the competition between the two ports. For Sunderland, the major advantage of the Civil War was that its coal exportation expanded rapidly while Newcastle lost its monopoly forever.

In today's peaceful modern age, both cities hold a Royal Charter and the coal industry is a memory, but strong feelings still exist. Sunderland and Newcastle are now partners in England's smallest county - Tyne and Wear, though the majority of Sunderland's residents will testify that there is far more Tyne than Wear in this partnership. In previous times, Newcastle was the main force in the county of Northumberland and Sunderland ruled the roost in County Durham, but a Government decision in the seventies clubbed the two together in an unlikely marriage.

Bitterness and rivalry between the two big cities of the North East will continue to exist until the blatant Newcastle bias shown by the various Tyne and Wear bodies and the local media ceases. Even when this unlikely day arrives, the football teams and fans will be going at each other hammer and tongs.

Now that I've got that out of my system, I'll continue. I'm walking around Northumberland Street thinking about the game that night. I wasn't going. You had to be lucky to get a ticket that day. There were only eight hundred tickets made available to Sunderland fans so you can imagine how quickly they were snapped up, or how many were left once the corporate freebies had been handed out.

The build up of those disgusting black and white tops were increasing all around me as I tried in vain not to brush against any of them in the crowded areas. Likewise my mind is playing tricks by saying don't make eye contact they'll know your a Mackem. It wasn't like there were hoards of twenty-somethings hanging around looking for trouble - there would be later as the *Gremlins* fought it out with the *Seaburn Casuals*. It's bad enough on Northumberland Street trying to avoid the religious nutters wielding their bibles and screaming at you if you dare to make eye contact with them, and *The Big Issue* sellers thrusting their publication in your face whilst shouting *"Bershoo"* as you hurry past.

What bothered me though in an amusing way was the overweight middle aged Geordies wearing their replica shirts, one size too small, and extra tight around their beer gut. I do feel sorry for them. It's pretty obvious that the top they are wearing is not only their pride and joy, but probably the only article of clothing they've got. No matter what time of the day or time of the year it is they will only wear their colours, faded and worn out. I suppose I feel sorry for them because they obviously spend each year saving up their dole money in order to purchase their fifty-pound tops that cost less than a fiver to make - if you believe what a certain Mags Director once said. Though I find their physique and dress sense rather humorous, I sense apprehension that once I'm middle aged, I'll be walking around all the time wearing a tight red and white strip with the same sized beer gut.

Nevertheless, I had a particular task to carry out that lunchtime and so I walked from Northumberland Street, past the Monument and towards the infamous Bigg Market. The task was to get hold of the telephone numbers of the two phone boxes made famous for being destroyed when the Mags rioted, not once but twice, the first time after failing to win the league in '96 and the second a week before the '98 play-offs when they lost the FA Cup Final and that hilarious picture on the front of the local newspapers of a tart on top of the phone box with her kegs round her ankles - I apologise to all other tarts!

Each time the two phone boxes in the Bigg Market were the victims each being totally destroyed and making headline news. From what I can gather, after the Cup Final defeat in '98, the Newcastle council installed new phone boxes sprayed with vandal proof paint. However following the Cup Final defeat the year after (yes I will admit it was heartbreaking to see the Mags qualify for back to back FA Cup Finals), more attempted scenes of violence followed, and if you ever get hold of any photos from this event, you can clearly see the Mags rioting covered in a black tarry substance which was actually the vandal proof stuff - obviously worked a treat then?

You're probably surprised I've never mentioned those defeats before, especially the '98 one which was one of the worst cases of public disorder the region has seen in many a year. I guess that as much as it meant relief them not winning anything I simply didn't feel they were worth writing about, after all, the Play Offs were the main focus of attention at that time.

Anyway I thought it'd be a laugh if I publish the phone numbers just in case we won, and see if any Mackems would ring them up and wind up whichever thick Geordie happened to answer.

The place was starting to heave with the heathens and I felt very uncomfortable mingling with the enemy so to speak. Quickly I write down both numbers from the boxes then headed off back to work. As five o'clock came I legged it as quick as I could to the car and drove as fast as I could to beat the horrendous traffic on the Tyne Bridge and get home. I had to put up the numbers on the web site before heading off to the Stadium of Light for the beam back. It was pissing down by now and I will admit that, stupidly, I drove too fast having a few narrow escapes with the bad weather, skidding and so on. But I survived, I got home with enough time to post the numbers on the Internet, grab some tea before heading off for the nerve wrecking beam back.

The rain kept on coming down and my jeans were soaking by the time I'd walked over the Wearmouth Bridge and into the main stand at the stadium. My seat was unfortunately low down and not covered by the roof so I was getting pissy wet. At half time it was 1-0 to the Mags, the rain had subsided a little, but I was still wet through and feeling rather sorry for myself. In fact I was wishing I wasn't there. I'd grabbed a ticket at the last minute so was sitting by myself. I had no idea if any of my mates were there or where they were sitting. There was over twelve thousand Mackem's inside the Stadium that night to watch the game. So here I was, *Billy Nee Mates* with an anorak on, soaking wet. What a sad sight that was.

The rain over us intensified into the second half but it was worse up the road in Newcastle. In fact the pitch was getting that bogged down, the game was looking more likely to be abandoned and seeing as we were losing at the time it would have been a welcome decision.

Suddenly however the rain in Sunderland stopped and Quinny scored an equaliser. All hell broke loose. Complete strangers started hugging each other. I hadn't witnessed such scenes or such feelings since the Play Off Final.

At that point I was content with a draw and wanted full time to come there and then. However better things were to happen. Nicky Summerbee who had taken the piss out of Newcastle's right hand side all night delivered a cross met by Phillips whose initial shot was parried away by the Mags keeper. The ball stuck in the mud in the six-yard area, Phillips turned on a sixpence to chip the ball over the keeper's head and into the net. We were winning. We were beating our arch nemesis with less than twenty minutes to go. I was soaking wet but couldn't give a fuck. We were fucking the Mags and I, like everyone else on Wearside that night, prayed we could hold on.

At that time Ruud Gullit was manager of the Mags, having succeeded the incoherent Kenny Dogleash, who had in turn dismantled the attacking flair of Keegan's side, and into one more boring than George Graham's Arsenal - if you could ever get that boring.

Even though Dogleash got them to the Cup Final, a poor showing in the League meant he either resigned or was sacked - I didn't care less so haven't even bothered looking into this - and was replaced by Gullit promising to turn things around. Apart from taking them to the Cup Final once again, which they thankfully lost - again, things had gone from bad to worse for NUFC, much to our amusement.

The Shepherd and Hall fiasco when they rubbished their own fans and stated that all Tyneside women were dogs or whatever still makes me chuckle to this day. And with all of this turmoil happening up the road while we were marching on and on meant things couldn't get any better being a Mackem, and I'm being conservative here with my judgement.

Of course things would get better if we held on for the win. Desperate to get something out of his swan song Gullit threw on Shearer who he'd had a major bust up with. The phrase *no one is bigger than the club* is true unless the club in question is Newcastle United.

Everyone knows Shearer is bigger than NUFC, just like when he played for England, his name was the only one pre-printed on the team sheets, regardless of form. Gullit thought he was bigger than Shearer and dropped him for the Tyne and Wear derby, and this along with defeat ended Gullit's reign.

As much as I loathe the Mags skipper, I was worried just in case the twat did score and we got the usual boringHitleresque one arm celebration - or is it the old elephant *"giz a bun"* impersonation when he scores.

Anyway with seconds remaining Bally sliced a clearance, which thundered over thirty yards towards Sorensen's goal. Bang, it bounced off the top of the crossbar with Sorensen well beaten. What a sigh of relief. Can you imagine if that had gone in? Without a doubt it would have been the most spectacular own goal ever had it been scored, and against our rivals it would have been talked about for years to come much to our annoyance.

But it bounced off the woodwork and to safety. It didn't go in, and seconds later the full time whistle is blown. We had beaten the Mags. The FTM had truly been performed - the first time since 1990. For me personally at that moment in time it was better than winning the Championship and I dare say I'm not alone regarding this.

Complete strangers hugged each other and everyone was chanting. *"We beat the scum 2-1"*, could be heard echoing all around the Stadium of Light, across the Wearmouth Bridge, and around the City Centre.

As I got home you could still here faint echoes carried by the wind *"we beat the scum 2-1"*. I logged onto the Internet and wrote the most outrageous match report you could imagine. It left nothing to the imagination, containing numerous colourful metaphors and was aptly titled, *"We Beat the Scum 2-1"*.

Better still was the amount of emails from celebrating Mackems who told of phoning up the Bigg Market telephones - which to their surprise were answered. Of course the person who answered the phone got a chorus of *"we beat the scum 2-1"*. I guess it's no surprise if I said I had one helluva shag that night too. They do say football is better than sex, but how do you describe sex after beating your rivals?

Next day I felt mentally exhausted. My throat was still sore from the singing and shouting, but that didn't matter. It's quite amazing how much stress a game like that can take out on your body, the adrenaline rush was wearing off and although you feel you're *'calming down'* you feel drained and empty - it's the old withdrawal symptoms again.

Walking around Northumberland Street at lunchtime eating a cheese pasty again wasn't so boring the next day. I wanted to make eye contact with everyone. I wanted them to know I was a Mackem and my team had fucked them the night before. I wanted a religious nutter to shout over to me and spout off some verse from the bible - I'd be tempted to shout back "but we beat the Scum 2-1". I even bought a copy of The Big Issue that day!

Building up to this game, some message board regulars who are known only as the Misfits asked people to email in poems themed around Sunderland and Newcastle's rivalry. The day after the 2-1 victory, a flood of them came bouncing in, as well as being posted on the message board. Two of my favourites were;

> "I'm only a poor little phone box,
>
> My glass is all broken and smashed,
>
> The Skunks invaded the Bigg Market,
>
> Their shite team the Mackems had thrashed.
>
> A transfer request I have posted,
>
> To the powers that be at BT,
>
> I want to live in a nice town,
>
> As I don't want to look like a tree."

And;

> "First game of the year and the Ref cops the flak,
>
> The second 's at Spurs where his team he will sack,
>
> At the Dell you score two but the Saints they score double,
>
> Your team and your manager are deep in trouble,
>
> A point against Wimbledon and the Mags are away,
>
> But nowt else matters 'cept Wednesday,
>
> Fifth game of the season brings the lads from the Wear,
>
> A defeat by the Mackems is what you so fear,
>
> And sure as it was God who brought all the rain,
>
> His son scored the winner, suffer in pain".

Then again, the shortest poem of all summed up the entire event. It simply read;

> Roses are red,
> Violets are blue,
> Newcastle 1,
> Sunderland 2.

The Sunderland Echo's front-page headline read, *"Stuffed 'Em"* and was accompanied by a picture of a lonely Mag, head in hands. The Newcastle media spat their dummy out though and said the Echo's headline was out of order. Pretty two faced considering the self same publication had no moral objection to publishing the Lee Clark T-shirt story. I reckon it was nothing more than sour grapes.

The only thing that spoiled the day was lack of banter at work. There were less than a handful of people working for this *'large'* Internet Company and there wasn't a football fan amongst them - well there was a Smoggy supporter from Hull, but he didn't count. I had no-one to annoy, no one to gloat to constantly, so as usual it was do your work in a strange but usual silence generated each day, only today I felt good inside.

The fans were now boosted by all of this; Ready To Go had another record day in terms of visitors. Would the moral of the team be sustained to move us up the table and away from the danger zone? It may have only been a few games into the season, but you have to remember the Premiership is a tough league, and if you get caught sleeping even at this early stage, you could suffer by the end of it.

XXI

The next few months saw Sunderland slowly but surely climb higher and higher in the league to positions the majority of fans had never experienced, and forthwith there were mass nosebleeds on Wearside.

The hit rate to Ready To Go slowly increased, the income was steady and things were looking pretty rosy or so it seemed. The month of September has poignant significance for me personally. There was the redundancy scare the previous September, prior to that we had that infamous 4-0 defeat away to Reading. This September, I'll be blunt here, I realised, I just fucking hated my job and I'd only been working there for about six weeks.

The daily routine of fighting my way through the masses of traffic heading over the Tyne Bridge to get to work, and fighting my way back over it to get home on an evening was burning me out.

I'd be exhausted by the time I arrived at work and needed increased levels of caffeine to keep going. Most days I'd end up waiting outside a locked office until the Boss arrived. It wasn't like he was stuck in traffic, he simply had a habit of swanning in when he felt like it, leaving me hanging around outside the office with the other employees waiting to get in to do some work. Sometimes I'd be waiting for almost an hour. It was a ridiculous and totally unprofessional way to run a business and treat your employees. That was only one of many things that slowly dawned on me and made me realise that I needed to get out as soon as possible.

In my first month at work I ended up getting paid by cheque even though I handed the Boss my bank account details the first day I joined the company. I put this cheque in the bank, and proceeded to write several rubber cheques - well I didn't realise the bloody thing would take ten days to clear. The hassle I had with money that month was unbelievable.

I never really thought much of it apart from blaming myself for making the mistake of paying in a cheque without covering it. The next payday came and on the way to work I called at the nearest cash point, entered my PIN number, and the words *"you must be joking"* appeared on the screen. Shit, funds were down to a minimum. PIN is one of those abbreviations that people always refer to as PIN number. It stands for *'Personal Identification Number,'* so to say PIN number; you'd be meaning personal identification number number. So really you should say just PIN. I thought I'd add that bit even though it's completely irrelevant.

Once again, I was given a cheque, but this time I get the cheque cleared through the company's bank and carry a wad of cash to my own bank, before the direct debits went AWOL again.

Overall I spent about seven or eight months working for this company. My salary was paid into my bank account about three times.

I felt like an employee of Ebenezer Scrooge, when it came to pay day, "Please Sir, are you paying me this month?"

"Barr humbug, here's a cheque boy, now piss off!"

As far as I'm concerned, it was unacceptable. There were also trivial things like not being able to surf during your breaks, having to account for every minute of the day on some stupid over-the-top worksheet that logged how long you spent designing a site, or registering a domain name, or spent offsite installing or fixing hardware and software. It showed a lack of trust between the Boss and the employees. It was messing with my livelihood as it meant I couldn't update Ready To Go during the day. I didn't dare look at the site or read any emails between nine to five for fear of repercussions. I'd probably be dragged into the Boss's office and given the birch for such behaviour.

I could go on and on about big things and little things that I witnessed and overheard at this place, things that added fuel to my own personal fire, but I'll have to be careful and draw the line. These employers would be the type bitter enough to sue.

My interest in being an online fanzine editor was dwindling, not through lack of motivation, but through not having the time. It showed just how much work I'd been doing during the day and attempting to do the same amount of updates after you've been to work, just wasn't possible. I did try, but soon realised I'd be ignoring the kids, or missing a favourite TV show, and I was slowly pushing the phone bills up higher and higher.

Christmas 1999 was a pretty shite time. I drew the short straw and was elected as cover for New Years Eve should the computer system's crash. What made it worse was the paranoia of the *'millennium bug'* and the controversy and panic it was causing to businesses around the globe.

I'd still end up going out and getting pissed as you do on New Years Eve, besides if the millennium bug hit as the extremist Sooth-Sayers predicted, the last thing on my mind would be to dash through to Newcastle and fix a broken server. I'd be looting the nearest Spar for supplies in case society, as we know it should break down.

The paranoid had predicted electricity failing, cash points not working, petrol pumps not pumping, lifts not moving and telephone lines going down. The ensuing chaos would mean we would go back to the dark ages within seven days.

Of course it never happened, and those companies who set-up business during 1999 to fix millennium bug problems made a killing out of what I consider to be a global con. Then again maybe the paranoid are correct and society will break down due to the millennium bug. Remember it's a bug so maybe there is a bug in the bug and the dates are all mixed up.

Over Christmas, Sunderland played Man. United. It was the last home game of the century and ended in a 2-2 draw. Victory was taken away from us by pathetic refereeing, and a cheating Ole Gunnar Solskjaer who conned the ref into thinking he'd been illegally tackled - Reidy would sarcastically joke afterwards that he'd tripped over one of the pitch watering sprinklers or there'd been an earthquake local to the West Stand - the resulting free kick gave them a late equaliser.

One of my partners had contacted SAFC prior to this game asking if Ready To Go could advertise in the match day programme. Being the last game of the millennium, it'd be quite a souvenir to have and we were quite willing to part with serious money to get an advert in it.

The Club turned us down. We were *'rivals'* to their own web site and of course *"scum of the Earth"* fanzine editors - they would not associate themselves with us. We did ask our sponsors, UFN, to try to win them over, but they failed as well.

It was disappointing to be turned down, but it demonstrated to me that we were indeed rivals, and they feared us. A supporters branch meeting a few months later indicated why they didn't want to associate themselves with us, when it was proved that we were number one on the Internet. Ready To Go was represented at this meeting and we managed to get John Fickling (one of the big wig Directors) to cough up the actual hit rate to SAFC's own web site. It was very satisfactory to know that we out-stripped them by about one hundred thousand page views each month (and that number was growing). Pity we weren't making the same money.

Returning to work after Christmas was ever so depressing. My New Year's resolution was to get out of there as quickly as possible before I became a recluse. The lack of human communication and military style procedures was too much. It was like being back at school and it just knarked me that's all. Come March, I finally got offered a new job. It was a similar role but based in Sunderland and about ten minutes drive from where I lived.

No more stressful Tyne Bridge crossings. No more wandering around Northumberland Street eating cheese pasties. Finally I was to escape this nightmare. I'd told them I'd been offered a huge salary and shitloads of incentives, which I knew they couldn't match. They offered a meagre pay increase to tempt me to stay but I declined.

As I was moving to what the Boss considered a rival company, I expected to be told to leave there and then. They'd still have to pay me my month's salary in lieu of notice and I was looking forward to a few weeks off before starting my new job.

However I had to work my month's notice during which hardly anyone talked to me. There was scarcely any talking to begin with, but the silence was even more deafening. A day or so before I left it was payday and you know what? That's right, I didn't get paid. They said they'd pay me the day I left, as that was the normal monthly payday anyway. What absolute bollocks, they were making the rules up as they went along. That took the piss, once again no money paid into my bank; once again the direct debits were potentially bouncing. After I pointed out payday had been on the same day every month I had worked there, they *'reluctantly'* handed over a cheque. Another round of lunchtime hassle followed, as I had to get the bloody thing cleared again. They obviously thought that if they paid me before the end of the month, I'd bugger off early and not work the rest of my notice. They're probably right. The next day was my last and quite a stressful one at that. My eldest daughter was really poorly during the last week at work, I reluctantly went to work, with my parents looking after the kids. I'm sitting at my desk, which by now was cleared of any personal belongings, with absolutely nothing to do except drink cup after cup of coffee. The Boss as usual wouldn't swan in until later on, and phoned a work colleague to check up on things. I overheard him say, "Yes he is," and I knew straight away he was asking if I had come in that day. The cheek, the nerve, the lack of trust was beyond ridiculous now, though I didn't care anymore. By eleven the Boss still wasn't in, then my mother phoned to say she'd taken the bairn to the doctor's and had been told to get her down to the hospital straight away as he suspected she could have pneumonia. Panic set in as I quickly shut down my PC and said, "See ya's". The boss walked as I was leaving. That was timed well. I told him what was happening and that I had to go. I also asked for my P45 but he hadn't bothered to make it out yet and wanted me to sign some sort of confidentiality agreement first, which said that I'd not spill the beans on any client information and so on to my new employers - the rivals.

I've often wondered if holding back an ex-employee's P45 is actually illegal, maybe I'll look into that one day.

I didn't sign it there and then, my daughter was in hospital with suspected pneumonia and that was the only thing I was focusing on at that moment. I took the agreement away with me, telling him I'd sort it out if he sorted out my P45 and thus ended my prison sentence on Tyneside.

After reaching the hospital in record time, news was good. It was a nasty virus but no pneumonia, thank God. However we had to stay in the hospital for about four hours until her temperature had dropped to a normal level.

When we did get home I checked my mobile for messages and couldn't believe the voice mail the Boss had left. It was asking if I'd make sure I got my car-parking pass sent back to them. No, *"how is your daughter?"* or anything. That showed just how insensitive and uncaring an employer he was. I was most definitely just a number while working there.

I've a theory that they didn't believe the hospital story and saw it as an excuse for me to leave early. I may be bitter and twisted and have strange and extreme views on life, but I wouldn't use my children as an excuse to get off work early.

Still, I didn't care anymore, I may not have liked the job, but it covered the bills until I found something more challenging and more comfortable.

A month into my new job and I was on emergency tax not having received my P45 because I didn't like the way the confidentiality agreement read and so hadn't signed it.

As you can imagine, my first months salary was piss poor and as much as I didn't want to sign the confidentiality thing, I did in the end just to get the last remnants of working on Tyneside out of my system and get paid the right amount - oh and it was now going into my bank account automatically, which was quite a novelty!

XXII

For quite some time we'd been getting correspondence from an exiled Mackem *'pensioner'* in Canada. I considered him a casual *'cyber-pal'* being an ex-Farringdon lad like myself and someone my gran knew as well - it's a small world.

I've lost touch with the bloke nowadays, as the 2001/2002 season unfolded into a disastrous nightmare - something which I'll touch on later if you'll bear with me - he stopped emailing his weekly views and opinions and I'd heard that he'd died, but he suddenly resurfaced, only to show his dissatisfaction at us being so negative about SAFC during the aforementioned shitty season.

It didn't half confuse me, after all I'd been writing bitter and sarcastic shit for quite a few years and couldn't fathom out his problem. I didn't lose sleep over it though. I was disappointed that someone you considered to be friendly was making me and the whole of RTG the scapegoats for the bad 2001/2002 season - I never knew how much influence we obviously had over the team, that is if you took his comments as being accurate.

Anyway the point I'm getting to is that at the time when he was regularly emailing in his exiled opinion on SAFC's amazing first season in the Premiership, he informed us he'd be coming over to Sunderland for a mini-holiday, and so we made arrangements to meet him inside the SOL's themed bar one night.

Now this bar was becoming a regular haunt for us RTG bods, being a quiet place (and clean), it was ideal to meet in private and discuss business strategy regarding the direction and steady growth of Ready To Go. Being slightly paranoid, when SAFC closed down this bar due to lack of sales (money, money, money), my initial thoughts were that they knew we met in there and it was an indirect attempt to sabotage our online commitments in sustaining our presence as the number one visited Sunderand AFC web site.

The closure was quite simply a disgraceful move if you ask me. It was a pub with American style diner food served all day, and was full of memorabilia, signed strips from many different eras, replica trophies, famous newspaper cuttings, bits and pieces from old Roker Park and so on, in fact, you could say it was a mini-museum. Closing it down meant denying access to anyone visiting the Stadium during the week.

You could only gain entry on match days and then only if you were a ticket holder in parts of the Premier Concourse.

The *Caring Club* image that SAFC had been pushing for many years was being tarnished with this act. Fair enough the place was always empty during the week, but it was a mini shrine. The *'Caring Club'* appeared to care only about income. Since when was running a football club based purely on profit making alone? We're not Man. United!

Now I made a cock-up by forgetting to take with me the guy's mobile number and likewise totally forget to give him mine. In the end you had just two RTG Dragon slayers sitting by themselves – that was me, and one of my partners.

Word had somehow got round that the bloke was in the region and a message had been posted on the site inviting people to come along and meet him - this made him sound like a real celebrity. Only one person replied to the invite, a regular who goes by the pseudonym of *'BiG'* who said to look out for a tin of Carnation Milk! He had a strange way of expressing himself, quite funny at times and weird. This outburst was one of his unusual subliminal type messages that no one would ever understand, me included.

After a few pints and realising we were alone we turned our attention to web site strategy and how we could consistently breach the one million a month page-views barrier. We agreed we needed a scoop, something we could publish online before SAFC and the media. That way we'd be seen as more than just gossip merchants.

Then this middle aged looking bloke walks in wearing a long rain coat, flat cloth cap, grabs a pint, sits downs, puts his hands in his inside jacket pocket, pulls out a tin of Carnation Milk and plonks it on the table he's sitting at.

I lean over to my colleague and whisper, "Don't make it look too obvious by turning around, but there's a bloke sitting behind us with a tin of Carnation milk".

Apprehension about approaching this stranger would soon be forgotten after we introduced ourselves and found out that this was indeed the message board regular known as *'BiG'*. He had an outlandish fascination with Bury FC after events the night we were promoted in Bury, and took it upon himself to tell us all about his antics following this lowly Second Division outfit. It was a subject we'd be tormented with for most of the evening.

I will say that *BiG* turned out to be just as strange in real life as he is in cyberspace, a guy I found fascinating, weird, frightening, yet harmless and very witty - quite a mix - and I don't think he'd take offence at any of these comments either.

I'd actually imagined him being a lot younger and a lot bigger - width wise. I guess that shows just how impossible it can be to perceive how someone will look when you only interact with him or her via a keyboard and a fourteen-inch monitor.

It is nice however to put a face to someone who frequently uses your web site, though I'd love to know what he was jotting down on paper all night. It was like he was in the process of writing his own book and the odd comment from us or something that caught his eye would be scribbled down in a secretive and sinister manner, all-very private detective *-ish* if you know what I mean.

One of these days, I'll probably turn up in his memoirs under the topic of *"sad and lonely bitter fanzine geek"*, or something like that.

Even though the night didn't go as planned we did formulate quite a few good ideas regarding raising the profile of RTG. Here we were the number one visited web site, but if you stopped anyone on the street or carried out a straw poll inside the ground on match days and asked people if they knew what *'www.readytogo.net'* was, they'd probably not have a clue and that's assuming they had Internet access or even knew what the Internet was.

We were providing a service to *the few*, those with the luxury of understanding the Internet and having the technology to surf the World Wide Web.

Percentage wise, I'd say less than a tenth of all Sunderland fans used the Internet and out of those we attracted eighty percent to visit our web site regularly. We still had a lot to achieve. We wanted to make sure everyone online knew who we were and where to find us as well as making RTG a household name to the fan on the street.

Through our sponsors we managed to get in touch with the living legend that is Gary Rowell. Now if you're reading this and don't know who Gary Rowell is, let me enlighten you. Gary played for Sunderland between 1975 and 1984, scoring a grand total of one hundred and two goals, becoming the greatest post-war goal-scorer to play for Sunderland. However his crowing glory came on February 24th 1979 when, at the age of twenty one, he scored a hat-trick against the Mags at St. James Park resulting in an historic 4-1 trashing of our rivals, elevating him to legend status. Gary is red and white through and through and will not say a bad word about Sunderland. The thought of persuading him to write for us was an inspired conception, and with financial backing from UFN, we managed to meet Gary prior to a game in a quiet location to tempt him to *'sign'* for us.

I met up with one of my partners early so we could get a rather antiquated laptop loaded up with an offline version of our web site. In *'English'* we wanted to show Gary our site so he'd understand how it worked and where his planned section would fit in. As we were in a pub we'd have no access to the World Wide Web so we copied the web site onto this dodgy laptop to simulate the surfing experience.

At that time, Gary knew nowt about the Internet, but after a few rounds of negotiating he warmed to the idea and became our first major signing. This lifted our recognition and level of professionalism. All we needed now was some publicity from the local newspaper. They didn't want to play though and rejected any article featuring our site whether Gary was part of it or not. Once again we would not be entertained and were still considered as major rivals to the all mighty official site. I wasn't sure whether to get paranoid or take it as a compliment.

We were actively promoting the City and the Club and yet we were still being ignored.

I had mixed feelings about the whole thing to tell you the truth. Maybe the Hadji wind-up, which the local paper fell for, had now come back to haunt us and thus the snub. It didn't put us off continuing to go in the direction we needed to go, or expressing ourselves in the way we wanted to. Nor did it stop us from launching the Gary Rowell section, even without *'external'* publicity, it became an instant hit.

However the transition from being amateurs to being *'professionals'* was made prior to transfer deadline day. A mate of mine had a friend who worked *'occasionally'* for SAFC. A few evenings before deadline day he rang me to say that this mate of his had been to the Stadium whilst this new signing had been having pictures taken. His name was Milton Nunez.

"Who the fuck is that?" was my initial reaction. "Is this a wind up? I've never heard of him," I say.

"No, it's true," he replies and passes on the information he'd been given.

I called one of my partners straight away to tell him and the two of us spend the evening communicating via email as we collected as much information as possible about this Honduran International striker, before putting out a story about this new transfer.

The next day it is officially announced by SAFC following what we suspect as being press pressure from the local and national media trying to find out if what this little independent web site was saying was in fact true. It did indeed turn out to be true and even though the player in question hardly kicked a ball in anger for Sunderland, we had managed to beat the press and the Club to this announcement. We had our scoop. Our credibility rating increased considerably following this and although we'd find it hard to get a sniff of future transfers before anyone else, people would turn to us first for what they considered to be up-to-date *official* news. I bet that narked the Club and the local paper, no the wonder they'd not acknowledge us.

XXIII

Seventh place in our first season back in the Premiership was the highest finish in the League for over forty years. We'd been on the brink of European qualification but one or two injuries, suspensions and rumoured player/manager bust-ups (one involving Nicky Summerbee, Chris Makin and a Sunday newspaper article about glamour girl Melanie Sykes) meant we just missed out at the final hurdle. It was still a great achievement especially considering that all anyone had wanted from Sunderland was to avoid the drop. That worry disappeared over Christmas when we breached the forty-point barrier, normally the minimum tally required to avoid relegation.

I still had a dig at SAFC for failing to qualify for the UEFA Cup. Call me fickle or hypocritical but when you look like achieving something, then to miss out due to lack of strength or quality you feel that gambles should have been taken in an attempt to ensure that going to Europe meant more than a fortnight in Benidorm for your average Sunderland supporter.

When you win more and more games, you want more and more success and if you can blatantly see where things have gone pear shaped, but there's nothing you can do about it, you air your views to see if you're either talking complete and utter shite or to see if anyone else agrees with your sentiments.

There was a lot of idle gossip going around that we had came close to buying Everton player Don Hutchison just before transfer deadline day. We didn't due to a wrangle over the transfer fee a margin whispered to be about 500k which in modern day football transfers is peanuts. The fact that we bought him anyway, after the season ended, allegedly for 500K less that the original *'asking price'* made me question if SAFC were being tight fisted. It also made me wonder if the purchase of Hutchison before transfer deadline day would've helped us qualify for Europe. If so, paying the extra would have been a drop in the ocean compared to what the Club would've earned by playing on the Continent. Sadly, this type of rumoured wheeling and dealing to save the odd penny or two would re-surface again in the future, this time regarding Emerson Thome.

Even if we didn't qualify, I doubt many people would have seen this as being money wasting, not when you look back at earlier in the season and the salary Thomas Helmer supposedly commanded, for playing less than ninety minutes football for SAFC.

It's been said that he questioned the training tactics used by the coaching staff, taking a football to Bobby Saxton and saying, "in Germany players train with these". This apparently was seen as dissent amongst the ranks and he was dropped then loaned out to a German team playing in the Champions League and prior to the end of the season or shortly after he was let go with a golden handshake.

I think the official story said his knees were *'shot'*. If you ever saw him play for Hertha Berlin in the aforementioned Champions League, you may have seen that his knees looked pretty good.

I also remember losing 1-0 at home to Bradford City of all teams, a game, which helped them stay-up and stopped us qualifying for Europe. I know many people who think the game was rigged and Reidy did his fellow Scouser Paul Jewell, a favour. Either that or the board were shit scared of qualifying because it meant they'd have to spend big and quite frankly they've never been big spenders. At times the board look as if they're quite content so long as forty thousand turn up each week and we remain in the Premiership.

But hey, don't take what I've written to be gospel; it's just all hearsay and a few rumours I'm merely sharing with you.

Of course I'm not being completely anti SAFC here, there was the FA Cup incident where we were beaten and quite frankly cheated by Tranmere Rovers. Near the end of the game they threw on a substitute as SAFC prepared for a final onslaught, but they failed to take off a player. Therefore they defended the closing minutes with twelve men, or was it that someone was sent off and the resulting chaos meant they defended the closing seconds with eleven men, when it should have been ten? Whatever, it was something the officials missed but Sunderland didn't and you could clearly see a smug grin on John Aldridge's face. He knew what was going on. Cries for a replay were thrown out as blame was put squarely in the face of the referee and not Tranmere. The event clouded the alleged player fall-outs and the lack of strength in depth that was clearly visible; well at least for a short period of time. At the end of the day however it was embarrassing to lose against a lower league team. Maybe it's just me, but I can't help but think at times that the substitute cock-up was used as the excuse for failing to beat Tranmere, when the big picture said we needed a stronger squad.

Putting aside my the initial concerns over these irritating issues and the gossip of all not being well behind the scenes, I do look back over the first year in the top flight with some pride. I recall the 5-0 away win against Derby County, the 4-0 away win against Bradford City and the 2-1 away win at St. James' Park as three of the many great victories accomplished. Kevin Phillips winning the European golden boot award for scoring thirty goals was another wonderful achievement, one that few would have dreamt of before the season had even started. On reflection it was a tremendously entertaining and satisfying period.

Internet wise, we were consistently exceeding a million impressions per month, we had Gary Rowell on board, but I was now getting tired of the whole fanzine editor thing.

Nothing controversial was happening, everything was rosy so to speak, there was no more online competition, no spammers lurking around, no online stalkers or individuals hell bent on personally slagging you off, all in all it was blissfully quiet and me being the fickle bitter type found it bloody boring.

It was also a tedious task having to pretend to be a Geordie once a month and update the resident Mag's section of Ready To Go. I mean I write plenty of negative shit about SAFC as it is, but doing it while trying to think how a Geordie would perceive SAFC was pissing me off.

The only bit of excitement I'd had in a while was prior to the home game against the Mags. I shouldn't really use the word excitement in this instance; it was quite an alarming experience when I look back at the event.

Walking over to the ground I hit a bottleneck of supporters going over the Wearmouth Bridge.

The congestion of fans was down to a large police presence slowly escorting a few hundred Mags across the bridge. They'd been rounded up around the City Centre and were being marched to the ground. Funnily enough they weren't wearing any colours all-casual like - I wonder what they had had in mind?

Well you can imagine the tone of the conversation being passed back and forth from Mackems to Geordies as the two groups of supporters got within spitting distance of each other. The thing is everyone had to go in the same direction. The police were marching the Mags on the road and the pavement area was being closely blocked by the boys in blue as the Sunderland fans were asked to move along quickly.

This bottleneck occurred due to the large numbers of Sunderland fans slowing down next to the Mags to hurl abuse, chanting the usual *"we beat the Scum 2-1"* and so on.

It was quite intimidating and being so congested you moved with the flow of bodies in whatever direction they swayed - much like the old surging days at Roker Park or some away ground when terracing ruled, and there were more fans than the standing area could take - these were the days before Hillsborough I'm referring to here - days when a Club would pack in as many fans as they could if it meant more gate receipts, regardless of how safe it was.

Being a small chap I felt quite smothered by this situation and wanted to get out of the tight spot as quickly as possible Although I found the *"we beat the Scum 2-1"* chants very amusing as I always do, I didn't like the amount of gob flying in the air and certainly didn't want any landing on me.

There was also the threat of the odd coin heading your way, and as it appeared the police were short changed in terms of numbers, you felt something serious could happen at any moment. A sudden surge took place which carried me towards the heathens as one or two of the Mackems had decided enough was enough and it was time to twat a few Geordie heads.

Sure enough a scuffle broke out albeit a minor one but I was in the fucking middle of it, and it was obvious I wasn't going to get out of there without getting involved. I could see the whites of their eyes, the stench of their body odour was getting unbearable as I tried in vain to move back over and out of the way. All I could manage was to turn full circle and was now being carried backwards towards the Skunks.

Now the whole thing happened in a matter of seconds but it felt like a lot longer than that at the time. I managed to get out of there pretty quickly, but not before receiving a whack on the head. I never saw where it came from. It may have been from a Mag, it may have been a stray punch from a Mackem but it fucking hurt and actually made me quite dizzy for a few seconds.

I'm glad I turned around otherwise it would have probably been a full facial twatting and my delicate yet beautiful face would have been scarred and damaged.

I just hurried away from the scene as quickly as possible before things got worse, not that they did, but I wasn't in the mood to hang around to find out even though a mass of police vans appeared from nowhere to separate the rivalling hoards.

I might be making a mountain out of a molehill here but in all the years of being a football supporter this was the first time I've been involved in violence resulting in injury. I'd been witness to the frenzied scenes at St James' Park in 1990. I'd been witness to the frenzied scenes at Stamford Bridge in 1985, but each time I was standing on the terraces protected by fencing and masses of police and the wife! This was outside the ground and perhaps the most dangerous place to get hurt if any sporadic outbursts of violence were to take place.

In the end it just made me hate the black and whites even more, Maybe I was hit by a stray Mackem punch, but I blame the Mags, after all why were they in our City Centre. Why were they dressed casual? Not that I need to tell you why, it's pretty obvious.

I guess you can imagine how I felt at half time during this match. Not only was I nursing a bump on my head, but we were losing 2-0. The joyous scenes near the end when Kevin Phillips scored the equaliser and final goal of the game were fantastic. I jumped up with joy, dived on one of my mate's in the row in front of me and ripped part of the skin off my leg as I slipped and dragged my shin down the back of one of the seats.

The game ended and I walked home limping with a scratched leg and nursing a headache.

Was it worth it?

Fuck yes it was, to snatch victory away from your rivals was a great feeling. I wished we could have beaten them though, the one thing I never saw us do at Roker Park was defeat the Mags. This was the first Wear and Tyne derby at the Stadium of Light, ending all square. I'd have to wait until next season before hopefully witnessing us beat them at home.

My match report of the game was surprisingly tame considering the events of the day, but maybe that was down to my lack of interest in continuing to preach Sunderland news and opinions on the Internet.

It also sounded the end of doing anymore Geordie updates for RTG. Regardless of how popular this parody was I wanted nothing more to do with it after all of that.

One of our feature writers wrote a brilliant alternative review of the game taking off the then Soccer AM's *"Spanish Aye"*.

It was something that spread outside of the Internet very quickly I dare say if you're a Sunderland supporter you may have even seen it too. One day my wife comes in with this tatty photocopied piece of paper and says, "read this, it's really funny".

I looked at it and said, "That's ours!"

Here was a *'Spanish Aye's'* view of the derby match being passed around from person to person. I was quite chuffed that some of our work had made it into the non-Internet public eye. At the same time though, the fact that it gave no mention of RTG annoyed me. It's all right saying something is yours and knowing inside it's yours, but anyone else getting a hold of this photocopied piece wouldn't know that. If you've read this *match report* before, enjoy it again, if not hopefully you'll find it amusing.

> Sunderland 2 Newcastle United 2
>
> El weekendos there was Muchos Bastardos Negros y Blancos en Estadio de Luz. El Barcodes vino a Sunderland on muchos scruffio coachos y try to 'Sing el arts oot for el lads' y 'There only uno Roberto Robsonio'. El muchos, muchos, grandes, Mackems (40,000) sing muhcos loudos 'There only uno Senile Bastardo' y 'Anal Shear-arse Illigimato'.

El Barcodes de Negros y Blancos el Roberto Robsonio el suyo bolso muy grande de las Originales de Werther y su Collostomy Baggos y pissos pantsio.

Mackems holdos heades en hands 21 minutes de 2-0 el Barcodes. Muchos Bastardos Negros y Blancos sing - 'Gannin alang de Scotswuuuud ruurrrrrrd'. El muchos, muchos, grandes, Mackems sing - 'Sunlunnnnn till I die, Sunlunnnnnn till I die' y shoutos 'HAWAYAWAYAWAYAWAYAWAY'.

En 22 minutes Estupendo Kev con knockdown de Muchos grandes Lepricorn El Quiniñho y 2-1. Muchos screamios - 'Estupendo, Estupendo Kev, Estupendo, Estupendo Kev, Estupendo, Estupendo Kev, Estupendo Kevin Phillips'. El Mackems torture el Barcodes con 'You not singin anymore, you not singgggginnnn anyyy-more!!!'.

El second halfes el Sunderland play like Matadorés y Newcastle es el weak bull.

Roberto Saxtone de Club del football de la asociación de Sunderland shoutos 'Ow Senior Summerbee - you weak as pissos' y 'That muchos minginos'. Senior Reidez make el subsitutioné de Irish pocket-rocketés - Michael Reddy.

El Mackems now franticos - 'Cuuuummmmm on Sunluuuunnnnn !!!' y 'We on our way, We on our way'.

En 82 minutes Estupendo Kev makes fools de defenciόne de Newcastle y scores magica equilizerós y Mackems go Cocoa-Loco y invades el pitch de Estadio de Luz. Muchos Mackem celebraciόnes y grande saddo Geordios. El wistel del finale blow y muchos reliefo de supportes de Sunderland y Newcastle.

Muchos pintes de cerzerva en Sunderland y Newcastle supportes en bars el la noche de sábado.

By Fernando Teodoro Manjarin.

XXIV

Euro 2000 kept the football addicts happy once the season had ended. All hopes were pinned on seeing Kevin Phillips play for England. However his thirty goals didn't warrant him playing at all during the tournament. The inconsistent Emile Heskey with pre-printed team sheet captain Alan Shearer along with England's only real goal scorer (apart from Super Kev) Michael *'little shit'* Owen was the strike force that would win us the competition - yeah right.

Of course we all know that England fell flat on their face, losing to Portugal who everyone underestimated, and although they beat a piss poor German team, they failed to get beyond the initial group stages.

Prior to the start of the tournament I'd hashed together another re-vamp of the site. It was a much-improved version of RTG and allowed me to do something that I still found interesting.

Our contract with UFN expired during the summer, and so attempts were made to sell ourselves to anyone interested in sponsoring or advertising on our *'popular independent football web site.'* We were offered a new contract from UFN who had now renamed themselves TFN, the Total Football Network.

We re-signed to them in the end as all other avenues of revenue making hit a dead end. We came close mind you. A deal worth ten quid per thousand impressions from a national football web site almost happened but, eventually we were given the usual shit about being seen as competition to their site and so on. The deal collapsed and I was pissed off. It would've meant a small fortune to divide amongst the three of us and could've provided some reward to our feature writers for all the work they volunteered.

But such is life and I should have known better trying to persuade some cheeky chirpy Cockney on the phone with my strong Mackem accent. At times I felt this twat was merely talking down to me not even bothering to listen to anything at all I was telling him about Ready To Go, its new features, plans for the future etc. It was like he'd put the phone down next to some pre-recorded audio tape that spurted out every ten or so seconds words like *"yes"*, *"uh-huh"*, *"right"*, *"go on"*, and *"sounds great mate"*, while he concentrated on jumping around his office doing a Dick Van Dyke dance in his pearly suit. He just didn't bother to do any serious negotiations with me.

I won't mention them by name though, I mean you never know they might at some point in the future change their mind so slagging them off won't exactly do me any favours now will it?

I do often wonder though if he ever had any intention of wanting to splash some cash our way or was he just full of shit, deliberately building up my hopes when his real intention was just to find out what our viewing statistics were. Why? Well I suppose it does no harm knowing how popular the competition is. I know given half the chance I'd love to know their monthly viewing figures compared to ours.

From this point onwards I would never give away our real figures and merely referred to the monthly hit rate by saying we attracted *"in excess of seven figures"*. If they wanted more details they'd have to put an offer on the table, that way I'd know they were being genuinely serious.

As the new season started, it became pretty obvious that we weren't exactly setting the world on fire in terms of record-breaking transfers that everyone was hoping for - me included. Reidy bought some unknown Slovakian defender called Stan Varga, in my view a replacement for Steve Bould who wasn't getting any younger. Club Captain, Kevin Ball, was let go on a freeby following his well deserved testimonial for the service he'd given the Club, and you could say his replacement in midfield was sorted with the purchase of Don Hutchinson for a price less than that 500k Reidy had been rumoured to be haggling over. Reidy also bought some unknown Argentinian wonder kid called Julio Arca.

Out of favour this season would be Nicky Summerbee who would hardly play a game and disappeared much like Allan Johnston. A case of déja vu or a *'curse of the Sunderland winger to fall out with the Manager'*.

The first game of the season was at home against Arsenal. We won 1-0, many thanks to one of the most incredible debuts I've ever seen from a player. Stan Varga looked like a dream buy as he single handedly took on Arsenal's front line, midfield and defence with a stunning performance. Now I'm not gay or 'owt like that but I swear there'd have been a queue to join for those who wanted to have sex with the bloke that day, such was the incredible exhibition he put on.

Of course it didn't last, we played Man City away and he basically fucked his leg, so much so that rumours spread that he'd lost over half of his lower muscles. The media were now asking *'us'* if it were true.

"How should I know?" was basically my stance, but following a tip-off from one particular source, I put out a story saying that Varga's career could be over.

God did I, or should I say RTG, get some stick over that. How dare we suggest a player's career was over with such rumours and what have you. Even *Kerching* re-surfaced for a brief spell slagging us off for suggesting half his leg was missing and so on. Jeez, all I was doing was passing on a rumour given to me by a respected member of the press. Wasn't it part of RTG's job as an independent source for news, rumours and gossip to air such information? Or had we grown that big that the audience could no longer distinguish between what was the official web site and our web site?

Either way I don't regret publishing that rumour, after all if you look at Varga when he finally got fit, he was a shadow of the player that held off Arsenal. At times he played so poorly that the Mags started to like him. I'm not trying to put him down, it was a shame he got injured so quickly into his SAFC career. Sunderland broke the bank though, in what I initially saw as a panic buy, as Emerson Thome arrived from Chelsea as either cover or replacement for Varga. By now Steve Bould had retired and so our central defence was made up of Thome and Jody Craddock a player who gets little recognition, but is a quality defender, and one who should've been given a chance in the England squad. If the likes of Wes Brown could get capped then so should Craddock. He is a much better defender than the Man. United player, but of course the difference is the Club. England is, and has always been primarily made up players from Man. United, Liverpool and London based teams. It sort of sums up to me why Phillips never got a decent run in the National squad.

Although we got off to a good start by defeating Arsenal, we then lost the following two games both to recently promoted teams, namely Manchester City and Ipswich Town. Playing at home against the likes of West Ham should really signal three points in the bag. But this game bore much frustration to many in the crowd. It was quite incredible that so early into the season frustrations were starting to boil over. This game ended in a one-all draw. I found Reidy's stance on not knowing how to use substitutes as very disconcerting. I reflected this in a report the next day, which I found satirical to say the least. Certain quarters did not, and once again the electronic flak came flying my way.

Fair enough I was whingeing, but come on, this particular round up of the previous nights events wasn't all that spurious. We'd slowly started to host some of the supporters branch web sites and one in particular must have taken my broadcast to heart and got rather heavy with one of my partners saying the branch wanted nothing to do with RTG and were more or less pulling the plug on the web site we were co-running on their behalf.

This led to a little bit of disagreement between my partners and myself over the whole write up. I refused to back down over what I had written. This was, after all '*my*' web site and I would not be dictated to by anyone nor would I bow down to any supporter's branch that may not like what I had written. If that was some sort of threat then I'd personally have agreed to let them have nothing to do with us. Remember the phrase *'freedom of speech?'*

It was a storm in a teacup, but I stand by my principles. I comment on how I see things or how I perceive how the majority of fans see things. I pick up on what's being said in the pubs, around the ground and in the bogs at half time - a great place to over hear what the *'true'* feelings are at any one time.

I know many will disagree but this is how I do my thing, I've done it for long enough so people should realise I'll not change in my pretentious methods of reporting on issues SAFC related.

The West Ham game was followed by defeat at Old Trafford. Nothing really wrong with that picture, we never ever win at Old Trafford, but it meant we'd played six games, won one, drawn one and lost four. We were heading in the wrong direction and heading there fast. We needed to pick up some points otherwise we'd be stuck in a relegation battle before too long. I've said it before but if you get stuck down the bottom too quickly you may end up remaining there for the entire season and we all know what that would mean. Peter Reid's abilities as a manager were being seriously questioned for the first time since the Reading defeat in 1997. Tactically we were looking ineffective. The lethal Quinn and Phillips partnership had been sussed out this term and the thirty-goal man was struggling to find the back of the net as frequently as he had done the previous season. Quinny, on the other hand, was not getting any younger and was seriously wrestling to last a full ninety minutes. But we had no real replacement on the bench. Our 4-4-2 system lacked a right-sided player following Summerbee being dropped.

The beginning of September was a pretty poor period, but at least the dreaded curse of the month didn't affect me personally, which was a refreshing change.

However things started to look up as SAFC slowly put together a ten match unbeaten run taking us into December before they tasted defeat again.

Impressive victories against the likes of Spurs and Chelsea at home, and Charlton away, paled into insignificance compared to the game on November 18th against the Mags at St. James' Park.

Now because I'd been giving away my season ticket vouchers for quite some time, I got an invite saying my loyalty points were high enough that I had qualified for a ticket for the Mags clash should I want to go.

I hadn't been to an away game since Wembley and hadn't been to an away game in the league since Swindon Town, but here I was officially classed as a loyal fan with a carrot being dangled in front of me. I do class myself as a loyal fan you know, just because I don't go to away games doesn't mean I'm not loyal. Loyalty often depends on availability and income.

The temptation to go to the game was too much to bear. I bought my ticket there and then.

I can't remember how much the actual price of the ticket was, but it cost me an extra twenty five quid as I'd gone overdrawn without realising it at the time I'd paid. Well, the wife wasn't at all pleased with that. It was also her birthday the same weekend, which upset her even more. The thought of me by pissing off to the game for most of the day when she wanted to go shopping annoyed her tremendously.

Therefore, the possibility did exist that I'd travel to Newcastle, watch the Lads lose, come home in a mood and be greeted by the wife in a worse mood. This outweighed the possibility of watching the Lads win. Either way I'd come home to the wife in a mood. I didn't feel confident enough that we could beat the Mags twice in a row in their own backyard. I decided it just wasn't worth going, so I sold off my ticket quite easily - at face value, I'm no tout or rip off merchant. I reckon I could've easily sold it for double the price - it would've helped pay the bank fee for being overdrawn, but I'm not that type of person, or I'm not that clever.

Of course after the game, it's easy to say, *"I wish I'd been there"*. I don't regret missing the game. Well I can't really say that because in the end I didn't miss the game. I watched it at a friends house on illegally chipped cable television. I won't go into the who, what, where, and why regarding stolen television programmes, I'm no grass and if pressed will recite the Fifth Amendment. It meant I could watch the game live without aggravation from the missus as she ended up watching it with me.

XXV

Instead of writing up my memories of the derby match, I searched through the many files I had backed up from the web site hoping I could find the original match report, in all its glory, full of spelling mistakes, and punctuation errors. I felt it was better to reproduce it as it was originally written, being only a few minutes after watching the game it holds more value when it comes to the passion and celebrations of the moment.

> Newcastle United 1 Sunderland 2
>
> Deja vu all over again?
>
> Of course and it's fucking lovely too.
>
> Today a draw would have sufficed, and having watched Beckham put Man U 1-0 up after 2 minutes in the so called "only Derby that counts", the main thought was not to concede early.
>
> What happens?
>
> A lucky and scrappy goal by Speed, rebounding off the post puts the Skunks 1-0 up after about 2 minutes.
>
> Oh dear.
>
> Panic struck, gutted and thinking stuffing is on the cards. You get this feeling even more so when the Lads look slightly off the pace by about 0.5 of a second. The midfield was at times struggling too much, but we held our own and a fine save by Judas denied Quinny mid way through the first half.
>
> Amazingly Sunderland started today with the same 11 that drew 2-2 with Southampton. No Arca automatically recalled meaning Hutchison playing right again and Kilbane on his natural left. Now without playing a broken record Kilbane is more affective for Sunderland on the right and Hutchison more affective as an attacking central midfielder and so naturally you expect a tactical switch from our illustrious leader at half time.
>
> No (as usual) and though we started brightly in the second half you felt more and more nervous that they would defeat us. But hey come on today is not the day to bitch and moan.

On comes Arca for Makin.

Kilbane switches to the right.

Arca on the left.

Hutchison now in the middle.

Phillips gets the ball down the left-hand side, crosses for The Don to *'half-volley'* it into the net.

1-1.

YYYYYEEEEEEEESSSSSSSSSSSSSS.

You're not singing anymore!

Right then that'll do, blow the whistle for full time I can't stand the pressure anymore - don't care how long is left. But then Mickey Gray bursts down the left crosses perfectly for Quinny to beat Judas and it's 2-1 (If you ever see this goal watch how Judas's head rebounds off the post as he hopelessly attempts to save the ball from going into the net - quite funny - ouch!)

OH MY GOD.

YYYYYYEEEEEEEEEEESSSSSSSSS.

You're not singing anymore!

Can it be? Can we actually defeat the Scum again?

But then disaster?

Quinny brings down Rob Lee and it's a penalty - what were you doing Niall? Oh shit.

And up steps Mary Poppins.

And Sorensen saves it you fucking hero!

YYYYEEEEEEESSSSSSSSSS.

You're not singing anymore and I've almost come in my pants!

Can you believe it - Shearer missed, no he did not - Sorensen saved brilliantly!

Five minutes to go. Speed hits the bar! Then four, three, two, one, then an agonizing three minutes of injury time. We keep possession nicely for a short period of time, then pressure from them, then the final whistle is blown and we've done it. Back to back victories!

An away double!

And so, the rather extreme *"we beat the Scum 2-1"* was instantly replaced by *"we always win 2-1"*. Defeating the Mags always signals over the top celebrations, well it doesn't happen all that often.

Sunderland was bouncing that night while rumours filtered through suggesting that BT were on red-alert in the Bigg Market.

Once again the sweet smell of success inspired the intellectual Mackem's roaming cyber space to put pen to paper and submit no end of creative and expressive poetic feelings. We're like git cultured us Wearsiders yer knar!

> I'm a poor defenceless phone-box,
> Tell me, what have I done?
> I was standing here so quietly,
> When it all begun,
> I thought they'd come to phone someone,
> But I couldn't really see,
> As they kicked all of my glass out,
> And speared me with a tree!
>
> Some people climbed on top of me,
> Others gathered around,
> They shook me up, pulled out my wires,
> I was too scared to make a sound,
> I was glad when it was over,
> And the policemen came my way,
> But imagine my horror the next year,
> The same thing happened again!
>
> I packed up and left the Bigg Market,
> I wanted to save my skin,
> At least I wasn't there yesterday,
> I knew Sunderland would win!
>
> And lest we forget;
> At the end of the day
> Tommy dived the right way.

XXVI

The dizzy heights of being second in the league unleashed no end of nosebleeds once again on Wearside. We had just destroyed Ipswich Town 4-1 on New Years Day 2001 and talk wasn't just being concentrated on the UEFA cup but on Champions League qualification. Everyone was getting excited. We had indeed built upon the seventh place finish the previous year, and as we started the year on such a high, it was obvious that now was the time to buy, attract big name players and top class quality to ensure that we could sustain our position for the remainder of the season.

I was bloody excited about the whole affair. I compared us to Leeds United a few years back when they had won the old First Division soon after being promoted. If they could do it then we could. We were only a few points behind the leaders Manchester United. The countdown was on until we played them at home in a few weeks in a top of the table clash. If memory serves, a win over Bradford at the Stadium would have put us top or at least joint top.

We drew 0-0 in a frustrating game and at the same time, Peter Reid openly commented that the 'E' word, meaning Europe, was not being discussed in the dressing room. Why was that? Too scared in case we didn't qualify, or too scared in case we did?

Either way our chance to improve and attract quality slipped by as silence emanated from within the ivory towers of the Stadium of Light regarding any fresh blood coming in. The squad we had was a good bunch of lads, but it would do no harm in to improve it, alas it was not to be.

To this day I look back at that period and think if only. If only SAFC had had the balls to speculate, but from my perspective they bottled it - yellow skinned.

When the season finished we ended up seventh just like the previous term. No Europe. Now it's all too easy to say that finishing seventh again was another success. In many ways it was, but cracks were forming within the ranks of SAFC, or so it was perceived by the average supporter like me. The shock sale of Chris Makin only led to more and more rumours about internal bust-ups, adultery and God knows what else. The Club in their season ticket renewal forms issued a statement that promised a push towards ensuring Europe and many looked towards the 2001/2002 season as being *"Europe or bust"*.

Was I satisfied? Overall, yes I guess I was. I mean we beat Chelsea at Stamford Bridge in an enthralling 4-2 victory. It really put us on the road towards reaching that European dream, but then we crumbled - so what's new - losing to Leeds, Spurs and Coventry, and drew against the *'rivals'* - Newcastle and Middlesbrough.

The Spurs game had to be the worse case of a Jeckyll and Hyde performance ever seen. We were two nil up at home cruising to victory and the next step towards Europe, but lost 3-2. Can you believe that? It was a disaster to lose a game you commanded for so long with such a healthy lead. Privately I feel that defeat cost us the spot in Europe. Losing away to Coventry was nowt new as we've always struggled down there but we would have relegated the *Sky Blues* that day if we'd have won. What sweet justice that would've been. Thankfully, Coventry did go down at the end of the season, which was most comforting. What goes around comes around. They had had the luxury of top-flight football for far too long. I wept with joy when they crashed out of the Premiership, content that they were too small to bounce back and that lower league football would haunt them for a long, long time.

Sentiments like this were echoed on the web site and yielded a barrage of complaints. We were accused by many a perplexed Coventry supporter of being sad and bitter individuals for holding a grudge over an event that had taken place so long ago. Tough shit. Sad and bitter is probably true but you cheating bastards relegated us in '77 and though it took longer than expected, watching you get relegated was exhilarating to say the least.

Other games bore little result. Blame was not focussed on SAFC but on the bloody referees. Step forward Graham Barber and Graham Poll. The former cost us victory at home against Liverpool by awarding a penalty after Gary McAllister was fouled outside the box. You blind bastard. Then there was Mr Poll in charge of the Man. United game, and as usual the most holiest of officials was to take centre stage. We lost 1-0 thanks to the bastard in the black also being blind and not seeing a deliberate handball by Andy Cole prior to the Red Devils scoring. Frustration following that incident cost SAFC two red cards. I was fuming over the blatant ignorance shown by the referee. I should've known better when it comes to Mr Poll. It wouldn't matter to him who was on the pitch. You could have Luis Figo, Rivaldo, or Renaldo scoring a hat trick and Poll would ensure he'd make the headlines instead of the Portuguese or Brazilian superstar.

In honour of his woeful officiating I set-up an online guest book for the *greatest* referee in the world. It took less than an hour before over five hundred messages had been posted *thanking* Mr Poll for his services to the football industry. I'd have loved it if any of these messages got through to him. You never know they may have, after all any news headline we published on RTG would get sucked up by online news trawlers that spider Internet sites for particular words that they've been programmed to look for, then copy those headlines onto their own news pages. To spider is geek speak meaning to scan, search and sift for information. As we had an agreement to be spidered from News Now who are the online equivalent of the Press Association, hopefully Mr Poll would be suitably embarrassed by his performance after reading the barrage of shit thrown at him. Then again he's probably that far up his own arse he'd probably enjoy it. I can well imagine he thrives on controversy and the publicity it generates for him. Most Sunderland fans look forward to him officiating games involving the Lads, it provides an outlet to hurl abuse at someone who is quite frankly another hated figure on Wearside.

I will point out though I deleted any crap that went too far, not that there was like any death threats posted or 'owt, but someone did find what looked like his home address and telephone number. I had little choice but to remove that guest book entry for fear of the potential legal implications that could have arisen. It wasn't meant to spawn malignant hate mail, more like seeing if others were just as circumvented as me over the whole encounter.

The presence of a female stripper during the second half of the Man. United game had helped ease the tension building up in the crowd. From a distance, running around the pitch wearing nowt but a knitted pair of red and white knickers she looked like a babe. Up close, well that's debatable. Don't take that the wrong way though; I'm no Prince Charming. Normally such behaviour warrants a ban from the ground. SAFC let her off after she appeared in court informing the authorities she had done it for charity. Was it that, or the fact that she may have stopped a riot taking place that made SAFC change their minds? Another conspiracy to brood over?

Then there was the home game against the Boro resulting in a very strange case of *'Groundhog Day'*.

Walking over to the ground I hit a bottleneck of supporters going over the Wearmouth Bridge.

The congestion of fans was down to a large police presence slowly escorting a few hundred Smoggies across the bridge. They'd been rounded up around the City Centre and were being marched to the ground. Funnily enough they weren't wearing any colours all-casual like - I wonder what they had had in mind?

Well you can imagine the tone of the conversation being passed back and forth from Mackems to Mutants as the two groups of supporters got within spitting distance of each other. The thing is everyone had to go in the same direction. The police were marching the Teessiders on the road and the pavement area was being closely blocked by the boys in blue as the Sunderland fans were asked to move along quickly.

This bottleneck occurred due to the large numbers of Sunderland fans slowing down next to the Smoggies to hurl abuse, chanting the usual *"small town in Yorkshire"* and so on.

Once again I was getting smothered by this unwanted case of déja vu and wanted to get out of the tight spot as quickly as possible. The amount of gob flying in the air and threat of the odd coin heading your way was far too much of a familiar scene and I didn't want the same thing occurring as with the game against the Mags. I couldn't believe this was happening again, and I certainly didn't feel like getting twatted again.

You may have realised by now that I've more or less copied word for word what I've previously written about the home game against the Mags. Up to this point everything that was evolving around me was identical to the Mags game. I therefore knew in advance what was going to happen next, so I made sure I got out of the way before any surge took place and subsequent outbursts of sporadic violence resulting in me getting thumped. Thankfully, this game would end without any personal injury.

On the web I was getting a lot of emails and phone calls from some bloke in Burnley who was part of a new network of independent football sites. He was constantly poaching for RTG to join them.

It was an interesting proposal. Our contract with TFN was about to expire, thus the new sponsorship offer was one worth further investigation. I managed to sponge one of the executive boxes at the Stadium of Light for nowt to invite this network's *'MD'* up one Saturday morning during the close season to thrash out a deal.

By obtaining the box, the idea was to show that we were professional people and not some back bedroom hobbyists. With print-outs of our new design, laptop simulations and waiter service with the tea and coffee, I think we did a marvellous job in presenting ourselves, so much so we shook hands on a deal that you could say doubled what TFN were offering.

This was great; it meant a second salary each month and money to invest in e-commerce - the ability to take credit card transactions online. We had no end of merchandising ideas to boost the site and this investment would enable us to offer our audience more than just news and gossip. We even planned on hiring someone to go to the training ground each day, take digital photos and keep the site updated with all the latest news, official or otherwise.

All we needed was a contract to sign and we were well on our way. It was the next rung on the ladder towards that illusive status of *dot com millionaire*.

Luckily we got a contract shortly after though the wording wasn't correct, but that appeared a minor obstacle and one to sort out on a planned visit to their headquarters in Burnley one afternoon prior to the start of the new season.

I arrived late having taken the long route to Burnley via the M62, ending up more or less at Wigan Pier before I realised that I'd missed the turning I should've taken about twelve junctions earlier. I was fucking annoyed with myself arriving late and all flustered as it looked unprofessional, but thankfully the meeting went well, much was agreed and a new contract was issued.

With income signed and sealed, I looked forward to booking an expensive holiday for next summer. The additional income each month would pay for it and would be just reward in my eyes. We'd also still have ample left to possibly employ a reporter and no longer had to worry about e-commerce as our new sponsors had their own set-up, which we were told we could utilise.

The new season was around the corner and optimism was high. I felt the forthcoming campaign would reap great rewards both on the pitch as everyone thought we would be easily challenging for Europe, and off the pitch in cyberspace as our popularity would hopefully soar higher, and bring in that pot of gold I'd worked so hard for.

XXVII

As the season got under way we were hit by a legal threat from the F.A. It appeared that the fixture list we were displaying on Ready To Go was copyrighted to the footballing authorities and we would have to remove them, as we did not have a licence. If we wanted a licence we would have to contact them. So we did. They then refused, as we were not an officially recognised member of the Press Association or whatever. Catch 22? It was sad to read their pitiful email. I mean here we were the small independent web site being threatened by the old gits who run football in the UK. How sad and how petty. I wish we had left them on and seen how far they would have gone. If they'd issued legal action against us, the publicity would have been immense, but cost wise it was too much to risk.

I have a suspicion, mind you, that we were shopped by a rival web site who didn't like the fact that not only were we on the ball by releasing the new fixtures before anyone else, but somehow we also managed to display the entire fixture list for every Premiership team before anyone else - including the likes of the BBC's web site. I believe jealousy set-in and that someone, and you know who you are you sad fuck, grassed us up.

It backfired as out of the blue *BiG* re-surfaced with his alternative fixture list, which many people found amusing. This list was in a way a two-fingered salute towards the sad twats that shopped us and to the footballing authorities.

What we put up was a daft cake eating tour of England, which for example would state that;

> March 2nd
>
> My enthusiasm fer cake *Spurs* me on. I particularly like chocolate. Especially *White*. *Hart* shaped bits of it stuck on the top of cake. That's right up my *Lane* that like.
>
> March 30th
>
> Yer knaa how aa said aa was gettin' fat? Well it's not just me belly. It's me *Arse 'n' all*. But cakes are great. Aa divvent need drugs. Meringue get's me *High*. *Bury* me with a tart aa told wor lass. She slapped uz.

Likewise our contract with our new sponsors meant that as they had the licence to show the fixtures we also had a licence to show the fixtures. In the end though we left on the cake-eating list.

Not long into the season Sunderland were drawn against Sheffield Wednesday in the League Cup. *BiG* emailed us a crazy idea which we decided to go along with it, and because of it, our publicity ballooned. The idea was code named *Operation Kazoo*.

Everyone knows how the *famous* Sheffield Wednesday band kills the atmosphere and any semblance of wit or banter between fans due to their incessant parping and hooting of the theme from *The Great Escape* all the way through a match.

BiG's idea, albeit through his alter ego *Stotty Tatlock*, was to get as many SAFC fans as possible to get their own back at the Worthington Cup game and echo a few of their tunes on the most irritating instrument known to man, the kazoo.

RTG helped spread the news of this operation, and with assistance from our new found *'associates'* ALS managed to arrange a radio interview one morning on the BBC 5's live breakfast show.

They wanted as many *'kazooers'* as possible to turn up in a stand off with the Sheffield Wednesday band, by alternating broadcasts between Sunderland and Sheffield, and between trumpets and kazoos. I went along to join in the fun ending up with a kazoo stuck in my gob due to lack of attendees. There was just me, one of the ALS lads, the BBC radio bloke, and *'Stotty Tatlock'* who turned up early and stood outside of Joan's Café wearing a false nose, tash, specs, rain mac, and flat cap - what a mad site, typical *BiG*.

When the signal came for the stand off to begin, I found I couldn't blow the fucking thing. I was giggling like a little girl with amusement over the whole scenario and *BiG* still wearing his false tash, nose and specs like an overweight Groucho Marx - we were on the radio, *BiG*. It was all good fun and just a big piss take, typical of the good-natured humour associated with SAFC fans. The lads being interviewed from the Sheff. Wed band didn't think so, and stated quite snobbishly that it was nothing new, they had done the same thing the previous season when the band was refused entry at Brammell Lane during the Sheffield Wednesday and Sheffield United derby. On that occasion they used kazoos. Fair enough, but I couldn't resist stating that it had taken Premiership fans to do this to get the national media to take notice. Sunderland were therefore the visionaries with this joke.

The radio interview wasn't the last of it, before I knew it local newspapers in both Sunderland and Yorkshire were on the phone or emailing for further information about the event. Toy shops around the region were fast selling out of kazoos and it appeared that everyone going to the match would be armed with this musical instrument. Then

Tyne Tees wanted to film a bunch of fans blowing their *'hearts out for the Lads.'* I went along to the Stadium to watch proceedings. A few people had turned up, mainly ALS lads, and one or two who had seen the invite from the RTG message board, but no *BiG*. No end of persuasion could get him to appear on television. He therefore remains to this day a figment of a few people's imagination.

As usual I wasn't going to the game, but I intended on listening to it on the radio to see if the few thousands Mackem's would be blowing to the tune of *"We Love You Sunderland We Do"* on these plastic efforts.

XXVIII

On September 11th 2001 events in the USA gripped the planet. Everyone knew somebody affected by what happened on that day. It was a black September all right and one of two events that completely changed my outlook on life.

I'd been on a training course at British Airways in Newcastle to learn how they develop their own web site, parts of which were being tendered out to web companies like the one I was working at. Half way through this course someone bursts in to say that all flights were being grounded due to rumours that the World Trade Center had been hit by a passenger jet, the White House had been hit, and basically World War Three was starting.

Attempts to log onto the Internet to see if any of this was genuine failed as web sites all over the globe went down due to the increased volume of traffic from people wanting to know if any of these rumours were in fact true.

As it became apparent what had happened, the training course was cut short. I got to the car and put on the radio listening to the horrors of the events unfolding in America.

I felt very strange, like we were on the brink of world leaders panicking and pressing big red buttons that would wipe out all of mankind. I was in the middle of Newcastle and couldn't get home quickly enough. The battery on my mobile was dead so I couldn't call the wife. She was at work, by now the kids would be at my parents after finishing school, and my thoughts were simply to round them all up as quickly as possible.

I sat glued to Sky News, BBC News 24, and CNN all night in total awe of what was happening across the Atlantic. I know I'm paranoid, I've said it many times but when news came that President Bush was now located inside the Cheyenne Mountain complex, headquarters of NORAD, It suggested to me he was deep underground in a bunker fighting the high moral ground between all out retaliation and some sort of sanity. The thing is I'm not sure anyone knew who had attacked the US at this time, so any launching of a nuclear strike would have meant targeting anyone and everyone.

I started to take the dining room door off its hinge and make a makeshift bomb shelter like I'd seen on some TV program that was shown in the Eighties.

The bairns were confused. Why was daddy making a tent out of a door? The wife told me to stop being so fucking stupid and put the door back on.

Inside, however, I was worried and apprehensive about the immediate future of our planet. I'm not taking the piss here over the events in the US on September 11th. It affected everyone, everywhere and this is merely how I absorbed everything that day.

I took a deep breath, calmed down and sat back down in front of the television.

Watching repeated re-runs of the towers collapsing was, to be frank absolutely fascinating. It was very frightening and horrific to think of all those people who were trapped inside those buildings.

I personally believe the planet came close to being wiped out in an avenging strike, but that's something we'll probably never know. My thoughts turned to a lad called Adam who was in fact RTG's very own exiled Mackem living in New York and a regular feature writer airing his views on life supporting SAFC in the U.S of A.

I sent an email to ask if he was *'alive'*. I got a reply that very night, yes he was *'alive'*, he lived outside of Manhattan but he never made it to work that day as the area was evacuated. For a few days he used the RTG news page to report on what was happening in New York following the collapse of the twin towers.

The first of his articles gave a first hand eye witness account of the tragic events, and the fact that it came from a Sunderland supporter, and one of our feature writers, showed just how small the world actually is when it comes to cyberspace.

This article reads:

> "A soldier stands surveying the damage, his rifle clutched loosely in his hands as he waves the crowds of mask wearing medical staff past him into the emergency triage centers set up by the local hospital.
>
> Around him the rubble continues to smoke, the underground fires still burning a whole day after the initial explosions. Rising from shattered buildings and debris it's hard to make out anything through the cloud that's further than a block away, but occasionally a gust of wind clears the air revealing the true extent of the damage ahead. It is obviously a war zone.
>
> Everywhere fire trucks and ambulances are lying empty and abandoned, some have their windows smashed, others are crushed under tons of rubble. Thick ash and concrete dust covers everything, in some places it's as much as an inch thick.

Behind him military trucks roll past in convoy. In the sky F-15 fighters circle, their jet trails mixing with the dense plumes of smoke hanging over the city.

This could be Beirut, it could be Sarajevo or it could be Mogadishu. But it's not.

It's New York and despite the light level it's only 11 am.

This is the scene that greets you in the lower area of town. One of the most memorable scenes that I witnessed was a tired looking national guard soldier standing in front of a poster from NBC's new WWII show Band of brothers stating, *"All we knew was that we're in this together."* On it two soldiers were helping a wounded man out from a battlefield, but in the City on that day several dust-covered paramedics had just walked past, their faces saying it all. Today I have been informed that tens of thousands of people have turned out to give blood (British subjects are not allowed to give blood due to BSE in the UK). Others are volunteering for the hospitals, the debris clearing squads or fire departments in such droves that the Mayor has formally asked people to register to be called upon when their particular skills are needed. They have enough, New York, although bruised, is pulling itself together.

The comparisons to a war zone are unavoidable and, I firmly believe, necessary. When I found out that they had attacked the pentagon with what the media called 'a human missile' I was asked what was wrong by a pedestrian near me, I told them and was flatly informed, *"This is war."*

It's what every American is thinking and this attack amounts to just that, a military strike against the heart of the USA, something that has not happened since Pearl Harbor.

Throughout the city, rescue workers are sitting around exhausted, their hair covered in that dust that I'm sure by now you've seen on TV. At the barricades on Houston Street, crowds of people are standing around gawping. It's not that they're staring at the horror of the scene, because there's nothing there, that's the point. From these scattered zones around the City there should be at leasing something visible: only a day ago New York had one of the tallest buildings in the world. Now there is nothing.

There is no denying the extent of the devastation here. It's truly terrible to behold, throughout Manhattan the normal crowds are missing, and even in the subway the usually packed carriages are subdued and silent. I have never seen or witnessed anything like this and I hope I never will again. "

This report was followed up a few days later by this update:

"It is now three days since a day that I will remember for the rest of my life. Three days and the chances of finding anyone are now narrowing dramatically.

Currently things are a little different in the City. Last night I awoke to a thunderstorm raging overhead, a mixed blessing as many people had been praying for rain to take the huge dust cloud that still hangs over the city, out of the air. An inch and a half of rain fell overnight and never forget that the World Trade Center goes some seven stories underground. It is there that is the last chance for survivors. It is hard to not think that such heavy rain will both hamper the rescue effort and endanger anyone left underneath the collapsed towers. I hope for everyone's sake that neither is true.

Another event is the *"wall of prayer,"* a wall of notification for people to post missing notices on, thousands are doing it (remember that at this time just under 5,000 people are missing). This wall is the pure human aspect of this tragedy, and to see these people yourself is distressing in the extreme. For the first day the relatives were calling the TV stations in tears begging for any sort of information. Now the TV stations are broadcasting long lists of names with photographs. What is most shocking about this is the realization of the youth of most of the missing. The sense of tragedy here is at a very personal level.

The effects on this great City have not just been physical; they have been psychological as well. All the time it seems now, reports are coming in of terrorist attacks, of explosives being found, and of people being stopped with devices. Many of these have been false, remember that the USA has never experienced a tragedy like this and terrorism here is a rarity. It is literally jumping at its own shadow but to be honest who can really blame them? I remember on the first day watching all the bomb reports come in, schools, hospitals, airports - I counted at least eight on the first day alone!

Another aspect of this terrible tragedy is the reporting. So far the media have been thanked by the fire fighters (many media personal over here have offices in the towers) but a lot of false reporting has led to false hope amongst the families of these victims, of people being found alive in particular. The only rescues have been on the two days. After this almost 100% of the reporting of rescues have been inaccurate. Last night a woman was arrested on site for convincing authorities that 9 people were still trapped underneath the building; it was not true. It is a sad fact of sensationalism, in a City that thinks it is under attack again because of a storm's thunder that every single rumour is picked up like gold. I cannot think what this is doing to those people I have seen giving out the leaflets with their loved ones faces on. You see them everywhere.

As this article goes out I wish again to thank the rescue crews. I have seen the extent to which they work, the hundreds of trucks on Houston waiting to go in and take rubble out, and the medical workers and firemen. "Ground Zero" at the World Trade Center as it is now known is a dangerous place, and people are being hurt there trying to rescue others. The disease risk is setting in among the ruins now, and risk of smoke/dust inhalation extreme. Yet work will not cease."

A few days later he sent in a final update:

"By now the crisis in America is slowly resolving itself, the City is burying its dead, the lost are being mourned and the vast majority of New York's civilians are waking up to a different world to the one that they knew only a few days ago.

Eyes have now ceased to look inward, and, like the rest of the world, are now fixed outside the boundaries of this country. People are asking what next? It is an important question to consider.

You might remember that in the last article I reported that people over here are getting jumpy, that there is a distinct feeling of unease hanging over the streets and that the attack is being seen as a military strike, one that was directed against military and civilian targets alike. I also mentioned a number of false reports regarding terrorists and bomb threats but to be honest I did not realize the full extent of this feeling until my visit to the City yesterday.

During the week I have visited central Manhattan pretty much every day but yesterday my eyes were opened perhaps far more then I would have liked. This was because I have seen many different sides of the arguments.

Now no one wants the attackers to go unpunished but although many comparisons to Pearl Harbor exist, this time there is no direct enemy to be punished. There are no foreign armies rampaging across the world and there are certainly no precedents for the kind of war that must be fought against this terror.

One message is very strong, that of the anti-hate crowd in the City. I was present in Union Square during one of these protests and the feeling was that of union and of optimism for the future. But there is a new type of feeling growing here that of revenge and no one is sure who it should be directed against.

For the first time yesterday I was informed that various foreign groups across the City are being targeted, in particular those from India, or Pakistan, or Afghanistan. Several of the people in these countries (of which there are many in this City) have been attacked for little other reason then their skin colour. To this extent hundreds of posters have appeared declaring that 'Muslims are not the enemy' or 'India is mourning too'. And to be honest they're right.

I was in a bar on 3rd Ave yesterday with some of my friends from Singapore/India when we were approached by a local and verbally attacked. The bar staff, although looking distinctly uncomfortable, did nothing and left the person in question alone. Not only were they mistaken for the wrong religion but also the wrong race, and country. And according to the news this sort of thing is happening more and more frequently.

Feelings are running high at the moment, and many people are talking about all out-war. I hope that they are wrong and that the real perpetrators of this can be found and dealt with individually. If they cannot then who knows where this might end."

    I felt it was worth reproducing those articles as it was history in the making, even though I'm writing about me and the Internet, the support and love I have for Sunderland AFC, September 11th 2001 is an event that cannot be ignored.

    The web site albeit a football fanzine ceased to be that for a few days following the event. The entire message board was focused on discussions about what was going on, people who knew people, comments, and speculation on what the future held.

    Sunderland had to play Sheffield Wednesday on September the 12th. The game should never have been played. I don't think that many people were bothered, or were focused on the match, and that probably included the players. The big kazoo thing never took off, and I'm not surprised after all it was to be a fun thing and September and fun didn't go together in 2001.

    The Lads lost the game, dumped out of the League Cup by a lower league team. It was disappointing but not seen as the end of the world, that happened the day before, or would be happening, in the coming months for all I knew.

But life goes on. Ready To Go needed to return to being a football site and normality, if there is such a thing did slowly return. At this point however, the *'American Psycho'* was born. Well that's what I call him. A regular poster on the message board who was always part of the holier than thou crowd appeared to lose his marbles about this time. Now I don't know who this person is, never met him, wouldn't want to, but from what I could gather he was some sort of merchant banker, working for some multinational corporation in London. He'd often find pleasure by posting on the message board that he was jetting off to the States and wouldn't be back for a few days. Nothing wrong with that I hear you say, but the thing is its the way it came across - like the guy suffered some sort of inferiority complex and had to tell all and sundry where he was going in order to prove how much of a big shot he was. Maybe I'm being too harsh here, or jealous of someone who was simply a successful businessman, I guess his views on SAFC compared to mine would never and will never be seen eye to eye, but I found his behaviour, albeit via words on a message board, very strange. The nickname *American Psycho* summed him up for me and following September 11th I witnessed him crack up online so to speak. First off he posted a heartbreaking message about the tragic events and how many friends he'd known and lost inside the towers - again nothing wrong with that, but to me the last thing on my mind if I'd lost colleagues on that day would be to post on a meaningless football message board to tell everyone about it. I guess that was his way of coping with grief. Yet a few days later the same bloke posts up a picture of a tourist standing on top of the World Trade Center posing for a photo with a doctored image of an airplane behind him.

Fair enough tragic events always spring up jokes and images that take the piss, but one moment he looking for sympathy about the loss of life, and before you know it he's taking the piss out the whole thing. Maybe I'll be viewed as misunderstanding the whole saga, but I wasn't alone in questioning this guy's motives. His anger was then suddenly directed towards RTG demanding to know our financial gains from exploiting Sunderland fans and that we were nothing more than parasites living off the back of SAFC.

> "Ready To Go will take no criticism of themselves and they take themselves far too seriously.
>
> Whilst they are completely happy to criticise SAFC they will not take criticism of themselves at all. Even when they criticise SAFC for reacting against criticism whenever someone criticises RTG they get banned or the posts get removed.

RTG are nothing more than parasites. Happy to criticise themselves but whenever someone criticises RTG they go all huffy.

Parasites, parasites, parasites."

What the fuck brought that on? Can't take criticism? Take myself to seriously? Go back to page one and start reading this book again please!

To me, it was a personal insult. Here is someone quite happy to use what is a free web site but wants to rip into you for some reason. I'm sorry but I'm only human and just a supporter who got lucky by co-creating a successful web site - successful in terms of popularity not financial gain. Even though the posts were from some git calling himself *'The Equaliser'*, our rather sophisticated hidden tracking system proved who the guy was.

I've still got copies of those logs, IP addresses that point to the organisation he works for. I kept them in case things got so out of hand that legal action was required.

Call it petty, call it pathetic, but my view was to protect my investment, and like previous flamers or Internet stalkers, it was viewed that the slagging off and name-calling would soon wear off. The fact is, it lasted a lot longer than I thought but each post made was added to the portfolio, kept safe in case it was ever needed in the future.

I'm sure if things had of got out of hand, his employers would be very interested in someone abusing their privileges while at work, to flame not only us but other regulars. The message board is very popular but it was slowly descending into a state of chaos.

Anyone new to the web who may stumble onto our site for the first time was walking on dangerous ground. They'd be victims of potentially posting a genuine comment, only to be instantly told to *"fuck off wanker"*, or something just as colourful.

I'm not saying these *"fuck off"* messages came from the *American Psycho*, there's far too many weirdo's using the message board, the holier than thou brigade whose views are the only views and if you don't agree with them you face the consequences. It's the power of the Internet, the ability to hide behind words and cause destruction, bad feelings, and other sinister activities.

I've got my own share of strong views, but I don't attempt to ram them down your throat until you submit. Too many posts were like this and even though they were signed by strange and unusual names, I could clearly see whom the culprits were. A dozen or so *'people'* were barred from using the message board as we attempted to make it a friendly place to interface once again.

Strange though that as I expected a flood of emails to come from people asking why they were banned, I never received any, and the message board slowly regained a level of decency.

Sunderland were having a shit season. Supporter's views were now in a state of disagreement regarding tactics, player attitudes, and keeping the faith. The beginning of the *'Reid-in'* camp and the *'Reid-out'* camp was emerging and slowly but surely RTG started to become victim of those who saw nothing wrong with the set-up at SAFC and that anything negative I, or we'd write, was seen as being unacceptable.

We were even accused of being nothing more than Mags in disguise, knew nothing about SAFC, and had only supported Sunderland since the new stadium had been built. We also had no idea what the *'true'* feelings of *'real'* supporters were, as we hardly went to any games, and lived outside the region. It was a great combination of conclusions, which were all shite.

I live in Sunderland but the fact that our P. O. Box address is based in Cheshire was enough for them to say we lived outside the area. It wasn't the *'American Psycho'* saying this and not so much the holier than thou brigade.

We were now being targeted by another so-called *'rival'* web site, well they see themselves as rivals.

Fact is, one day they announced their daily statistics, which I found mildly amusing as they matched at times our hourly statistics so in terms of visitors, you can hardly say they were rivals. Yet they seemed to be fascinated by anything controversial we'd write.

They'd only stick to pro-Sunderland stories, probably down to privileges installed on them by SAFC, and for some reason kept on mentioning us and our web address.

We've never mentioned them by their real name nor publicised their web address, much like *'Kerching'* in the early days we were getting no end of free publicity and they were in turn driving traffic away from their site and onto ours. So in my best Elvis voice, *"Thank you very much."*

I tried my best to keep calm over all of this, as it was bad enough watching Sunderland play shite but the finger of blame was slowly being pointed towards RTG for their *'negative'* attitude.

It was probably only my attitude that was negative, but since when was I ever positive? I've stated many times before that no matter how good life is or no matter how well your team is playing there's always room to moan and have the odd dig or two at someone or something as you search for prefection.

However, putting my editorial head on, I attempted to remain neutral, I didn't want to lose it big time and push any self destruct button on the web site. Our new contract with our new sponsors meant bigger things were on the horizon for RTG and hopefully SAFC would get over the predicament they were in, jump that next hurdle and onto more stable things.

Well we all know that the season slowly got worse and I too slowly sank into a state of negativity and sort of lost my own marbles, not through idiots having a pop on the web site, not through SAFC playing like a bunch of fannies, not through the stress endured globally after September 11th, but through my mother!

Before I get onto that though, and as a supplement to this chapter, here is the Oxford English Dictionary definition of the word parasite, which of course Ready To Go and I are collectively charged as being. What do you think?

> Parasite *noun:* an animal or plant living on or in another; a person living off another or others and giving no useful return.

XXIX

When I sat down to compose this next chapter I was in two minds as to just how much I'd end up saying and how personal I'd get. I found by writing down my feelings it helped ease the pain and shock of the personal events following the September 11th disaster.

I'm talking here about my mother, and how she managed to throw back in my face all the respect her only child, that's me, had ever given her. I'm not going to get too detailed, but I was stunned when, at the age of sixty, she told me she was leaving my father as she had been having an affair with some fat bloke for the past six months. This was the same woman who had always taught me that this sort of thing was the devil's work and that a marriage should be for life. She had even chastised a member of her own family for doing the same thing several months earlier. She had, until that day, always been the most moral person I had known. In fact she was moral to the point of stupidity sometimes. I had noticed a bizarre change in her attitude of late. For example, she'd been having her hair dyed a silly shade of ginger, I mean come on, and had been going out regularly drinking with these friends she'd known for years but had recently bumped into in town, coincidence? I think not! She seemed to think I'd be interested in hearing how many times either she or one of these friends had been sick in the taxi on the way home from the pub. Of course I was not. I just wanted to shake the silly woman and say, "you're a grandmother for God's sake, act like one!"

As she's speaking, or rather telling me this unwanted news, my mind's a blank. You see, part of my problem is I always know the right things to say after an event has passed, and never at the time it happens. I'm either at a loss for words or talk absolute shite. When she'd finished talking, I sat in silence not saying anything of any sense really. I should've blown my top or something, but you see that's not like me. I am a timid person; I hate confrontations and have always strove towards keeping everyone happy if a crisis should arise. I also show respect to my family - my immediate family that is, other than your parents, brothers, sisters or grandparents, remaining family members are merely relatives and there is, in my opinion a distinct difference. All my life I've never crossed my parents nor done anything untoward, yet all of a sudden here was my mother telling me something I didn't want to hear.

If a person's attitude can change overnight then I guess mine did. Everything I'd learned about family commitments and respect was being questioned. I'd seen families break apart before, after all separation and divorce is commonplace these days, but never expected it to happen to my family. At least I have the comfort of knowing that my marriage is solid and I think the missus and me are a dying breed. We're dinosaurs because our marriage remains so intact; we have a bond that cannot be described. We are soul mates.

As for my dad, well as you could well imagine he was devastated. He initially couldn't speak, nor contemplate anything I was trying to tell him. He turned to the bottle to numb the pain, well only for a short time. I soon nipped that one in the bud. I had now become the parent. He was this little lost boy with hardly any knowledge of how to look after himself. I'd slowly have to teach him many day to day activities we all take for granted such as, paying the bills, washing his clothes, buying food, and withdrawing money from the bank. It was a burden and very stressful, but he had no one else to turn to and no one else was offering much consoling.

The mood swings I developed following my mother pissing-off could be clearly seen. The tone of RTG went very dark, very bitter and very resentful. My anger was vented towards SAFC and their shitty season. So if you ever wondered why RTG went downhill, it was because my own state of affairs had been fucked up. I'm not going to dwell on my mother anymore; I've said what I want to say. Anything else and it'll be like Eminem and the relationship he has with his mother. She sued him for his outbursts regarding her. If this book gets published my mother will have to join the queue of people suing for what I've written.

I like harmony but all that changed leaving me perplexed, mortified, exasperated, resentful, incensed, unsettled, agitated, frustrated, hostile, wounded and any other words you can think of that could express my anger, pain, hurt, and disappointment. I'd been lied to for God knows how long by a deceptive and deceitful person, someone I thought I knew but now no longer know, someone I had affection towards but now have none, an empty shell, a relative not family.

I reckon that's enough looking through the thesaurus for alternative words to help describe my feelings or lack of them over all of this.

As you may well imagine my appetite for football dwindled considerably resulting in missing numerous games leading up to Christmas. I could say I never missed much really apart from the home game against Leeds, which was probably one of the few highlights at the Stadium of Light that season.

The stress endured throughout all of this was at times too much to bear, but I managed to soak up much of it inside my sponge-like persona. On top of this it became apparent that all was not well with our new sponsors as we'd been paid fuck all. Well we did get a gesture payment, eventually, but that was peanuts compared to what we were owed. No end of phone calls resulted, during which I was given no end of utter shite from the twat that ran the company *'sponsoring'* us.

Post September 11th also meant that I had a holiday to pay for which neither my wife nor I particularly fancied going on. Flying was now a fearful journey to undertake for many people around the planet resulting in one or two major airlines collapsing. We had booked to go to Tunisia, which is a predominantly Muslim country, and we therefore became uncomfortable about going there. You see even I had been duped by the media hype about world terrorism and reading that the odd British Muslim going to Afghanistan to join the war against the West, meant it was all too easy to classify people of a particular race to be one to be wary of. I think the phrase is *"being tarnished with the same brush"*.

We had to pay our deposit; we were bound by it and did so. We decided that what we would do was to attempt to transfer the holiday elsewhere, but I held off enquiring if that was possible until I had spoken to the bloke who was supposed to be paying us, as per our agreement.

Unfortunately I can't really go into too much detail about the contract made with the new sponsors for legal reasons or indeed for hopefully future legal reasons. I will say that many, many telephone calls were made; sometimes I spoke to him, other times he pretended he was the receptionist and took a message because he wasn't in the office. You may fool some people but you didn't fool me.

By March 2002 we had exhausted all avenues of trying to recoup some, if not all, of the payment that we were contracted to receiving. Our only other course of action was to take the bastard to court, but we had no money and I wasn't willing to cough up out of my own pocket to fund something from which the outcome would be unknown and cost wise could spiral. I will say this to the bastard; I will have my day with you. I long to win the lottery or have some kind soul fund a court case which, if it did ever happen, I'd take you to the cleaners. If say I made a canny profit from this book, then once again I'll take you to the cleaners. If not then what goes around comes around. You'll get yours and even if it's twenty or fifty years time before you die, I will visit your grave and piss on it you fucking pathetic excuse for a human being. You ripped me off; you ripped my partners off. You made me book a holiday I could no longer afford to pay for. You put a halt to the ongoing progress of our web site and in a way you've set us back by over two years in my reckoning. I will not forget this.

Too strong I hear you cry? I'm sorry but I just loathe the guy. In fact I'm not sorry at all come to think of it. This disappointment on top of the carry on my mother caused was stressing me out far too much. SAFC were shit, and there was nowt good happening anywhere.

Over Christmas, I looked back over the past few years, personally, football wise, and Internet wise. I concluded that I had one or two stories to tell and so I began the task of writing this *'novel'* of mine and slowly but surely it took shape. Maybe it was my own personal therapy. Writing helped ease the anguish. It gave me something to focus on, something that cleared my head of all manners of concerns and irritations. The computer became the shrink, typing my words was the same as lying on a couch yapping away to the psychiatrist, only it never replied, so I assumed what I wrote was an acceptable method of treatment for my mental disorder. Am I making sense here? I hope I am. I hope you know what I mean by all of this. Sometimes I talk that much shite that it makes no sense whatsoever so God knows if any of this will be interpreted the way I'm trying to express it.

In the meantime, life carried on as normal, whatever normal is, all things considered. One of the RTG feature writers came up with an idea about organising an online poll about whether or not Peter Reid should stay or should go. Over the course of one cold weekend in January, jut after we'd been beaten in the F.A. Cup at the first hurdle by a lower league team, the *'www.reidytogo.co.uk'* web site and its counterpart *'www.reidytostay.co.uk'* were born and unleashed to the roaming Mackem hoards in cyberspace.

XXX

The publicity surrounding the *Reidy To Go* and *Reidy To Stay* web sites was immense, generating more record viewing figures for Ready To Go, an unbelievable amount of feedback, but unfortunately not all positive. In fact, I've never had so many abusive emails thrown my way. I was upset but I attempted, where possible, not to bite. I was dumb founded partially because I saw this online poll regarding how the fans saw the future with or without Reid as being pro-active. Part of the existence of a fanzine, be it an electronic one or paper based, is to generate topical interactivity like this, isn't it? The anti-Reid brigade far outweighed the pro-Reid brigade but the anti-Reid brigade didn't have the ferocious voice the pro-Reidy lot had when it came to clutching at any straw that pointed towards the positive side of Sunderland's dwindling season.

At times the pro-Reid voice was quite amusing, playing the predictable, *"look where we were five years ago,"* and, *"look what we've achieved since then"*. Did it ever occur to anyone where we might have been and what we might have achieved without him?

As things were starting to get very uncomfortable in terms of the tones of the messages and emails being directed toward us regarding these peripherals, I decided to attempt to write one or two editorials to calm things down - no such luck!

I couldn't comprehend why so many people couldn't see past the nose on their face. The results and playing style of SAFC were embarrassing. The FA Cup defeat took the piss - we lost 2-1 at home to First Division West Bromwich Albion was a major disappointment, especially as we were 1-0 up after about five minutes. I went to the game with the missus, the bairns, and my dad. It was the first time he'd ever been to the Stadium of Light, likewise the first time for the little 'un who up to then had always gone on about going to watch the *Red Army* with daddy.

She hated every moment of it. She sat on my wife's knee, fingers in her ears, because of all the shouting going on. When we scored I think the poor kid nearly shit herself with the roar that erupted. She burst into tears, dropped her crisps, spilt her hot chocolate and wanted to go home. My dad still enjoyed the day though, regardless of the result. But the boos and atmosphere amongst the fans made me realise the assumptions I was writing on the web site were spot on - a majority view. I reflected the moaning and the booing I was witnessing first hand.

I wanted to write something positive, some glimmer of hope, but couldn't for the life of me find any inspiration from anywhere to do so. Yet online my words were condemned, probably down to the fact that the majority of online surfers are exiled, no disrespect but they don't see nor feel the tension, atmosphere and sense of direction, or lack of it, at each and every home game, like I do.

SAFC was slowly, but surely self-destructing before my very eyes. I had watched Bob Murray turn from hated to saviour in the five years since taking Reidy on board as the Boss. I'd seen my beloved Roker Park disappear through waves of protests only to see the magnificent Stadium of Light come to life. I'd gone from watching shite for twenty years in front of eighteen to twenty two thousand fans, to suddenly watching sexy football in front of over forty thousand. Life as a Mackem couldn't get any better, I mean it was only a matter of time before we would buy big, play big, and win something.

However some things just don't happen. I was now watching a side whose form mirrored that of the teams I'd watched mid-Eighties to mid-Nineties - teams who got relegated (statistics do not lie). Bob Murray was now becoming a hated figure once more as the deafening silence coming from the ivory towers of the stadium bore much frustration to many.

Footballers with skill and determination warranting the honour to pull on the red and whites were mysteriously disappearing. It gave me the impression that SAFC couldn't have players with attitude - only *'yes men'* would suffice!

The hard work in establishing Sunderland AFC as a top class team had been achieved prior to the start of this dreadful season. Sustaining it was another matter and SAFC were now a rather boring side with little skill and little to no creativity.

We were leaking goals and not scoring goals - *"If Phillips does nowt the team does nowt"* was a line I read on the message board which in a nutshell sort of summed up everything happening on the pitch. I couldn't see the team putting together a run of good results nor challenging for anything. There were many rumours circulating Wearside stating that Martin O'Neil would drop Celtic and walk on broken glass to manage SAFC. If this were true I'd have sacked Reidy on the spot. O'Neil is allegedly a self confessed Mackem, he may indeed want to manage Sunderland - but probably only if a consistent amount of money is made available. The chances of that happening are as remote as Newcastle United winning any silverware.

Reality said we were stuck with Reidy and at that time maybe there was no one else better to manage the Lads and attempt to steer us away from the drop. It was his cronies that needed dumping and a change in the coaching methods wouldn't have done any harm.

Something had to happen - something more than just words, but as the season got closer and closer to its grand finale, nothing happened and things did indeed get worse. Transfer deadline day came and went with no new blood coming in. We were badly missing the injured Emerson Thome in defence and had never really recovered from selling Don Hutchison earlier in the season, when the money grabbing Geordie git walked out on SAFC for a bigger wage packet with West Ham. Sunderland should have bent over backwards to keep *'The Don'* from leaving. He was a quality player; we let him go and replaced him with no one. Reidy saw strength in depth of the squad and the *'crab'* (my own personal and affectionate term - yes I am taking the piss) Paul Thirlwell was drafted in on far too many occasions for my liking. Crab means passing sideways or backwards, no forward thinking creative midfield play at all. Stefan Schwarz also disappeared due to another rumoured training ground bust-up. He may not have been getting any younger, but his experience was sorely missed. We then had a mystery injury to Julio Arca prior to the vital home clash against the Mags, which also prompted rumours of a training ground bust-up. What the fuck was happening to my team? They were being eaten from the inside out. They were rotting away into the First Division. If we went down, I saw no way back. We'd be stripped of that many decent players we'd find it nigh on impossible to achieve instant promotion. I was thoroughly pissed off, more so when the Mags turned us over at the stadium. The atmosphere that day can only be described as non-existent. There was little fight in the fans chanting and there was certainly little fight in the team. Where was the bite that derby games bring? There wasn't any. Why? Because most fans, like me, were disillusioned by what was happening that season. I've never witnessed such a dull atmosphere at a derby match, especially one against Newcastle United. It was like lambs to the slaughter, you know how people accept the inevitable and just lie down and die. Too many journeymen and spineless players wore red and white that day. They embarrassed the name of Sunderland Association Football Club, yet there was little to no anger from the crowd, just acceptance that it wasn't to be. Similarly we'd lost a few weeks earlier in another dull derby match against the Boro. We may have been top dogs in the North East for the past two years - that's top in terms of games played between us, Newcastle and Middlesbrough, but we were rock bottom this time around, and I hate to say it, but we deserved to be there.

Thankfully I missed the Smoggies match. I was on my way out but another family crisis put a halt to me attending the game.

My eldest daughter had been seriously affected by the splitting up of my parents, more than I care to admit. She's quite a shy and timid child at times, but following my mother's antics, became even more withdrawn into her shell. She's never been herself since really and so to try to cheer her up a little I decided to buy her a kitten. Well it was to share between the two kids, but I guess I was focusing on my eldest to try to elevate her own heartbreak. Ideally I wanted to get two kittens, one each for the bairns, but in the end managed to track down just one for sale, at an animal rescue place. Now to keep all those pro-Reidy conspiracy theorists happy when it comes to accusing RTG of being Mags in disguise, the kitten I bought was, wait for it - black and white! I was told it was a girl kitten so my main thoughts were on getting it *'done'* before I ended up with a dozen or more cats darting around the house, which would inevitably end up smelling of piss, and my missus would be forever known as the smelly cat woman of the street. You know what I mean right? Every street has some sort of dirty old woman that loves cats and has hundreds of them in her house, which stinks. Well most places I've lived there's been one. I guarantee there will be a dirty smelly cat woman where you live; you may not have noticed her that's all. Anyway as I got ready for the Smoggy match, which is basically grab my season ticket, pull on my jeans and my stripes (red and white ones - honest), the kitten decides that she likes the look of this yellow flame flickering in the fire in the living room. She decides to jump on the flame. I now know where the term *"curiosity killed the cat"* comes from. Eight lives left as it bounced off the fire and darted around the living room, probably trying to cool-off with its singed arse, and burnt whiskers. My eldest was in complete hysterics - not the laughing variety but totally distraught. Well I couldn't go to the game with the house in such disarray now could I? I bought the little twat to cheer up my daughter and it was causing just as much grief as my fucking mother had.

It was fine in the end and the whiskers grew back in next to no time, though the kitten, now a cat was scarred for life - inside mentally that is. In fact it's probably completely fucked up now as the girls christened her Annabel, yet one night a few months later I'm lying on the settee watching television, cuddling into the missus (like you do) when the cat comes bouncing in purring in front of us, only for my wife to notice she had a pair of balls - the cat not my wife. So, all of a sudden, this female kitten was a male, called Annabel! - a she-male! Poor thing has issues now, it's confused as to it's own sexual orientation.

Back to football again, and as the final few games approached, the Lads lost three in a row following important wins at home over Bolton and Leicester and away to Derby County. They crumbled at Arsenal, were unlucky to lose against Leeds and Liverpool and played up to their spineless reputation away to West Ham, folding far too easily. Two games remained; we needed to win at least one. For some reason the pro-Reidy supporters still felt he was the right man for the job. Their stubbornness mirrored that of Peter Reid who also insisted that only a minority of fans wanted him out. The online poll from the *Reidy To Go* and *Reidy To Stay* web sites showed that fifty four percent wanted Reidy out, that amassed to around three thousand people. If Internet opinion reflected the opinion of attendees at the Stadium of Light then you could say that the fifty four percent of people, who wanted Reidy out, amassed to over twenty five thousand - still a minority? Regardless of the abusive emails and other shit thrown at RTG for being allegedly anti-Reid, I still stand by everything I said and proposed. Things got so out of hand that people assumed anti-Reid meant anti-SAFC. The problem is everyone is pro-SAFC, which doesn't make you pro-Reid or pro-Murray & Co. The two camps were at war with each other, though it's pretty clear, and history will show the feelings towards Peter Reid and Bob Murray were non-existent.

I read a comment on the message board suggesting that a protest should take place at the last game of the season, should the team manage to defeat Charlton away. I decided to echo those comments on the news page, suggesting that people should turn up late, or leave at half time, or turn their backs for fifteen minutes, or stand up at a certain point and wave their match tickets or season tickets books, in the same way Spanish supporters wave white handkerchiefs to show their anger towards their Clubs. Having said my piece on the news page, the Internet trawlers and spiders picked this up; the press loved the idea turning it into media hype. RTG had once again supplied the ammunition for the pro-Reidy voices to shoot us down.

XXXI

"You'll be pleased with the publicity you got from your little stunt", was one of the sarcastic comments to appear on the message board following the media's over-the-top reaction to the proposed protest idea. It seemed that a certain element saw everything we did as being nothing more than a publicity stunt to get ourselves in the papers. I could say they were partially right but most of the rants made were never intended to be an excuse to put Ready To Go in the spotlight. Then again, how were we to know whether or not the press would ever make a song and dance out of anything we'd write, especially the proposed protest? Even though I only hinted at the possibility and even though I said it should only happen if we defeated Charlton, the word was that this protest was definitely going to happen, even though we drew with the Addicks meaning SAFC still needed at least one more point to be mathematically safe. I had a few radio stations call me up, and a couple of newspapers wanting to know more details about *'the protest'*. Hello, are you fucking stupid? When you become a journalist do they teach you to read every other fucking line or something? The protest was only a proposal and then only if we beat Charlton. We didn't, thus there would be no protest. Did the press follow this? Oh no, of course not, you've heard of people having selective hearing, well you now had selective reading.

It was quite funny really. I'm not having a dig at the pro-Reidy camp for still sticking with the man even though we were about to be relegated. Who the fuck are they to bitch at me or my web site if I was not happy with our position in the Premiership table, squad, and playing style? I am sick to death of those who suck up to the Club, openly state they'll renew their season ticket no matter what, and profess to know for a fact Peter Reid would turn things around. These people also stick up for too many players who are no better than average First Division players. Where is the ambition? These supporters lack the ambition the Club has shown. Yes, I will more than likely renew my season ticket regardless – to a certain degree - but I won't openly state it. I will do so at my discretion should I feel my money warrants paying obscene wages to footballers who in my opinion disgrace the red and white, and not when the Club issues season ticket renewals, with a deadline to pay for it otherwise I'll lose my seat. If I lose my seat so what? The way Sunderland were headed meant that there'd be many an empty seat the next season, and I'd be spoilt for choice.

The press still insisted a protest was to take place though. That was amusing, to the point that it caused the Club to come out and make a statement about it all, asking for calm, then Niall Quinn came out via the local press and also asked for calm. If my proposal caused them to openly make these statements, then I feel quite proud, because for once,

an average supporter's disgust and resentment, an average supporter's feelings and concerns were being addressed and not ignored. There was no longer silence from the ivory towers at the Stadium of Light. I believe the Club were shitting themselves about all of this. Well it was about time. It took them long enough to realise the anger, frustration, falling attendances, and disappearing crowd noise was not because Reidy insisted on playing Kevin Kilbane instead of Julio Arca. If they thought a protest was happening then I decided to keep up the momentum and let them think that. It's quite scary how powerful your influence can be using the Internet as your medium.

As the final game of the season dawned, Sunderland needed a point at home against Derby or needed Liverpool to beat Ipswich Town. It was us or Ipswich to play lower league football the following season. I will admit that I felt quietly confident that there was nothing to worry about. People think to this day that RTG would've loved it if SAFC had been relegated. What absolute bollocks. If you thought that you're not worthy of licking the dog shit off the sole of my shoes. I've no idea why I said that, but it makes me feel better and rams home my point, I think. Those who think RTG are Mags can go fuck themselves. Why the fuck should I sit back and take constant abuse from fans that don't like what I, or my fellow web site *journalists* are writing? It's not like I'm a professional airing '*official*' news or owt, just a fan's view, and if people want to disagree, then I'm entitled to disagree back.

What I wanted was the Lads to stay-up then the Club to say sorry and hold an investigation into why the season went completely pear shaped, and make up for their previous broken promises. I wanted them to show some fucking ambition, by buying some decent players, not has-beens or spineless gits. Likewise I prayed we'd stay up and could hold onto our prize assets, the few we had left.

By half time the season was over. Sunderland were safe, not down to their own performance but that of Liverpool who were two or three nil up at Anfield. With our halftime one goal lead, it meant Ipswich were effectively four nil down. For us to lose and them pull back that deficit in the next forty-five minutes was impossible. Some people say nothing is impossible, but that was without a doubt. You could cut the atmosphere with a knife, it was so tense during the first half, but as news filtered through the crowd that Liverpool were winning the atmosphere returned to its normal boring self as fans breathed a sigh of relief that we would still be in the Premiership next season. The Club however didn't display the Liverpool score on the scoreboard at half time. A few boos rang out because of that. Then again the Club for some childish reason had adopted a policy of, if the Mags are winning don't show the score and upset the already volatile crowd. This policy obviously extended to showing the score from Anfield that day. I'm sorry but refusing to show the Mags score just because our season was shite and they were headed towards the Champion's League stinks of immaturity. Obviously embarrassed by our own season and jealous of theirs, did they honestly think we're so fucking stupid as to not notice this childish act?

With the season now finally safe the second half became a passing game, Derby equalised but could've won the game, it made no difference. What got to me, and showed just how out of touch the Club was with the fans, was the emergence of the boys in blue towards the end, encircling the pitch in a wall of defiance. I laughed when this happened. Obviously SAFC read every other line as well and were prepared for the protest that they'd obviously assumed was to be a pitch invasion. For fuck's sake, what was their problem? Their attitude stank to high heaven. Then to top it all they had the nerve to bring out a banner carried by the Club mascots saying *"thank you for your support"*. Thank you for my support? Where was the *"we are sorry"* banner? The players emerged onto the centre circle to clap the few remaining supporters inside the ground. I do hope they were ashamed of themselves. In my opinion, they too didn't deserve to lick the dog shit off of my shoes. Peter Reid never came out onto the centre circle though. I wonder why?

All of this meant an explosion of criticism directed towards the Club by me and many other contributors. Like dogs on heat, the venom was getting close to becoming epidemic. However I still feel to this day that what we were writing was a general consensus of feelings amongst the vast majority of supporters. There were, as always, those who bombarded RTG with their own propaganda, their own shite, contradicting anything we said no matter whether it was controversial or factual. In fact a so-called rival web site started to become paranoid with anything said on RTG - something I've already mentioned earlier. It wasn't *Kerching;* then again I dare say he'd have had a dig at us for the *Reidy To Go* campaign and the alleged protest idea. I stopped my abnormal tendency of mistrust towards him and his site a long time beforehand, so never bothered looking to see if he was bitching at us or not. I was more concerned with this other web site, a so called professional one, one whose sponsors had wanted RTG to join them a few years earlier, one whose authors also ran a printed fanzine and one whose editor is Sunderland's number one supporter, allegedly, the true voice of the fans, or so it's said!

Yet this so called professional couldn't resist but to join in with the *"lets slag off RTG because they are nowt but Mags in disguise"* routine. We were questioned as to what our hidden motives were and pointed out again, that our P. O. Box was in Cheshire. Fucking hell here we go again. Does that mean if you're not based in Sunderland you cannot be a Sunderland supporter? How many of you does that point towards? Upsetting isn't it? As for the hidden motives, hey we've got none; I've got none, if anything I just want success for my team. Privately I questioned their motives for having such a dig at us. Then again they were shooting themselves in the foot blagging on about us, which would merely drive more and more traffic to our site again, as surfers who may not have known of our existence, would home in on us to see what all the fuss was about. I bet they were disappointed. What I mean by this is they'd have noticed a distinct lack of the one sided totally anti-SAFC stuff, which was being alleged. Instead they'd have found a web site full of mixed comments, openly airing anyone's views no matter annoying or insulting some of them were.

I do remember this web site's editorial finishing by saying we must rally around the team, wait for the season to end then have a post mortem. Strange how they never asked or pushed for the aforementioned post mortem, instead, over the summer months, they pulled out of the Internet market. Apparently they wanted to concentrate on their paper fanzine, which was fine by me as it meant there was absolutely no online competition whatsoever.

XXXII

With our Premiership status still intact – just, and a huge *"thank fuck for that"*, and having screamed *"for fucks sake,"* practically all season, it was time to reflect on the recent disappointments as well as ponder the future of RTG, while starting work on yet another site re-vamp, a simple clean version this time, with less graphics, and less content - of the static type (in other words pages that never get changed or are hardly ever looked at). Where I got the enthusiasm from I still don't know. I guess working late hours on the web site drew my attention away from the sheer anger and frustration the season had brought as well as a few months of personal turmoil that I still couldn't shake.

The big change in all of this geeky re-style was creating a new message board, making it more user-friendly as well as collaborating with the ALS fanzine to combine our online forum with theirs. Our relationship with ALS was getting stronger. They knew our site traffic far surpassed their own, though we were never in any way shape or form a competitor to them. They had their market, we had ours. However their message board was suffering in terms of hits, so a collaboration was formed which hopefully would help them increase potential subscriptions while help us increase our awareness offline. Well that was the theory, thus one night prior to the end of the season I sat down with a few of the ALS lads and one of my partners to discuss how the system would work, as well as giving it a new name - the Sunderland Message Board. A simple title and maybe somewhat boring - that is until you abbreviate it - it then becomes SMB.

Now we all know SMB is the Mags poor attempt at getting to us Mackems following years of abuse via our FTM slogan. SMB - the *Sad Mackem Bastards*, had already been manipulated around Wearside becoming **_Sexy Mackem Bastards._** To take ownership of someone else's slang was a clever move, or so I thought. So once again, I'd be burning the midnight oil to get the new look ready to launch - the date being the start of the World Cup tournament - which I'm going to skip over. Well, England were never going to win it, though I guess the victory over the Argies was very satisfying, but for me the time difference made it nigh on impossible to watch properly and besides, I've never really gone into any of England's tournaments throughout this book, so why start now!

Prior to the World Cup, however was Niall Quinn's testimonial match, a massively publicised charity event with Quinny determined to break the one million pound barrier and donate all money to charity - something along those lines. Those who could not make it to the match were offered non-attendance tickets as a way of giving to charity whilst at the same time having a souvenir of the game in question.

II've never been to a testimonial. To be honest they don't really bother me all that much. This time around wasn't any different. The game was spoiled coming just days after the end of the season and of course a time when many fans were very still disillusioned with the Club. I just wasn't interested in going and likewise wasn't interested in purchasing a non-attendance ticket. Sorry for sounding selfish here, but charity begins at home in my book. I'm not getting all high and mighty here, but I pay my taxes, and I therefore donate more than ample to the charities of the world. In the end however I did go, but only after being offered a ticket for nowt! My partner from Manchester had a spare ticket, so I thought what the hell, why not go along and see a SAFC XI take on the Republic of Ireland.

The game as you'd expect was nothing special. The event was good. Quinny played for both SAFC and Eire, while Kevin Kilbane playing for the Republic put in a performance that defied logic - he actually played good, and showed he had talent! Why couldn't he play that well when he played for us?

One highlight from the match was seeing Nicolas Medina actually playing. Yes he was real after all and though slightly thin, looked cool, calm, and comfortable playing a somewhat defensive midfield role. Well that was hopefully a sign of improvements to come at the start of the next season.

As for Ireland it was disappointing that Roy Keane wasn't playing. In fact he wasn't there at all, which in hindsight was no real surprise with what was to happen during the World Cup and his much-publicised fall out with Mick McCarthy.

I was sitting amongst a few of the Manchester Branch supporters in the West Stand, and got talking to the bloke sitting next to me who turned out to be a Man. United supporter (you Man U you). Now I think its good when you can talk to fans of opposing teams without any bad feelings or bitter resentment (apart from the Mags). This particular bloke surprisingly had a Manchester accent and wasn't a typecast Cockney Red Devil that most people poke fun at when it comes to Man. United supporters.

The conversation I was having was nice and to be honest more interesting than the game itself. However some chain smoking piss head Sunderland fan in front didn't agree and at the end of the first half stood up to verbally abuse the Man. United fan telling him to fuck off and eat some prawn sarnies! That was uncalled for. This was after all a friendly and he was taking the game far too seriously. Attitudes like that really get to me. I know I've got attitudes, but I don't carry on like that. His girlfriend or wife was obviously embarrassed the way he was shouting and screaming. Her attempts to calm him down made no difference whatsoever. There was a match on and this Man. United fan had no right to talk to me or any other Sunderland fan, let alone be there.

At times like this you expect the Sunderland stewards to come over and sort things out especially considering he was smoking on the terraces. As usual they were nowhere to be seen, probably too busy watching the game or picking on someone twice as small as them.

The verbal onslaught got louder and louder until some unsuccessful head butting was attempted, though no blows were ever made. The Man. United supporter just fucked off in the end probably to find another seat and I don't blame him. The piss head made me feel quite ashamed to be a Mackem at that moment. The way he went on was quite pathetic to be honest. My partner from Manchester pointed out that he was on the same coach as him and normally his behaviour is not like that. Maybe so but that did not excuse his current behaviour. He then told me that the Man. United supporter was also on the same coach. Well I bet the journey home that night was interesting.

Sunderland lost 3-0 - no real surprise I guess, good job it was just a friendly run out. As I walked home that definitely meant the season was over. I prayed the Club would hold some sort of investigation as to what went wrong, and that we would see some major improvements to the playing staff and coaching staff, buy some quality and sell off the dead wood and journeymen. I also hoped some twat living inside the ivory towers would come out and say sorry. How can one word be so difficult to say? Alas it wasn't going to happen, in fact if I recall there was very little in terms of an inquiry into the shitty season, more like the odd brief statement full of the usual crap as if we the fans are so fucking stupid that we'd believe anything the Club tells us. Maybe some supporters are sheep or lemmings blindly following the blind so to speak, but I'd say the vast majority of fans are intelligent souls who had had the piss taken out of them for far too long and thus warranted slightly more respect than the statements the Club were issuing.

Nevertheless working on this new message board lifted the doom and lack of interest I had been feeling regarding the tedious job of being an online fanzine editor. I don't know, I change like the wind me. One minute I'm fed up of it all, the next thing I'm all excited and addicted again.

So as the World Cup kicked off, the new look message board was launched, and greeted with much acclaim from the vast majority of users. All we needed now was some good news from the SAFC front.

Without any sponsors, Ready To Go's income was almost zero. It was like the good old days where money didn't matter and passion to offer a service and share views with others was taking precedence. Unfortunately times change and money did matter. Bandwidth was rising and rising. The SMB simply increased traffic to RTG and the charges were starting to get quite scary. I had tried advertising via a US dollar system, which initially looked good. With a few weeks we had earned in excess of two thousand dollars, which was supposed to be paid by cheque. For a long time, and I mean a long time, the money never materialised. It was like I had the un-Midas touch if that makes any sense. Everything RTG touched or had contact with went eerily silent, folded, or as in SAFC's case had a shitty season.

Even though running the web site was costing a serious amount of money each month, without any return, I somehow felt something would turn up and hoped like SAFC fortune would favour us all. A web site that now attracted over two million impressions per month was surely worth something. If anything all I wanted was to break even, sentiments my partners agreed with. Actually I should alter that last sentence and just say partner. It was quite sad but not surprising that one of my partners decided to call it a day. I wasn't shocked because he had been quiet for a while and no longer went to any games. Then again he did work away from home and travelled abroad quite a bit. In the past however he had always made the effort to go to a game when he was back in Sunderland. Now that aspect was no longer part of his schedule and for all the hard work he had initially put into RTG - the initial concept of the super site was his - I was both saddened by his decision to leave RTG yet somewhat relieved at the same time, after all me and my other partner in Manchester had for far too long ran the site between us. It did signal the end of an era, though I will say I'd welcome him back with open arms any day should he ever want to be part of the dream.

His resignation came at a time when our legal partnership expired, that meant I'd sort of gone full circle from starting out doing my thing on the web as a hobbyist to becoming a fully fledged partner earning a little extra pocket money, and had now returned back to being a hobbyist. It sort of gave a raw edge to things and a sense of purpose once more being free from the shackles of legal paperwork the taxman demanded every year.

Not long after the launch of the new message board - the SMB - I received an anonymous email apologising to all *"involved with RTG"*. The tone of it and reference to the word *'parasite'* made me conclude that it must be a confession from none other than the American Psycho. I would never have expected such a holier than thou person to ever say sorry for his many previous immature cyberspace acts.

"It's time to say I apologise wholeheartedly to everyone involved at RTG for the stupid comments made several months ago and the use of the word 'parasite'. I knew what I wanted to post at the time, the point is I didn't post what I wanted to say and what I did post was bollocks and spiteful. I wouldn't want to say that I apologise for any offence felt as that's not really an apology; as what I did post did cause offence and for that there is no excuse and I wholeheartedly and unreservedly apologise to all the RTG bods and to all fellow posters."

Well that was fair enough, from my perspective, apology accepted. His sentiments however didn't last. Before long he launched an attack on ALS trying to get people to boycott their publication because of the nature of some new merchandise that had been put on sale. I have to admit I cringed when I saw what was being sold - Reid-In and Reid-Out t-shirts with the characterisation of a monkey printed on the front. That was way too close for comfort in my opinion, even for someone as radical and as extreme as I am. ALS did see the error of their ways and quickly removed them, replacing them with a more subtle way of showing where you stood in terms of Peter Reid remaining as manager of Sunderland or not.

That move just wasn't good enough for the American Psycho though. Instead he started to re-phrase ALS as *"Another Lost Subscription"* commentating on how as a subscriber he would be cancelling in disgust. It's easy to say one thing and get people wound up into believing it, especially when you're an anonymous entity living in cyberspace, but in reality the subscription in question was never cancelled. He was merely causing trouble and shit stirring for the sake of it. All his arguments and constant ridicule and so on had no place anymore on RTG. Another ban of IP addresses, nicknames and so on was put into place and the cat and mouse chase started again as RTG attempted to track him and delete anything he posted regardless of whether it was contributable or not.

XXXIII

For a while the club had been announcing exclusive news online via their own web site or via email. Not too long after the end of the season, the Club announced their first *'major'* signing - online, teasing the worldwide audience by releasing a silhouetted image of a footballer, a few hours before the unveiling was to be made. This obvious publicity stunt was a good gimmick and a great incentive for surfers to go to the official site and wait for the big announcement. On close inspection the silhouette looked like Patrick Kluivert to me. However once the news was out I had to check the date to make sure it wasn't April Fools Day. The signing was non other than Phil Babb, ex-Liverpool, and ex-Ireland and bought on a freebie from Portugal. What a let down, something others roaming in cyberspace found disgraceful. For once the online outcry wasn't directed at Ready To Go but to the Club. Did they honestly think that people would be pleased with the signing of another central defender, Phil Babb of all people and the way in which the signing was unmasked? Someone somewhere fucked up if they thought this little prank would perk up the majority of still disillusioned fans.

Still that was nothing compared to the next effort they tried. This time they announced - again online - that Sunderland had agreed a fee with Leeds United for striker Robbie Keane. Now this was more like it. In fact it was so exciting that the Ready To Go server blew up! It cost a good few hundred quid to get our hosts to turn the site back on; such was the intensity of visitors that the bandwidth went beyond danger levels. However, before any Sunderland fan could catch their breath, Robbie Keane released a statement more or less saying he didn't want to sign for us, and he didn't, and so we were let down again.

Well who do you blame in a situation like this? Do you focus your anger towards the player in question, or Sunderland Football Club for mouthing off so prematurely, or do you deduce some sort of conspiracy theory, one in which the Robbie Keane news was leaked the same week season ticket renewals were due? I know quite a few people who immediately spat out their cash, renewing without thought, when the news first broke - well before Keane had opened his mouth. I didn't, regardless of whether we signed Robbie Keane or not I refused to renew. I knew I would, maybe I am a bit of a lost sheep, blindly following the blind, but my stance this term was to renew when I decided to and not when Bob Murray and Co demanded me to.

And so with the transfer activity getting both exciting and disappointing at the same time and with the Club shooting themselves in the foot constantly, life as a Sunderland supporter was anything but dull during the summer.

My stance of not renewing lasted about three days beyond the renewal deadline, and to my surprise - not - my seat, according to whoever I was talking to on the phone, hadn't been taken. Of course it hadn't been taken. If you believed the rumours, less than ten thousand people had renewed - which believe me was a pitiful number. But as I've just said who was to blame?

Now I will openly state here I wished I had never renewed. Shortly after splashing out my hard earned cash an incident occurred which indirectly had consequences for me as an employee and as a fanzine editor. Now lets just say that some fool decided to use the message board to post some defamatory remarks about someone who worked at SAFC, and those remarks landed me in trouble, and though it will be denied, I felt like I'd been victimised and intimidated by the powers that be. On one hand I saw what was being bestowed upon me verbally and via a legally *'threatening'* letter from SAFC as an attempt to shut down Ready To Go - you know what I mean - silence the outspoken ones. On the other hand this bloody fool I've just referred to, in my view, had a grudge against SAFC, be it the Club, the players, or someone who worked there, and had used RTG to vent out his or her frustration by posting sordid remarks on the SMB. I apologise here because in the original draft I used another word, not fool, to describe this person. It is the foulest of swear words, but it fits this scenario, though the word was in fact barred from use on the message board - replaced by online slang - *'hallway'* – those of you who visit the site will know what word I mean, the rest of you can guess. Actually, in the North East the use of this word is rare and used only when venting real anger towards someone or something, whereas, from what I can gather, down south it's commonly used, more commonly than your average good morning greeting. However, as far as I'm concerned, whoever posted these remarks, caused an emotional wave of disillusionment to hit me and that hurt. I was the scapegoat, and I was severely downhearted. I was low, in fact lower than the lowest position you can imagine - even lower than being six feet under. I lost it big time, you could say I was verbally warned and all because of some unknown fool on the Internet. I tried my best to trace this person, but their IP address lead to nowhere, though what I did trace made it look like an inside job if you want my honest opinion. It was also strange how having meticulously looked through the archived logs on the web site, logs that kept a record of all IP addresses that accessed the message board, I couldn't find any duplicates. It has also never appeared since, even after unblocking it for a while in an attempt to catch the felon. Then there was another one (hallway) that had decided to join in with the libellous remarks made. I actually tracked this *'person'* down and, after banning his IP address; he had the nerve to email me and asked why he was banned. I resisted the urge to reply to him. Well what would I say - *"you're banned because you nearly cost me my job you 'hallway'"*. His petty pleas about being done, and his university studies going up the spout, didn't wash with me. If anything I hoped he would fuck up in his studies. He and the original anonymous one had fucked me up, inside and outside. And to make matters worse this all happened the same day my mother decided to send me a threatening text message. Now all of a sudden I had nowhere to run to and nowhere to hide. Because of my personal problems, I couldn't settle at home and would often switch off the phone on a night, locking myself away giving a two fingered salute to the outside world - *"just fuck off and leave me alone"*. I just hated the phone ringing – as it meant round after round of verbal onslaughts, accusations, consistent lies, and of course my own aggressive anger being thrown back down the line, leaving me so agitated on a night that I was suffering severe insomnia. Now I couldn't hide at work either because not only was my mother fucking with my perception of certainty, Sunderland AFC were too. What had I done wrong? What? Someone please tell me as to this day as I don't know why I was the one who took the brunt of all of these threats that were being poured out. Like boiling tar, it was burning my flesh - but from the inside out.

How could the Club do this to me considering all the work I'd done for them in creating and developing some of their own web sites? That's something I've never mentioned but something I've actually done in my real job (I haven't mentioned it due to confidentiality agreements I've signed in the past). I wanted to pick up the phone and demand a refund for my season ticket. My partner in Manchester wanted to go to the press, local and national, with the story, while at the same time legally sorting out the whole mess. As for me, I was turning into a schizophrenic psychotic if that makes sense, everyone had it in for me, the world became a blur, I was on automatic pilot, my body moving and functioning independently from my brain. I was lost in a labyrinth, screaming for help but my crying was to no avail as they were silent cries. I'd lie dormant inside my head cowering in a corner of my conscience daring not to look up in fear of some sort of retribution. This was not helping. I was fading. My life was being torn apart and the stress was turning into rage.

I suddenly decided that my life, my health, my job, and my well being far outweighed any loyalty to a web site that I'd help build and help prosper. Likewise all of this outweighed twenty odd years of undying support to Sunderland AFC. I know sentiments like this will be hard for some to accept, but I can categorically state that there are things more important in life than football, especially when your support is thrown back in your face. I had enough on my plate with my parents splitting up without having to endure the legal threats from Sunderland AFC.

In the end, my partner sorted out the legal implications with the Club and built a new message board - in record time, which was most admirable. This new system required registration in order to post comments, and would only accept real email addresses and not potentially falsified Hotmail or Yahoo online free email accounts. That meant any repeat of the defamatory incident would lead to us knowing exactly who had posted it, and if we were sued, then they would be too. These *'secure'* steps were ultimately *'accepted'* by SAFC. Well, maybe they weren't trying to close down RTG, it's a possibility but one that's hard to tell - my paranoia had taken over my sense of reality.

However, if anything, the new message board would create a somewhat better relationship with the Club, but in my case the damage was done. And as for the perpetrator behind all of this, well I'd love to be brutally honest with you, but I'll resist bringing myself down to your pathetic trashy and despicable level, but whatever your reasons for your slanderous remarks, fuck you – *'hallway!'*

XXXIV

I needed a holiday, some time to escape from everything and everyone. So I took the family to Scotland for a week, to some remote outpost accessible only by ferry and completely cut off from civilisation. It was back to basics living in a log cabin, away from the hurt I had suffered, away from football, family, and work.

The pre-season up to that point was turning into a complete disaster. We were showing no signs of improvement. If anything we were getting worse since the end of last season. Fair enough Bobby Saxton had retired but Reidy's partner in crime would be Adrian Heath who was not exactly a *'successful'* coach, though if you believed everything the Club told you then his *'European credentials'* and other comparable Labour Party hired spin doctoring would make you think otherwise (that is until you removed the rose tinted glasses).

The team by now had ventured off to play a couple of friendlies in Europe, and those loyal souls who travelled to watch the Lads play in these games were tested to the extremes of their loyalty. During one pre-season game things boiled over to the point where Kevin Kilbane showed us all just how much of a model professional he was by giving a two-fingered style - *"fuck off"* - salute to those supporters who had made the long journey abroad. Some say he had been subjected to a torrential downpour of abuse, and that he's only human and lost his cool for a split second. Others will say he should not insult supporters with such a gesture, supporters who pay his obscene wages, wages a month that many are lucky to earn in a year. He should never have pulled on a red and white shirt again. His apology was weak in my opinion and if the likes of Allan Johnston, Nicky Summerbee and Chris Makin could get the cold shoulder for lesser crimes, then Kilbane should have too. But he never did. I may sound a bit over the top with what was a young man showing frustration due to the abuse he was receiving, but in the past, Sunderland players who have given a fuck off gesture to the fans have been immediately dropped from the team - anyone remember Terry Curran under the McMenemy years? He was shite as well, got booed a lot, finally decided to give a fuck off gesture to the paying public and never played again.

Anyway, prior to going away Sunderland had splashed out on the purchase of Stephen Wright from Liverpool, which I saw as a great buy. I'd seen Wright play for Liverpool on the television and he looked a very promising full back - a replacement for the disappointing Bernt

Haas. Well we hadn't had a decent right back since Reidy mysteriously sold Chris Makin, and the signing of Wright as far as I saw would strengthen a very weak area of the squad.

Sunderland had also signed a young winger from Leicester called Matt Piper, who according to a friend who worked in Leicester was a good player, young, and full of promise. These signings along with a goalless draw away to Blackburn at the start of the season sparked life back into many disillusioned supporters, me included to some degree.

My break away from to all meant I'd miss the first home game which was against Everton, that meant my first match of the new season would be the home tie against Manchester United, something to look forward to then - more so when Sunderland broke the bank prior to the end of the new transfer window and signed two strikers - Tore Andre Flo from Rangers and Marcus Stewart from Ipswich in a deal reportedly worth around ten million pounds.

For a long time Sunderland supporters had been begging the Club to think big and spend big. I. like many, wanted us to buy players that would make the rest of the league stand up and take notice. Flo was in my opinion such a signing. It also meant an end to Quinny's reign in the number nine shirt, which although sad was also welcomed as he was well past it. Besides it was a shame to watch such a great player struggling.

The previous week's home defeat against Everton, a rather unlucky one was soon forgotten when the Man. United game got under way. The Stadium of Light was full, the crowd very buoyant even though we were one down at half time. Now Tore Andre Flo had scored on his debut for every club he'd played for and Sunderland would be no different. Midway through the second half he grabbed the equalizer. However that wasn't going to make the headlines in the newspapers the next day. Towards the end of the match a tussle (one of many throughout the game) between Jason McAteer and Roy Keane exploded with Keane losing his rag - well there's a thing! Out came the red card and no end of protest from the entire Man. United squad and Sir Alex Ferguson screaming from the touchline would make any difference. To this day I still wonder what Niall Quinn was trying to do as he went over towards Keane trundling off the pitch - shake hands or jest something - something that obviously had to do with the World Cup bust up? Quinny however was told in no uncertain terms where to go from a very gut busting red faced Sir Alex - very amusing if you ever see the television replays.

With four games gone, we had two draws, one win and one defeat. The squad looked tidy, nothing special in terms of winning anything but good enough to better the previous seasons fourth bottom finish. A few days prior to the Man. United game we won 1-0 at Leeds United, a victory we had not achieved at Elland Road in the top flight for over thirty years. We were certainly on form and for a moment it looked like the previous terms problems had been sorted out and to coin a phrase *"things could only get better"*.

However for me personally thing would only get worse. As I left the Stadium following the Man. United game I suddenly felt a chill unlike anything I'd ever felt before rush through my body. As I got home I was so cold, I thought I had some form of hypothermia. I immediately filled a hot bath in an attempt to warm up, but to no avail. As the weekend drew to a close my health was rapidly deteriorating, but I put it down to catching a cold or at worse a mild dose of the flu. Come Monday I lasted one hour at work before going home and back to bed. My wife kept telling me to go see a doctor, but I resisted and just fed myself hot lemon drinks, pain killers and cough medicines. Unfortunately they didn't work.

On the way to work the following week, my wife finally convinced me to go see a doctor. I said I'd make an appointment once I got into the office, which I did, and for the same day. My wife also suggested I tell the doctor about my personal problems, the issue of my parents splitting up and the recent work related incident. I was apprehensive about talking to a stranger about issues that I felt I was coping with admirably in my own unique way. That however was far from the truth. In hindsight I look back on this period and realize just how much I wasn't coping with this turmoil that I was somehow trying to block or bury deep within my consciousness hoping it would just go away.

As I sat down to discuss my health with the doctor, I opened up and told him exactly what had been happening to me, around me, and how I felt about it. To sum up this appointment, I left the surgery with a bottle of Prozac and a sick note that declared I was suffering from depression. It would be three months before I would pull myself together and return to work and to an extent reintegrate myself back into society, something that I'm not going to discuss in detail as those three months would fill an entire book by itself. Maybe one day I'll write it all down, but there's just too much to say, too much pain, too much mental anxiety.

Football wise I never went to a game throughout this period of ill health. Some will say I was fortunate not to be present during the Fulham defeat at home following on from the Smoggies turning us over in *'Chemical-Land'*.

I watched us lose to the Mags and just wasn't bothered about the result. So what if the black and white scum turned us over with ease, life was more important that a football match, something that I discovered while in *'rehab'*, something that previously would have left me feeling bitter and angry, always moody for days after the result - unless of course we turned them over then I'd be the complete opposite.

I logged off the Internet for a while, ignored my emails, ignored text messages on my phone. I just didn't have the strength, or motivation to update RTG, besides plenty of others would be quite capable of running things without me being around.

Results did pick up following two derby losses, yet it was just too difficult to enthuse about it all, my focus, what little I had was centered squarely on getting better. I had what I believed was a dose of the flu for over a month and just couldn't shake it. Frequent visits to the doctor made no difference as I was told it was purely a psychological affect. That was worrying. You could say I felt ill, but I wasn't so I must have been hallucinating! I also suffered an allergic reaction to the antidepressants I was popping, hardly slept, and sat around the house or lay in bed like a total zombie. My wife showed incredible strength during this period to keep me *'alive'* whilst assuring the kids that their daddy was merely poorly with flu. Looking back on how she coped, I must say what a tower of strength she was, and yet I don't think she knows just how much I appreciated what she did for me during this time. I'll also say how a lot of people showed immense sympathy for my condition, but at the same time too much advice was being thrust in my face.

"I've been through what you're going through and you should do this, and do that."

Such sentiments may have been genuine but I didn't want anyone's advice. I just wanted to be left alone with just myself, my wife, and the kids. I needed to dig deep inside and search for my soul and try to work out how someone like me, a sponge who absorbs emotions, never showing any concerns could suddenly leak. I wasn't the superman I thought I was. The ability to cope with all manner of problems life would surprise you with, had now relinquished itself from my fleshy carcass.

I know some people will see my condition as just **being** miserable, feeling sorry for myself and looking for self-pity. It is quite astonishing just how many people see depression and mental stress in this way. *"You're no man if you cannot handle the simple things in life"* is a phrase I overhead at one time. If you want my opinion real men will express their feelings, share their experiences, and above all admit to their failings. I think I better stop here and focus back on football. Like I've already said the three months I was off ill is a story in itself.

So anyway by now, SAFC's mini revival would start to go pear shaped, or would that be inconsistently inconsistent! The team did scrape a win at home over Aston Villa, before cruising to a 7-0 win in the League Cup over Cambridge United.

Then came the match away at Arsenal and Reidy's farewell! We crumbled 3-1 and lost Tommy Sorensen with a pretty bad injury that would keep him out for around three months. A few days later to much surprise and much relief Reidy was shown the door. The *Reid-Out* brigade celebrated while declaring that it had taken long enough. The *Reid-In* brigade were devastated and declared the Club was making a huge mistake. My mobile started going berserk as no end of local newspapers and national radio stations were trying to get in touch to get my opinion on Peter Reid's departure. I ignored them all. The publicity for RTG would have been good, but I didn't want to talk to anyone about anything, thus the calls went unanswered.

XXXV

I clicked onto the football pages of Ceefax one morning shortly after the sacking of Reidy to notice that Stoke City's manager has resigned to go off to an unnamed club. Nah! No way would Sunderland take on board a manager from a lower league club, and one that was struggling at the time as well - would they? Later in the day it's announced - Howard Wilkinson is the new manager, his assistant Steve Cotterill, the bloke who had resigned from Stoke. Well bugger me!

I logged onto the message board to see what the reaction was. A *'Wilko Out'* campaign had started, and it looked like SAFC had pissed off the pissed of fans even more. Personally, I was surprised by the appointment. My choice would have been George Graham - it's easy to say that such an appointment would have led to a boring football team, but at the time watching Sunderland was exciting wasn't it?

I didn't join the *Wilko Out* campaign. Jeez, the bloke needed to be given a chance. A fresh man in charge, fresh ideas would hopefully see the team morale pick up and points also be picked up, or so I thought.

Watching Wilkinson's press conference was indeed refreshing. The bloke oozed confidence, was blunt and to the point. That alone would hopefully be enough to keep us up. At the same time, all roads pointed to Wilko grooming this unknown (well to me he was and I dare say I wasn't alone in this particular conclusion) Mr. Cotterill into becoming SAFC's new manager at some point in the future, with Wilko possibly retiring upstairs or moving on.

My email box started to fill and my phone stared ringing. The press from everywhere was trying to get in touch with me, wanting a quote from the webzine about the surprise appointment. My phone was on divert. I was on the sick, I wasn't well, wasn't thinking straight and the least of my concerns was giving a quote on something that I was rapidly losing interest in.

I still wasn't well enough to go and watch the first game that Sergeant Wilko's red and white army played - a home game against fellow strugglers West Ham. Instant miracles don't work when SAFC are involved; they were dispatched 1-0 right at the death, a situation most fans would come accustomed to leading up to Christmas and the New Year.

Jeckyll and Hyde performances would creep in again becoming the norm and resulting in some erratic outcomes, from a 2-0 win at home over Spurs followed by a 0-0 draw at Anfield, then crumbling 1-0 at home to Birmingham, 3-0 at Stamford Bridge, getting knocked out of the League Cup by First Division Sheffield United, and to top it all a spineless performance losing 3-0 at home to Man City.

Was Peter Reid still in charge? The initial improvements shown at the start of Wilko's reign had all but disappeared by now. As for our league position, well we were slowly becoming relegation fodder with difficult games looming – not that there is such a thing as an easy game in the Premiership.

Out of all of these games, I only managed to watch the Birmingham defeat. I was slowly starting to feel well, though somewhat forced to pull myself together due to finances. I saw going to this game as the beginning of integrating myself back into society, before bravely going back to work.

A dose of flu knocked back my comeback as I ended up missing the impressive win at home against Liverpool, the first win over the Scousers in the league since the fifties. That said something and was a massive spirit lifter. Drawing 2-2 away to West Brom coming back from 2-0 down also showed signs that team spirit was up for the fight.

But then Lady Luck who had rarely been available for the previous two years, finally packed up her bags and left us for good, as the last minute heartaches started. We lost 2-1 at home to Leeds, Robbie Fowler scoring a penalty near the end of the game. We lost 2-1 away to Southampton in the 94th minute and then having lead 1-0 at Old Trafford for over 75 minutes we lost 2-1, Paul Scholes grabbing the winner in the 90th minute. Let us not forget, though I'd rather *'we'* did, the record breaking 3-1 home defeat by Charlton. Sunderland scored all four goals, the three Charlton ones being own goals all comically put into the back of our own net within a space of thirty minutes. Its easy to say *"we were unlucky"*, but there has to come a point where you draw the line and luck has nothing to do with the fact that you're just not up to the standards expected or to be frank you're just shite. I mean you cannot be unlucky for almost two seasons now can you?

The New Year started with Sunderland third bottom, but League games were on hold as the third round ties of the F. A. Cup began. Initially I felt that we'd put out a team of fringe players as Wilko had stated that Premiership survival was the primary goal. I couldn't agree more. By now the Sunderland squad was rapidly approaching skeletal levels due to the amount of injuries being sustained. The team was effectively down to one qualified midfielder and if anything sustaining more injuries would put us into a state of crisis. A 1-1 draw in the Cup away to Bolton was achieved at the expense of losing two right backs. Stephen Wright was taken off injured early in the game and replaced by some reserve team player named Mark Rossiter. He lasted ten minutes before being stretchered off.

Our injury list had grown to ridiculous proportions. Someone somewhere had put a hex on the team. I know I resented many parts of the SAFC set-up on and off the field, but any curse I'd made towards the Club wasn't meant to affect the playing staff like this. So please don't blame me!

By the time details of the Cup replay were announced, the injury list consisted of:

Julio Arca (midfield),
Mart Poom (goalkeeper),
Thomas Myhre (goalkeeper),
Stephen Wright (right back),
Mark Rossiter (right back),
Michael Gray (midfield),
Gavin McCann (midfield),
Emerson Thome (central defence),
Claudio Reyna (midfield),
Jason McAteer (midfield),
Nicholas Medina (midfield),
Thomas Butler (midfield),
David Bellion (striker),
Matty Piper (midfield).

Add to that the players who as far as I was concerned were being snubbed for some unknown reason, Marcus Stewart (striker), Joachim Bjorklund (defence), and Stefan Schwarz (midfield). In total, seventeen players, who you may or may not have heard of, that's not important, what it showed however was that the Club was in trouble and with the board still insisting no money would be made available to strengthen the squad, Wilko's task in keeping us up was getting more and more difficult and slowly becoming an impossible task.

If the team morale wasn't low, the fans morale was and made more so by the Club issuing ticket prices for a Cup replay at twenty quid a shot. I'd attempted via the web site to demand free entry. I wanted the Club to show some support to the fans who were disappearing in their thousands. But I now often feel that the Club is a business and no longer a community vessel and money and income takes priority over loyalty.

Prior to the Cup replay and a poor goalless draw at home against Blackburn Rovers, one of our overseas feature writers (from Hong Kong) posted a very sentimental, yet thought provoking article entitled *"living the dream"*, which in a nutshell really summed up life revolving around supporting Sunderland AFC.

Living The Dream (or should that read nightmare?)

There was a programme on ESPN in Hong Kong last night, a Peter Reid special, made when he was in Singapore recently. A surprise, as it wasn't advertised. It took us through his playing career, and his management career, which was of course Sunderland-dominated. It showed us the scenes from 1996, when Reidy took us up with the ragbag of the squad that was nearly relegated the season before. The relegation that followed didn't quite extinguish the hope that the fans had in the club and Reid. Despite some harrowing moments the following season (Norwich at home, the spitting incident and the infamous Reading away are given good coverage by Quinny), the club went from strength to strength.

The main reason for this was undoubtedly the move to The Stadium of Light. From the paltry Premier crowds at Roker, we were now getting 40,000 plus every week for Tranmere, Crewe, et al. Through either luck or judgment, Reidy had found a team that were playing superb football and scoring wonderful goals. Only the bad start prevented automatic promotion. Despite the traumatic loss at Wembley, we had played our part in the best-ever match there, which for me, along with the fact that we had to be odds-on for promotion the following season, was a big consolation.

The goals flowed the next season too. We made light of Kevin Phillips injuries. We went up in style. We were wearing the best ever Sunderland home strip in my lifetime. Proud to be a Mackem more than ever.

People wondered if we could do as well in the Premier. We knew it wasn't going to be a 1996 job. We knew these players had it in them. And, boy, did they deliver, especially in that fantastic first season back. Who can forget the storming Scum win, the 5-0 hammering of Derby, the Kevin Phillips led demolition of Chelsea? We were deservedly in the top three. Sell-out crowds. Great football. Everyone liked us. Reidy was a hero, could do no wrong to most people.

The season petered out (pardon the pun), and the next season saw perhaps a less exciting style of play, but the results kept coming. The home clash with Man. United, first against second, in January 2001, was perhaps a turning point. At the time, we were seen as the perhaps the only realistic alternative to Manure winning the title. Poll saw to it that we were kept in our place, and free-fall commenced. In retrospect, yes we should have bought then, if not before. We didn't, we fell. Whose fault? Don't care, it happened, it's history.

The point to this article is that for a period of at least four years, we were living a dream. A dream playing itself out in real-life. I wonder if it will happen again. Whatever happens to Reidy in future, he was in charge during the dream period and that can't be taken away from him. I had never experienced anything like it in my thirty-seven years of supporting the Club. This is not meant to be a Reid eulogy. It is simply a fact. Blame him for the subsequent disasters if you want.

This is why I think people were so reluctant to get rid of Reidy. He had taken us to the promised land, on a wave of attacking football; we had the respect back we lost decades ago. By sacking him, the dream died. I was one of those who said, at the end, and most reluctantly, he had to go. The Stadium of Light is now a moribund place, it seems to me. We still get behind the lads from time to time, but once again we are the perennial relegation strugglers. Reid admitted on television last night that he overstayed his welcome, he had taken the team as far as he could (echoes of many on the SMB) and that he should have left before he did. He didn't, because, as he said, he loved the Club, and perhaps shouldn't have. In his words, perhaps he should have been more cynical. Well, loving the Club is no crime in my book. He wanted the dream to continue, as we all did. For me, it would have been sweeter for us to have won the League or Cup with Reidy as opposed to any other manager. Despite everything, it's just not the same.

Good luck to Wilko and the Lads for the rest of the season. I will support Sunderland until I die. I just think a little bit of me has died already.

As the replay came around the attendance bearing in mind the 46,000+ capacity of the Stadium of Light was a pathetic 14,000 and bit. It wasn't a surprise, such games normally attract low attendances down to timing e.g. not long after Christmas as well as motivation e.g. fans pissed off and refusing to go out of principle or annoyance or whatever. The game was won on penalties a great confidence booster for all involved on the pitch, off the pitch, and the stayaways - like me! League wise such a victory didn't help improve status as we kept on sinking lower and lower - the next match being the usual defeat we always sustain at White Hart Lane. The next home game however would be a fifth round cup-tie against First Division Watford at home, and victory would put us in the quarter finals. League wise we may have been shite and heading for certain relegation, but if the team could continue their winning ways in the Cup it would at least give the suffering supporters something to cheer about.

The Watford game attracted over 26,000 people - still small in comparison to league attendances but a stark improvement over the last tie. A win was a certainty right? Wrong. We lost 1-0. We didn't even play well, struggled to test their defence, and if relegation was to happen, my fear was that bouncing back would not be a dead cert. If anything we'd struggle in mid-table and for who knows how many years before any return to the top flight would be made. I suppose I could blame the referee as we all know we were cheated in this game - a penalty awarded to The Hornets, which Sorensen saved, only for the referee to decide that the penalty had to be taken again, which this time wasn't saved.

The Club had by now announced some financial difficulties, a sign maybe that preparations were under way to batten down the hatches for the millions to be lost through demotion. Well they couldn't blame falling attendance for that situation could they?

Apart from the Club's financial cry, Ready To Go was now in deep shit – in respect to turnover. With no revenue coming in at all, with the Internet advertising industry having burst it's bubble a long time ago, and to a certain extent the collapse of the likes of ITV digital, the chances of a piddly little web site making any income had two hopes - Bob and no!

My deranged vision of becoming a dot com millionaire had also disappeared by now. Revenue for the web site meant one thing - survival of the web site. It was costing a considerable amount of money each month to host the site across numerous servers, numerous domains, and with the bandwidth now reaching detonation levels, excess over-use charges were also on the up, on top of a threat by the hosting company to permanently switch us off (due to slowing down the performance of hundreds of other web sites). We had effectively put out long-term cyberspace road works causing serious tailbacks.

The money RTG had made in the past was almost dry. By Christmas 2002 we had about a month's worth left before the site either closed or me and my colleague in Manchester had to fork out from our own pockets dosh to keep the site going. I'm not that flush, never have been, and probably never will be. My colleague at that particular time was unemployed. We therefore decided to take a risk and ask our readers and SMB (message board) members for voluntary donations to help keep RTG up and running. It did feel somewhat degrading going out cap in hand, well to me it was, but what else could we do? No one wanted to advertise with us. You'd think that a site attracting the hit rate we were creating would attract someone somewhere, but it never did. Maybe it was the subject matter. Maybe Sunderland AFC are not as big as they or we think they really are. Maybe outside the region nobody gives a fuck about this *'sleeping giant'*, this *"phoenix waiting to rise from the ashes"*, this *"big fish in a very small pond"* or would that be *"a little fish in a very big pond?"*

With a little bit of investment, we set-up an online credit card transaction service so people could donate with ease, and keep the site bustling. I say we, but my partner in Manchester did all of the work here. Slowly but surely the contributions came in, and therefore I'd like to take this opportunity to personally thank everyone who made the effort to help us out - the lurkers, the dedicated, the occasional, the paranoid, the holier than thou brigade, the comic geniuses, the philosophical gurus, the political spin doctors, and as quoted on the message board; *"members of an incredibly deep, inventive and creative resource that even the United Nations should begin to use as a guide to world peace and harmony."* To be blunt and brutally honest, without your support Ready To Go would not have prevailed.

This helpful and generous income meant we could move to a dedicated server where bandwidth no longer became an issue. We had our own private motorway, one that meant access only by our audience - a wise move in the end, as to my amazement, we were now pushing an incredible four million impressions per month and the target now was to reach a magical ten million.

The only thing that mattered now was if Sunderland could keep going? Next up was the *derby* that is not, namely a home match against Middlesbrough, a vital, yet *winnable* game that the team could hopefully use as a proverbial springboard to survival.

XXXVI

For fuck's sake! There you go again, my wonderful foul opening line to this book, but words that sum up the home game against Boro. Well I could've added journeymen, spineless, gutless etc, but I'd be playing the broken record again. It was just so bloody frustrating. I actually thought we would win that game, even if it did mean false hope and that we'd lose the next three in a row. But the way in which we crumbled, being two down after about twenty odd minutes, both identical goals, both from corners, do we ever learn? Sunderland had by now adopted the tactic of all hands on deck. Corners to the opposition meant everyone back in the box defending. That didn't work and didn't help. They were falling over each other in their hideous efforts to clear the ball. It was no wonder we'd concede more than we could clear. The Boro game signalled relegation. I know we were already struggling, but if anything I saw that game as our last chance to avoid the drop. Alas it was not to be, even though Phillips pulled one back with a spectacular goal early in the second half, Kevin Kilbane foolishly attempted a back pass which gifted Boro with the opportunity to make it 3-1 - the final score. It had to be Kilbane didn't it, a player who far too many people praise and stick up for? Yeah he may have been subjected to the abuse of the boo boys for a long time. But he had had almost three years of football to prove himself and he still played like a fanny. Another player I sense whose heart was in his wage packet and not the colours he'd pull on, apart from the green jersey of Ireland that he obviously worshiped, often playing to levels unseen in a Sunderland shirt. Mind you, that meant nowt to me. I couldn't see Sunderland changing our colours so that one player could miraculously transform himself into a super star. Besides I still haven't forgiven him for this two-fingered salute during the pre-season. He should never have played again in a red and white shirt as far as I was concerned. There you go again I'm playing another one of my many broken records. Time out!

Another point about the Boro match before I relentlessly move on was the sporadic outbursts of violence. Frustration boiled over when Boro scored and a half dozen or so Smoggies decided to celebrate - these half dozen or so sitting in the Sunderland end. Well as you can imagine, no sooner had they jumped up to applaud than a dozen or more Sunderland fans piled on top of them to give them a good twatting.

And you know what I thought? Good on the Sunderland fans. On one hand I deplore football violence be it on the terraces or running battles in the streets, yet on the other hand I saw a bunch of supporters defending the name of Sunderland Football Club, with their efforts to evict invaders who had unashamedly trespassed onto their turf. The fact that they decided to pour hurt onto the antagonists had nothing to do with me, that was their decision. However what I found daunting was the time it took the boys in blue to arrive in certain parts of the ground. I saw one such tantrum last for over ten minutes in the upper section of the North Stand before the police turned up to assist the stewards who were outnumbered, overwhelmed, and unable to cope with the torrential vilification the Sunderland fans were laying on the imbecilic Smogmonsters.

Then there was an alleged coin-throwing incident, which hit a steward. Apparently the steward looked around, and said something along the lines of, *"If I find who threw that coin I'll have you thrown out and your season ticket confiscated"*. Within a split second or so the story goes, around one hundred and fifty people owned up to it! Sad but true!

That game was it for me. We were down. There was no need to wait for the mathematical certainty and no need to hang onto any thread of hope that said we could still avoid the drop. No matter how much Sergeant Wilko showed defiance with his continuing post match defeat interviews, and no matter how much Steve Cotterill kept mute and stood on the touchline writing down on note paper who knows what (maybe he was moonlighting as the OPTA statistics representative), it made no difference to my disillusioned and broken heart.

Back where we belong is something I hate to say but often believe is so unfortunately truthful. We'd had a good run between 1998 and 2001, the board, the Chairman and other high profile employees of SAFC made some horrendous mistakes though, failing to capitalize at the right time, making rash and hasty decisions at the wrong time, and it now felt like the good old bad old days of Roker Park. How naive of me to think such days, such referrals as a yo-yo club would return back to haunt the name of Sunderland Association Football Club. Unanswered questions and a seething anger was growing and growing. The echo of *"Murray Out"* chants was slowly getting louder and louder. Feeble attempts to calm down this growing faction by re-employing Kevin Ball for example, was a gesture that was simply too little too late, and then to make matters worse our delirious Chairman states that we're not a big as we think we are, we cannot compete with the likes of Newcastle and what was really hurtful - Middlesbrough! Maybe Bob Murray is a genuine supporter of Sunderland, but his business attitude was not, and these comments, the exact words of which I cannot remember nor dare I look them up due to their hurtful tones, put my feet firmly in the camp of the growing band of *"Murray Outers"*. Yes he had helped bring us from the depths on more than one occasion, yes he had built a wonderful stadium, but he had also held the reins throughout numerous heartbreaking relegations, numerous heartbreaking defeats at Wembley, and not putting his money where his mouth was at the right time. He was firmly pressed into a corner and his time was now up.

But Uncle Bob had one card left up his sleeve, and in my opinion shrewdly deflected attention away from himself with the surprise sacking of Howard Wilkinson and Steve Cotterill. Two wins from a half season in charge, we were rock bottom, heading towards a record number of points not gained in the Premiership, lowest scorers on the planet, but the departure of Peter Reid's replacement was quite simply painfully farcical. It made us a laughing stock. What was the point of the appointments in the first place? We'd have been better off sticking with Reidy, or if you believe the rumours, Uncle Bob originally wanted Mick McCarthy to replace Reidy, and phoned up Wilko when working for the Football Association for advice only for Wilko to sell himself instead. Two days after Wilko's sacking Mick McCarthy was appointed manager! McCarthy was immediately compared as being another Reid, which I'm not sure is a good thing or a bad thing, someone who may or may not have saved us if he'd been appointed in the first place - should you believe the aforementioned alleged stories circulating.

Having said that, wasn't McCarthy manager of Millwall, top of the league when we stuffed then 6-0 at Roker Park from which they astonishingly nose-dived and got relegated? At least Big Mick would be spared any backlash from the fans once relegation was sealed. With nine games to go and at least five wins needed he admitted the task was nigh on impossible but showed his own level of defiance by not giving in unlike many others - and me - until it was mathematically certain. Whatever the outcome, his consolation would be that of being free from any blame the fans would charge the Club.

Wilkinson for all his failures did inherit an injury riddled team and under strict instructions that no spending would be made available regardless of the situation. Who knows where we might have been if the likes of Reyna amongst others had not been sidelined?

At the time Reidy's departure was the right thing to do. There's no point reflecting on the past and *what if* or *if only* style conjectures. The fans, the people of Sunderland had to face the facts that being let down was a compulsory emotion attached to our beloved football Club. England may have gone through thirty odd years of hurt according to the song. Sunderland bar the '73 Cup final had gone through almost sixty years of hurt and we are still counting!

XXXVII

Throughout this book I've more than often mentioned the SMB in its various stages of development - the Sunderland Message board, the online forum, a breeding ground for surfers to merge and air their feelings, their opinions, and their general nonsensical meandering waffle.

The constant reference to the message board is not only down to the fact that it is the most popular area of the RTG web site, but that message boards in general are a pivotal focal point for bringing together people across the globe into one central pot where they can communicate in a comprehensive yet simplistic method.

It's also a very addictive tool that can have people constantly posting hundreds if not thousands of messages, topics, and general rant. In my time I've gone through numerous incidents of total addictiveness, spending almost all of my waking hours communicating tidings that may or may not have had substance. Likewise I've gone through countless periods of despise towards this online community due to episodes that have caused anger, hurt, intimidation, legal threats, and other such instances that have meant a thankful or forced withdrawal from the monitor and the keyboard, and thus a *'Borg'* like integration with other cyber surfers.

These days, I usually just lurk, that is to say I read the occasional message that looks interesting without responding. I guess I find myself too busy to actually participate in any discussion no matter how worthy it is of a reply. My interests have now moved on, and like many people before me, the time when total saturation is reached, it becomes boring. I do act in my role as an administrator, that is a *Big Brother* style overlord having the power to remove unwanted messages that have either no relevance on a football web site, or comments that may offend or be libellous (and we've been down that route before, thus personally I have a policy of zero tolerance). Posters who over step the mark are barred from the site. They are unable to contribute further until an apology is made. However, in extreme circumstances they will not be unbarred due to the nature of their acts.

Previously such banning techniques involved blocking a users IP address or hunting down their PC's cookie, placing its references into a text file containing other cookie IDs that would be checked each and every time a messages was submitted for contribution. All of this had to be done manually to keep the integrity of real time communication going. In the past such simple techniques were adequate in preventing abuse of a system that you could relate to as being the electronic version of pen pals, writing messages to fellow people which are then placed onto the world wide web for all to read or from a personal point of view to be read on a one to one level.

As the Internet audience grew, people became more PC aware finding ways around the blocking of an IP address or a cookie. This meant many hours would be spent in a fox hunt tracking down new cookie IDs to keep an unwanted person from contributing further. In many cases they just couldn't comprehend or accept their banning - maybe down to their own addictiveness - and had to keep posting regardless.

Following on from the legal threat SAFC thrust upon RTG, a new and more sophisticated message board had to be built, one that required registration before messages could be posted. Such registration required a legitimate email address and other generic details that gave us breathing space if it ever came to future legal issues. Basically we would know exactly who had breached the rules and if I or RTG were taken to court, then I would take the person who caused the breach to court - my stance is what comes around goes around, an eye for an eye, do unto others as they would do unto you, do what thou wilt shall be the whole of the law and so on. My warped personality holds grudges and they remain buried deep within my soul until such time I can bring them to the surface and act out my own form of self-justice, my own level of revenge to satisfy my tormented being.

Message boards for all their simple principles are a complex environment for a naive person to venture into. With large forums such as Ready To Go's SMB, you find thousands of registered users, thousands more lurking in the background and a somewhat difficult place at times to come on board and join in with the fun. This difficulty is more down to the ranging personalities of the posters that exist in cyberspace. From my prospective, they fall into five different categories, namely; *"The Holier Than Thou Brigade"*, *"The Serious Beyond Reason Brigade"*, *"The Lunatics"*, *"The Cyber Hooligans*, and *"The Level Headed"* entities. You can easily sub categorize all of the above as being either pessimistic, or optimistic, or fickle, or radical, or philosophical, all or more. Before rendering my interpretation of the five categories, there is I suppose a sixth - if not many more - the surfer who occasionally attempts to invade the message board with intent to harass, or those lost fans from other clubs that prefer to reside on the SMB rather than their own club forums. Most of these are of course Mags, but then it's easy to summarise this particular pedigree, after all, *"they're scum and they know they are!"*

Whether or not you use the SMB or other message boards I dare say your personality, be it the online version or the *'real-life'* version will fit into one of the following descriptions.

The Holier Than Thou Brigade

This bunch of Sunderland Association Football Club supporters have only one opinion, namely theirs. Dare you try to reply with a differing view, no matter how constructive and meaningful it is to the thread or topic posted, you will be shot down in flames. You will be judged as being either a Mag in disguise, or anti SAFC, or you'll be simply told to fuck off and mind your own business if your views do not match theirs. These people are so self-centred; do not have any balanced opinions other than their own which quite often are anything but balanced. In real life they may indeed be decent people, online however they take on board a whole new identity, maybe as a result of an unhappy childhood, or they were probably bullied at school and use the web as a means of purveying themselves as arrogant and brash, in other words becoming the online bully in some sort of retribution. They cannot fathom out why others disagree with their views, be it realistic or just a humorous piss take. They are far too lost in their own little world of harmony, which simply comes across as impetuous and condescending.

Most holier than thou people are blokes and as I lurk in the shadows reading their one sided views, I do often wonder if any of these scornful supporters are married or have children, and if so what type of upbringing are they providing for their family? Or, are they ordinary well-behaved citizens in real life and their somewhat despicable online behaviour is a secret unto them. Yes, there are many out there roaming the information super highway getting up to all sorts of misdemeanours without their other-halves ever finding out about their Jekyll and Hyde personality and their belligerent attempts to provoke argument for the sake of it, their sick little games of disagreeing to disagree and other similar and rather pitiful acts.

Any articles that any member of the RTG staff write which the holier than thou brigade do not agree with, term the feature as *'bollix'* in other words offer no constructive reply to whatever argument or notion has been relayed.

The Serious Beyond Reason Brigade

These people unfortunately take on board many of the characteristics of the holier than thou brigade. The only difference being that they will participate in a discussion, counter arguing their opinions that are thankfully not one sided. However they take themselves far too seriously and get easily provoked by any messages or views than sway from the general and overall purpose of a message board. The SMB is primarily

Sunderland AFC related, but its success has come about mainly due to the good bantered nature of the vast majority of users who will discuss other than the day to day support of SAFC, non football issues including world events, last nights telly, your favourite book, film, song, album or person - male or female - you'd most like to shag.

Basically this pot pourri of discussion has made the SMB the huge success it now is. When there is no football to discuss, be it the close season or weeks without a game due to international fixtures, then the general topic of conversation will - quite rightly - sway away from football and in general Sunderland AFC. The serious beyond reason brigade however find such non-football and in particular non-SAFC topics disgraceful and will attempt to continue to discuss conversations that have basically been flogged to death, but they do it because it relates to the Club. When given the online two fingered gesture from a friendly and comical point of view rather than extreme one (unless the two fingered salute comes from the holier than thou brigade), they become defensive, start biting instead of taking a chill pill and timing-out. I've no idea what they're childhood will have been like, maybe a school swat with spots and *'jam-jar-gegs'* who grew up to be merchant banker or solicitor wearing pin stripe suits, reading The Times rather than The Sun, and if fortunate or unfortunate to have a family (though it's often inconceivable how people like this could ever marry - sex is surely an embarrassing taboo subject that is performed by the lower echelons of society) will neglect them. Work is paramount; their loyalist support for the Club is also on par.

They are indeed the blind sheep the Club can rely on no matter how bad things get. If told to jump off the Wearmouth Bridge they will do so without question no matter how absurd the gesture. Where they get the time from to post onto a message board run by such lower echelons of society is one question I find hard to answer, unless the overall good-natured fun of the message board counteracts the loneliness of their real life.

The Lunatics

Without the influence and participation of this group of people any online forum, not just the SMB would be doomed to failure. Their wit, their ability to sway from the serious to the silly, to calm down online arguments and the occasional full-scale thermonuclear cyber war has to be admired. They never overstep the mark. They can be either totally addicted to posting or will only post when the need arises. They can turn a message board on a quiet boring non-football day into a hive of active discussion about anything and everything. Their ability to type such wonderful mini pieces of literature are a talent in themselves and one that I take my hat off towards. Their support is never questioned.

People know they are *'Sunderland till they die'*, but they will if the need arises criticise the players, the Club, or fellow fans if issues arise which they are not happy with.

This faction however soon gets bored. Maybe they were the class joker at school, or the Jackass style college student, a person who knows when to take life serious, but also knows when to chill or have fun. However their constant search for something new or refreshing means they far too easily disappear from the online community. They will quite often create alter egos, cyber characters that have a life of their own to keep themselves entertained, but when it becomes dreary this character will be killed off - in style of course - like your soap star that leaves the show because their feet are too big for their shoes. There is an abundance of characters that have come and gone on the SMB, humorous posters who I will say with hand on heart are sadly missed.

The Cyber Hooligans

These wary bunches are unwanted. I don't understand the mentality of a hooligan and its difficult to relay how the online version works. Quite simply they come and go in short periods usually depending upon who the opposition are, or will surface only when an international takes place, or an incident of actual football violence happens. Quite often they are difficult to spot as they have developed their own language, relaying coded instructions regarding meeting places for fights and so on. They have no real allegiance to any football club and abuse online forums as a way of communicating without attracting the attention of the local constabulary. Sometimes they will expose themselves usually via their avatars (*'geek'* term for message board users who post up within a profile of themselves a small image that to them represents some part of their personality or characteristics or loyalty). The cyber hooligan who exposes himself online will post up an avatar containing some form of Burberry imagery, be it just the tartan itself or his priceless baseball cap. For an Internet administrator, keeping a watchful eye out for cyber hooliganism is a very time consuming and difficult job. It could unintentionally cause the web site to be sued or worse case closed down due to their antics. Cyber hooligans who in real life are not hooligans spend their online addictions pursuing the pleasures of bullying other people for the sake of it, using Neanderthal language, normally typing in upper case - which to the online nerd means YOU'RE SHOUTING - without any real understanding of Internet terminology or basic English grammar. One they've worked out how to type *"fuck off"* or *"you're going home in a fucking ambulance"* - that is once their pea sized brain has managed to send a signal to their arms to pick up their knuckles off the floor to incredibly type such wonderful colourful metaphors, then they disappear normally to recuperate such was the strain of using something so incomprehensible as a computer and an instrument they cannot use as a hand held weapon for their next outing.

The Level Headed

Some might say level headed people are boring because their input cannot be argued with, be it intentionally or not. Their feelings and comments on whatever subject matter is under discussion are extremely sensible, more than often accurate and under normal circumstances will be highly applauded. Unfortunately this breed is rare, in fact an endangered species more down to the ever increasing pace of modern life, thus increased levels of stress and anxiety causing level headedness to slowly depart from their bodies plunging them into another state of existence.

Levelheaded people are leaders, visionaries who don't demand praise nor seek it. They will sit back and admire the chaos that unfolds before them and if applicable will step in to *'put things right'* though they will fail miserably in any attempt to find common ground with the holier than thou brigade.

I can safely say that you will fall into one or more of these categories and if not your personality - online - will mirror some of the traits I've expressed here, whether you admit to it or not. Likewise what I've failed to mention so far which is a trait that all categories share is that of illegally surfing during office hours. Most site traffic around the globe takes place between the hours of nine in the morning until five in the evening. Many new employment laws have come into being regarding Internet usage whilst at work. And again, whether you admit to it or not you will have or you are using the Internet for your own personal satisfaction when at work during whatever length of skiving you ritually undertake. I've yet to come across any Mackem who has lost their job due to online surfing that has no relevance to their jobs, though I've seen many message board users come and go, the go factor when they get caught out and the web site is blocked via a firewall (self explanatory *'nerds'* term), and thus can no longer actively participate as a member of the online community.

Then there are the online affairs, weirdos and love cheats who without physically committing adultery will flaunt themselves and sexually tease the opposite sex whilst in cyber character mode. You see such antics let the mind roam and the fat spotty faced yeast ridden witch you're talking too in your perverse mind is a fit tanned blonde with big tits. Such playful antics are however anything but playful. Such people should feel deep remorse for tapping up someone online especially when their other half may be unaware or will feel deep heartache if they ever found out - not that you should be either doing it in the first place nor trying to hide something that is quite sad really. You're still cheating by being so sly and that degrades you. I could go on and on, as the subject of human behaviour within the realms of the World Wide Web is a mind boggling analytical subject that sadly cannot be concluded in a single chapter.

XXXVIII

Pride is something that bonds together complete strangers sharing a common goal. Pride is something to cherish and something we've all felt, witnessed and believed in on many, many occasions. I look back at 1990 and the pride I felt leaving Maine Road having watched Sunderland go down. Such pride was felt at Wembley in '85, '90, and '92. Pride was missing initially, but found its way back into my heart following the '98 Play-Off Final and relegation at Selhurst Park in '97. Pride leaving St. Andrews was however not present nor I feel will it ever be.

Of course Sunderland were already relegated before this game, the only difference being that it wasn't a mathematical certainty. Such crucial games - usually the last game of the season - brings out the pride in the Sunderland faithful resulting in thousands travelling to support their team and help them to survive a devastating drop into obscurity. Such a following didn't emerge at Birmingham and to a certain extent the thirty quid a ticket charge didn't help.

At the end many cried out in vain *"Sunderland Till I Die"*, that war cry that echoes much pride, but also much sorrow. I couldn't find anger following the final nail being hammered home. Anger had been present for far to long to suddenly swell over one game, a game that ended the dream.

However annoyance did emerge two days later when our beloved chairman Bob Murray issued a press release that I considered patronising, somewhat insulting the intelligence of the supporters and above all badly timed. The term *"same old shit"* sprung to mind, excuses without merit, lamenting without apologising. Using part of a phrase immortalised by the permed one - Mr. Keegan - *"I'd have loved"* to have re-printed Uncle Bob's comments and tear them apart word by word. However when you write a book, you need to obtain permission to use articles published elsewhere - something which I have done so for the articles included in this book (bar the anonymous psycho emails). Therefore I approached SAFC and asked for permission, though something released as an official statement in my view didn't warrant permission once it's circulated in the public domain, and so when I was *'politely'* refused by SAFC, I should have or could have contested it.

Instead it showed just how caring the so-called *Caring Club* is. Always closed doors to anyone associated with a fanzine, or an outspoken supporter or one who is publishing a book that quite frankly they (the Club) may be shitting themselves over. I don't think that there are any startling revelations in this book, but I shouldn't have been surprised when I was turned down. I guess my cheek got the better of me so I asked if I could print the reply I got from my initial approach that said *"no."* Guess what they said? No again! Still it doesn't stop me from putting forward my anger at the statement. On one hand it was so comical I wonder if the Iraqi Information Minister had wrote it. On the other hand I could see a slight glimpse of remorse and indeed Mr Murray's own sadness at our plight.

But then who is to blame? Of course you start with the players, but then you can go back to who picks the players and the tactics they are told to use, but then you can go back to the person(s) who pick the manager and run the Club. Fault and blame has to lie squarely on the shoulders of the chairman and that is Mr. Bob Murray, the man who allegedly said when Reid goes I go, and that Wilkinson would be in charge of SAFC regardless of the season's outcome. These alleged remarks have not come to fruition; thus it begs the question was someone lying when such rumoured comments were made? When Mick McCarthy was appointed *'Uncle Bob'* was absent, apparently ill with stress or something along those lines. Stress as quoted by one of the RTG feature writers is for poor people not rich people. I've suffered stress and more from a personal point of view, but I have no sympathy for anyone who suffers stress that is basically self inflicted. If a person cannot handle the responsibility then they should walk away.

I've said it before in an earlier chapter but the respect the chairman of Sunderland AFC had gained following the Play-Off Final had all but disappeared. I'd love some day to be able to sit down with Bob, not to argue with him or start a bitching session, but to have him apologise one on one, so that I can see that way up inside the ivory towers of the Stadium of Light is a genuine supporter who is genuinely upset about the relegation of the 2002/2003 season, rather than the figure we witnessed discussing gold taps on Premier Passions while Sunderland slid into obscurity in 1997 – *'and Nero fiddled while Rome burned'*.

I never really intended on writing too much more after the Birmingham result, besides the losing streak just kept on going - 1-2 at home to West Brom, and 0-1 at home to the black and white heathens. However the Skunks game opened my eyes a bit and made me realise a lot of what I've said previously about my fellow Sunderland supporters will to a few, be somewhat insulting. My reference to blind sheep renewing their season tickets regardless is one such potential insulting statement. I suppose what I didn't mention nor ponder were those who renew regardless but in fact do have a life; they will complain when the need arises and as such they are loyal supporters who without a football club would quite simply die. My attempted interpretation of blind sheep is stemmed towards those who don't see anything wrong with the set-up. They cannot or will not complain towards players who are spineless or management who are inept and executives who dare I say lie. The thing is you see these *'holier than thou'* types will often scorn people like me who have quite simply had enough and have decided to go to games on a match by match basis, even if it is more expensive, but like me they cannot justify giving the Club their own hard earned cash up front in return for *'nothing'*. In a recent phone-in on local radio, a female supporter vehemently expressed how she'd be renewing her season ticket, as now was the time the Club needed our support. Before I comment on this she went on by saying quite ostentaciously that once SAFC were top of Division One, the *'stayaways'* would soon be back. Well referring to the latter, yes I totally agree that the *'stayaways'* will be back, but I ask what's wrong with that? If the Club improves their diabolic performances people will be back in their thousands - to be entertained, until then, they'd probably prefer to paint a white wall white and watch it dry. As for now is the time the Club needs our support, well support has always been there and will always be there. Our support is undying even if attendances and renewals drop, the Club will still pull in more than they could in the latter days of life at Roker Park, and more than often the combined attendance of whole leagues. There is a thin line between blind loyalty and stupidity, by all means support your team with undying love, but without making stupid noises or comments that justify the pathetic performances over the past two seasons. The Club should show more respect to the supporters and actually say the word *'sorry'*. I know I've mentioned this before, but how hard can it be to say one word?

    The Skunks game brought home such differences that up until now I've painted as one scenario, and to an extent, some of this retraction was down to the rather sad sight of Sunderland fans bickering and verbally assaulting each other with their differing views or attempts to force other supporters to do as they do. The sad thing is it was everywhere to be seen. At times people were more concerned with arguing than watching the game, though as a friend of mine said, "you pay your money you're entitled to your own opinion". I suppose that is a simple and accurate assumption to make, after all this book is my opinion and my view, though as I write these sentences, I look back over the two years I've spent putting it all together and realise just how contradictory I have been. I think I probably am fickle, two-faced and will alter my opinions based on recent results. I've also got issues towards the Club from a personal point of view, which has probably made many of my comments very one sided.

I still think that many will echo much of what I've written. It takes courage to open your heart and pour out your true feelings no matter how much they can hurt or haunt you once revealed. However I'm no glory hunter, so even though I rarely go to away games, even though my stance on renewing my season ticket has changed and I intend on going to watch the Lads on a match by match basis - if I feel like it - I still perceive myself as a fan, a loyal supporter. I don't believe I need to pump my own money into SAFC before a ball has been kicked to prove my loyalty. I've pumped money into SAFC for twenty odd years and that alone is proof enough as far as I'm concerned.

But at the end of the day we are all human beings, that species of this planet that is unique, has the ability to think, act and survive out of its normal habitat and thus should be allowed to express opinions whether agreeable or not - free will.

I've focused on myself because this is what this book is primarily about - me, my life, my dedication or recent lack or it towards my football club, my bitter resentment towards aspects of society, my rather naive attempts at becoming a dot com millionaire and so on. I never intended writing a match by match summary or unofficial history of SAFC over the past six or seven years, just my tale, unique maybe, but nevertheless a truthful account from one lonely person's aspirations towards something better in life, something more rewarding or secure whilst dreaming of success, that sadly has not come to pass. Instead the circle is complete. I started with relegation and have unfortunately ended with relegation. Such is life, the roller coaster ride of supporting Sunderland Football Club that at present is on a downward spiral. It remains to be seen exactly when we shall rise again. I hope I'm wrong but presently I just cannot see us bouncing back. People say we are capable of *"doing a Leicester"* but I'm more concerned with us avoiding *"doing a Sheffield Wednesday"* especially if we remain stuck with some of the playing staff that have contributed to the demise of the Club from England's elite league.

Players come and go, some attain hero status, others become boo boy victims. The Premiership has seen an avalanche of mercenaries playing for money rather than club loyalty. Clubs have come and gone from the Premiership most of which will splash out obscene and silly wages to keep or attract star names. Sometimes such decisions will haunt a club as they take on board a mercenary rather than the star quality they crave. Some players, many of which I have seen pull on a red and white shirt over the past two seasons are mercenaries or over-paid has-beens. At times, like my initial perception of a blind sheep supporter I've probably put across the entire team as being spineless or overpaid journeymen. Sometimes I think I was spot on, other times I've been wrong.

The match against the Skunks restored a certain level of pride and passion in the team, something sadly lacking over the latter months of the 2002/2003 season. Some players tried hard but were out of their depth. Some players I pray will never wear *my* colours again. I could slowly go through each and every one picking faults, something which I am perfectly entitled to do so regardless of how many goals or great performances they'd put in the past. The present is what counts and these millionaires have devastated thousands of Wearsiders, bled our Club dry and I hope they find some remorse when they look at themselves in the mirror each day (instead of thinking *"oh dear, how sad, never mind, but at least my new Ferrari is shit hot"*). On the other hand, some players have never been given a sniff, or have made it into the first team late in the day, when the damage was done, or players like Jody Craddock who has to be admired for his courageous attempts at playing football in a season not only full of defeats and the bitter disappointment of relegation, but also more importantly, the grief of losing a baby. Jody showed incredible strength and is one player I hope will remain to help SAFC escape from the Nationwide at the first attempt. Then we have Sean Thornton, a breath of fresh air, but for far too long snubbed by Reidy and Sgt. Wilko. Others like Marcus Stewart have been bought (maybe a panic buy) and yet were never given a decent run in the team to prove themselves. Fan favourites like Julio Arca have been missing for long periods while Kevin Kilbane still played, and deep inside I still question whether or not Nicholas Medina is real and that maybe I'd had one too many when I thought I saw him play in Quinny's testimonial. Emerson Thome for some reason (apart from long term injuries) never played much during the relegation season though it's common knowledge now that if Thome reached a certain milestone in terms of games played for SAFC, then the Club would have to cough up an additional fee to his former club namely Chelsea – around £250,000. I think the Craddock and Thome partnership was one of the best defensive line-ups of recent years. Who knows if Thome had played more often where we could have ended up? The same can be said of Renya and the *'if only'* he hadn't been injured. Thome however is a mystery that few know the truth and the masses will probably never find out, but I wonder if not playing Thome for a few quid was worth the potential twenty million lost by not retaining Premiership status? There are other numerous conspiracies and thoughts regarding the synonymous *'if only'*. I mean some will say if only we hadn't dropped wearing the *'lucky'* black cat on the sleeves of our shirts, or if only we hadn't brought out a strip with a plain colour on the sleeves instead of the traditional striped look - plain sleeved shirts have always resulted in relegation. Then there's me putting my foot in it by declaring to a few friends after the home game against the Boro that we'd probably not win another game for the rest of the season - I didn't mean it you know - honest. Sadly Sunderland now wear with shame the record of being the worst team in the history of the Premiership, how the board must sleep soundly at night with that tag attached to them, including Mr. Murray who is adding quite nicely to his collection of relegations under his belt - five is it now?

What happens now? Well as I've previously said, I've gone full circle, like the team, and I'm now back to square one, from being a hobbyist, to establishing a company via a legal partnership, to making half decent money, only for new contracts not to be honoured, the partnership expiring, and so back to being a hobbyist. Likewise feature writers have come, and I'm eternally grateful for their voluntary input, though I'm glad the resident *Geordie* has been dropped (you know I look back and can't believe I spent a few months pretending to be a Mag, writing shite about Sunderland until we found a *real* Mag who wanted to offer his wise opinions about how great the Skunks were and how sad us SMB's were). My devotion has suffered greatly and I've gone from being enthusiastic to being burdened, too many issues I do not want, nor deserve to have clouding over me.

I've also got a helluva lot more to say, as well as a helluva lot I haven't said. Sunderland 0 Arsenal 4 being our last game in the top flight for God knows how many years, Bob Murray refusing to step down, rumours that the Club could go into administration, mass redundancies of ordinary folk while players continue to draw twenty-odd grand a week to name just few. But you've got to stop writing at some point - right? I guess my other tales will have to wait until a follow up - should I manage to write one. Why do I do it? I have no idea, but I will still keep doing it whatever *'doing it'* actually means - it probably means many things, most of which will have been explained somewhere within these pages.

Hopefully by the time you read this, the troubles, the torment I've suffered personally and that we've all suffered as supporters will be a distant memory and that we will have or will be *"doing a Leicester"* and not *"doing a Sheffield Wednesday!"*

What does the future hold?

How the fuck should I know, if I did I'd be stinking rich, but I'm not - not yet, well you can dream can't you? I mean those elusive *'dot-com'* millions are out there somewhere, if I can find them, and after I take time-out, pop a chill pill, and stop being Mr. Angry!

I guess all that needs to be said now is to quote from an ancient proverb I once read. It says, *"Once you read the last word on the last page, close the book!"*

Sunderland Till I Die?